Travelling
— The —
Turf

Editor Julian West

KENSINGTON WEST PRODUCTIONS LTD

HEXHAM ENGLAND

Acknowledgements

Kensington West Productions Ltd
5 Cattle Market, Hexham, Northumberland NE46 1NJ
Tel: (0434) 609933 Fax: (0434) 600066

Front Cover: Claire Eva Burton At The Last *Courtesy of Rosenstiels*
Back Cover: D.M. Dent *Courtesy of Private Collection*

Print catalogue avilable Tel: 0434 609933 Fax: 0434 600066

Editor Julian West

Design Kensington West Productions Ltd

Cartography Camilla Charnock, Craig Semple

Typesetting Tradespools Ltd, Frome

Origination Trinity Graphics Hong Kong

Printed and bound by Firmin-Didot (France),
Group Herissey, N° d'impression : 25493

Contents

Introduction

Travelling The Turf has been published for some nine years. It is the leading racecourse guide and for much of that time has been the only racecourse guide of any merit! It now has a young stable companion which we know will grow to become a valuable addition to the yard.

Travelling The Turf In Your Pocket is an attempt to combine the twin virtues of quality and value. The editorial spans the racecourses of Britain and Ireland but we also have included a list of hostelries of various descriptions to help you complete your memorable day out. The hotels are listed under the heading Local Favourites.

We are extremely grateful to the many racecourse officials, hoteliers and others who have helped us in the compilation of this pocket guide first time out. In future years, we will expand the book to ensure that you can find winners a plenty as well but for this, the first edition, we wish you many happy days on and off the racecourse while travelling the turf.

Featured Racecourses

Perth

Hamilton Park · Edinburgh

Kelso

· Ayr

Newcastle
· Hexham

· Carlisle

Sedgefield · Redcar
· Catterick
Cartmel · Ripon · Thirsk
· York
Wetherby · Beverley
Haydock Park · Pontefract
· Aintree
Doncaster · · Market Rasen
· Chester · Southwell
· Bangor On Dee · Nottingham
· Fakenham
· Uttoxeter
Great Yarmouth ·
Wolverhampton · · Leicester
Ludlow · · Huntington
· Warwick
Worcester · · Stratford · Newmarket
Hereford · Towcester
· Cheltenham Windsor · · Kempton Park
Chepstow · Ascot · Sandown Park ·
· Epsom
· Bath Newbury · · Folkestone
Taunton · · Salisbury · Lingfield Park
Wincanton · Plumpton · Brighton
Goodwood ·
Devon & Exeter · · Fontwell Park

Newton Abbot ·

January	Race name	Racecourse
8th Jan	The Anthony Mildmay, Peter Cazelet Memorial HandicapSteeple Chase	Sandown Park
8th Jan	The Baring Securities Tolworth Novices' Hurdle	Sandown Park
8th Jan	The Newton Steeple Chase	Haydock Park
15th Jan	The Dipper Novices' Steeple Chase	Newcastle
15th Jan	The Victor Chandler Chase (Handicap)	Ascot
22nd Jan	The Peter Marsh Steeple Chase (Handicap)	Haydock Park
22nd Jan	The Premier Long Distance Hurdle	Haydock Park
22nd Jan	The Bic Razor Lanzarote Handicap Hurdle	Kempton Park
28th Jan	Rossington Main Novices Hurdle	Doncaster
29th Jan	The Wyko Power Hurdle	Cheltenham
29th Jan	The West of Scotland Pattern Steeple Chase	Ayr
29th Jan	Great Yorkshire Chase (Handicap Steeple Chase)	Doncaster
29th Jan	River Don Novices Hurdle	Doncaster

February	Race name	Racecourse
5th Feb	The Agfa Diamond Steeple Chase	Sandown Park
5th Feb	The Scilly Isles Novices' Steeple Chase	Sandown Park
5th Feb	The Marston Moor Steeple Chase (Limited Handicap)	Wetherby
5th Feb	The John Hughes Grand National Trial	Chepstow
9th Feb	The Reynoldstown Novices' Chase	Ascot
12th Feb	The Tote Gold Trophy (Handicap Hurdle)	Newbury
12th Feb	Game Spirit Steeple Chase	Newbury
19th Feb	The Persian War Premier Hurdle	Chepstow
19th Feb	The Tote Eider Handicap Steeple Chase	Newcastle
19th Feb	The Nottinghamshire Novices Hurdle	Nottingham
24th Feb	The Kingwell Hurdle	Wincanton
26th Feb	The Racing Post Steeple Chase	Kempton Park
26th Feb	The Rendlesham Hurdle	Kempton Park
26th Feb	The Greenalls Gold Cup Steeple Chase	Haydock Park
26th Feb	The East Lancs Steeple Chase	Haydock Park

March	Race name	Race course
2nd Mar	The Cavalier Steeple Chase	Worcester
12th Mar	The Sunderlands Imperial Cup Handicap Hurdle	Sandown Park
12th Mar	The Swish Hurdle	Chepstow
15th Mar	The Smurfit Champion Hurdle Challenge Trophy	Cheltenham
15th Mar	The Supreme Novices' Hurdle	Cheltenham
15th Mar	The Arkle Guinness Challenge Trophy Stple Chase	Cheltenham
16th Mar	The Sun Alliance Steeple Chase	Cheltenham
16th Mar	The Sun Alliance Hurdle	Cheltenham
16th Mar	The Queen Mother Champion Steeple Chase	Cheltenham

Date	Race name	Race course
17th Mar	The Bonusprint Stayers Hurdle	Cheltenham
17th Mar	The Tote Cheltenham Gold Cup Steeple Chase	Cheltenham
17th Mar	The Daily Express Triumph Hurdle	Cheltenham
19th Mar	The Tetley Bitter Midlands National (Handicap Steeple Chase)	Uttoxeter
24th Mar	The Doncaster Mile	Doncaster
26th Mar	The William Hill Lincoln Handicap	Doncaster
26th Mar	The Cammidge Trophy	Doncaster

April	Race name	Race course
2nd Apr	The Bonusprint Easter Stakes	Kempton Park
2nd Apr	The Bonusprint Masaka Stakes	Kempton Park
4th Apr	The Rosebery Handicap Stakes	Kempton Park
4th Apr	The Magnolia Stakes	Kempton Park
7th Apr	The Martell Cup Steeple Chase	Aintree
7th Apr	The Glenlivet Anniversary Hurdle	Aintree
8th Apr	The Mumm Melling Steeple Chase	Aintree
9th Apr	The Martell Grand National Steeple Chase (Handicap)	Aintree
9th Apr	The Martell Aintree Hurdle	Aintree
9th Apr	The Martell Aintree Steeple Chase (Limited Handicap)	Aintree
12th Apr	The Shadwell Stud Nell Gwyn	Newmarket Stakes
13th Apr	The Earl of Sefton EBF Stakes	Newmarket
13th Apr	The European Free Handicap	Newmarket
14th Apr	The Craven Stakes	Newmarket
15th Apr	The Gainsborough Stud Fred Darling Stakes	Newbury
15th Apr	The Scottish Champion Hurdle	Ayr
16th Apr	The Stakis Scottish National (Handicap Steeple Chase)	Ayr
16th Apr	The Edinburgh Woollen Mills Future Champions Chase	Ayr
16th Apr	The Thirsk Classic Trial	Thirsk
16th Apr	The Singer & Friedlander Greenham Stakes	Newbury
16th Apr	The Lanes End John Porter EBF Stakes	Newbury
22nd Apr	The Gardner Merchant Mile	Sandown Park
23rd Apr	The Whitbread Gold Cup Handicap Steeple Chase	Sandown Park
23rd Apr	The Thresher Classic Trial	Sandown Park
23rd Apr	The TGI Friday's Gordon Richards EBF Stakes	Sandown Park
27th Apr	The Insulpak Victoria Cup	Ascot
27th Apr	The Insulpak Sagaro EBF Stakes	Ascot
28th Apr	Madagans 1000 Guineas Stakes	Newmarket
29th Apr	The Jockey Club Stakes	Newmarket
30th Apr	2000 Guineas Stakes	Newmarket

30th Apr	The Palace House Stakes	Newmarket
30th Apr	The Staffordshire Hurdle	Uttoxeter
30th Apr	The Thirsk Hunt Cup	Thirsk

May	Race name	Racecourse
2nd May	The Jubilee Handicap Stakes	Kempton Park
2nd May	The Swinton Handicap Hurdle	Haydock Park
3rd May	The Dalham Chester Vase	Chester
4th May	The Ladbroke Chester Cup (Handicap)	Chester
5th May	The Ormonde EBF Stakes	Chester
7th May	The Lingfield Derby Trial Stakes	Lingfield
10th May	The Tattersalls Musidora Stakes	York
11th May	The Dante Stakes	York
12th May	The Yorkshire Cup	York
12th May	The Duke Of York Stakes	York
13th May	The Juddmonte Lockinge Stakes	York
17th May	The AR Dennis Bookmakers Predominate Stakes	Goodwood
18th May	The Tripleprint Lupe Stakes	Goodwood
21st May	The Daily Mail Leisure Stakes	Lingfield Park
21st May	Coral Handicap Stakes	Newmarket
28th May	The Crawley Warren Heron Stakes	Kempton Park
28th May	The Tote Credit Silver Bowl	Haydock Park
28th May	The Sandy Lane Rated Stakes	Haydock Park
30th May	The Zetland Gold Cup (Handicap)	Redcar
30th May	The UB Group Temple Stakes	Sandown Park
30th May	The Cementone Beaver Henry II EBF Stakes	Sandown Park
31st May	The Brigadier Gerard Stakes	Sandown Park

June	Race name	Racecourse
1st Jun	The Ever Ready Derby	Epsom
1st Jun	The Diomed Stakes	Epsom
2nd Jun	The Ever Ready Coronation Cup	Epsom
3rd Jun	Northern Dancer Stakes (Handicap)	Epsom
4th Jun	The Energizer Oaks	Epsom
4th Jun	John of Gaunt Stakes	Haydock Park
4th Jun	The Horse & Hound Cup Final Champion Steeple Chase	Stratford
11th Jun	The William Hill Trophy (Handicap)	York
14th Jun	The St James's Palace Stakes	Royal Ascot
14th Jun	The Prince of Wales's Stakes	Royal Ascot
14th Jun	The King Edward VII Stakes	Royal Ascot
15th Jun	The Coronation Stakes	Royal Ascot
15th Jun	The Jersey Stakes Royal	Ascot

15th Jun	The Queen's Vase Stakes	Royal Ascot
16th Jun	The Gold Cup	Royal Ascot
16th Jun	The Cork and Orrery Stakes	Royal Ascot
17th Jun	The King's Stand Stakes	Royal Ascot
18th Jun	The Handicap Stakes	Ascot
22nd Jun	The Gala Stakes	Kempton Park
23rd Jun	The Veuve Clicquot Champagne Stakes	Salisbury
24th Jun	The Northern Rock Gosforth Park Cup	Newcastle
25th Jun	The Newcastle 'Brown Ale' Northumberland Plate	Newcastle
25th Jun	The Van Geest Criterion Stakes	Newmarket

July	Race name	Racecourse
1st Jul	The Royal Hong Kong Jockey Club Trophy (Handicap)	Sandown Park
2nd Jul	The Lancashire Oaks Stakes	Haydock Park
2nd Jul	The 196th Year of the Old Newton Cup (Handicap)	Haydock Park
2nd Jul	The Coral–Eclipse Stakes	Sandown Park
2nd Jul	The Sandown Rated Stakes	Sandown Park
5th Jul	The Princess of Wales's Stakes	Newmarket
5th Jul	The Hillsdown Cherry Hinton Stakes	Newmarket
6th Jul	The SBJ Group July Stakes	Newmarket
6th Jul	The Falmouth Stakes	Newmarket
7th Jul	The July Cup	Newmarket
7th Jul	Ladbroke Bunbury Cup (Handicap)	Newmarket
9th Jul	The John Smith's Magnet Cup Handicap	York
9th Jul	The Champagne Jacquart Silver Trophy	Lingfield Park
16th Jul	Weatherbys and Sales Super Sprint Trophy	Newbury
18th Jul	The Tennents Scottish Classic	Ayr
23rd Jul	The King George VI and Queen Elizabeth Diamond Stakes	Ascot
25th Jul	The Federation Brewery LCL Pils Lager Beeswing Stakes	Newcastle
26th Jul	The William Hill Cup	Goodwood
27th Jul	The Sussex Stakes	Goodwood
27th Jul	The Richmond Stakes	Goodwood
28th Jul	The Tiffany Goodwood Cup	Goodwood
29th Jul	The Schweppes Golden Mile (Handicap)	Goodwood
29th Jul	The Leslie & Godwin Spitfire Stakes Handicap	Goodwood
29th Jul	Schroders Glorious Rated Stakes	Goodwood
30th Jul	The Vodafone Nassau Stakes	Goodwood
30th Jul	The Vodac Stewards' Cup	Goodwood

August	Race name	Racecourse
6th Aug	Brierley Investments Handicap Stakes	Newmarket
12th Aug	The Gardner Merchant Hungerford Stakes	Newbury
13th Aug	The Ibn Bey Geoffrey Freer Stakes	Newbury
16th Aug	The Juddmonte International Stakes	York
16th Aug	The Great Voltigeur Stakes	York
17th Aug	The Aston Upthorpe Yorkshire Oaks	York
17th Aug	The Falmouth Stakes Handicap	York
17th Aug	The Scottish Equitable Gimcrack Stakes	York
17th Aug	The Tote Ebor (Handicap)	York
18th Aug	The Lowther Stakes	York
18th Aug	The Keeneland Nunthorpe Stakes	York
18th Aug	The Bradford & Bingley Handicap	York
19th Aug	The Solario Stakes	Sandown Park
20th Aug	The Tote Great St Wilfrid Handicap Stakes	Ripon
26th Aug	The Prestige Stakes	Goodwood
27th Aug	The Beefeater Gin Celebration Mile	Goodwood
29th Aug	Bonusprint Champion Two Year Old Trophy	Ripon
29th Aug	The Virginia Stakes	Newcastle
31st Aug	The Lawrence Batley Handicap	York

September	Race name	Racecourse
1st Sept	The Sun Life of Canada Garrowby Rated Stakes	York
2nd Sept	The Milcars Temple Fortune Stakes	Kempton
3rd Sept	The Bonusprint Sirenia Stakes	Kempton Park
3rd Sept	The Bonus Print September Stakes	Kempton Park
3rd Sept	The Hazlewood Foods Sprint Cup	Haydock Park
7th Sept	Park Hill Stakes	Doncaster
7th Sept	The May Hill Stakes	Doncaster
7th Sept	The Tote Portland Handicap	Doncaster
7th Sept	The Doncaster Bloodstock Sales Scarbrough Stakes	Doncaster
7th Sept	The EBF Fillies Nursery Handicap	Doncaster
8th Sept	The Doncaster Cup	Doncaster
8th Sept	The Kiveton Park Stakes	Doncaster
9th Sept	The Laurent—Perrier Champagne Stakes	Doncaster
9th Sept	The Abtrust Select Stakes	Goodwood
10th Sept	The Ladbroke Racing Sprint Stakes Handicap	Goodwood
10th Sept	The Tripleprint Flying Childers Stakes	Doncaster
10th Sept	The Coalite St Leger Stakes	Doncaster
17th Sept	The Ladbrokes Ayr Gold Cup (Handicap)	Ayr
17th Sept	The Rokeby Farms Mill Reef Stakes	Newbury
17th Sept	The Courage Rated Stakes	Newbury
24th Sept	The Royal Lodge Stakes	Ascot

24th Sept	The Queen Elizabeth II Stakes	Ascot
24th Sept	The Fillies' Mile	Ascot
24th Sept	The Tote Festival Stakes	Ascot
24th Sept	The Ascot Handicap	Ascot
24th Sept	The Diadem Stakes	Ascot
28th Sept	The Shadwell Stud Cheveley Park Stakes	Newmarket
29th Sept	The Newgate Stud Middle Park Stakes	Newmarket
30th Sept	Supreme Stakes	Goodwood

October	Race name	Racecourse
1st Oct	The Timeform Hurdle	Chepstow
1st Oct	The Jockey Club Cup	Newmarket
1st Oct	The Sun Chariot Stakes	Newmarket
1st Oct	The William Hill Cambridgeshire Handicap Stakes	Newmarket
8th Oct	ANC Rockingham Stakes	York
13th Oct	The Challenge Stakes	Newmarket
13th Oct	The Tote Two Year Old Trophy	Redcar
14th Oct	The Dewhurst Stakes	Newmarket
14th Oct	Tattersalls Rockfel Stakes	Newmarket
15th Oct	The Dubai Champion Stakes	Newmarket
15th Oct	The Tote Cesarewitch (Handicap)	Newmarket
15th Oct	The Charisma Gold Cup (Handicap Steeple Chase)	Kempton Park
20th Oct	The Desert Orchid South Western Pattern Steeple Chase	Wincanton
20th Oct	The Vodafone Horris Hill Stakes	Newbury
22nd Oct	The Castrol St Simon Stakes	Newbury
22nd Oct	The Racing Post Trophy	Doncaster
29th Oct	The Ladbroke Autumn Handicap	Newmarket
29th Oct	The Charlie Hall Steeple Chase	Wetherby

November	Race name	Racecourse
1st Nov	The Plymouth Gin Challenge Cup Steeple Chase	Exeter
2nd Nov	The Erdman Lewis Classic Novice Hurdle	Uttoxeter
5th Nov	The William Hill November Handicap	Doncaster
5th Nov	The Tote Silver Trophy	Chepstow
5th Nov	The Serlby Stakes	Doncaster
5th Nov	The Remembrance Stakes	Doncaster
9th Nov	The Aga Worcester Novices Steeple Chase	Worcester
12th Nov	The Mackeson Gold Cup Handicap Steeple Chase	Cheltenham
19th Nov	The H & T Walker Gold Cup Steeple Chase	Ascot
19th Nov	Crowther Homes Becher Chase	Aintree

22nd Nov	The Peterborough Steeple Chase	Huntingdon
26th Nov	The Bellway Homes 'Fighting Fifth' Hurdle	Newcastle
26th Nov	The Hennessy Cognac Gold Cup Handicap Steeple Chase	Newbury

December	Race name	Racecourse
3rd Dec	The Rehearsal Steeple Chase	Chepstow
3rd Dec	The William Hill Handicap Hurdle	Sandown Park
3rd Dec	The Mitsubishi Shogun Tingle Creek Trophy (Handicap Steeple Chase)	Sandown Park
10th Dec	The Tripleprint Gold Cup Handicap Steeple Chase	Cheltenham
10th Dec	The Lowndes Lambert December Novices' Steeple Chase	Lingfield Park
17th Dec	The Betterware Cup (Handicap Steeple Chase)	Ascot
17th Dec	The Long Walk Hurdle	Ascot
26th Dec	The Rowland Meyrick Handicap Steeple Chase	Wetherby
26th Dec	The King George VI Tripleprint Steeple Chase	Kempton Park
26th Dec	The Tripleprint Feltham Novices' Steeple Chase	Kempton Park
26th Dec	The Lincolnshire National	Market Rasen
27th Dec	The Bonusprint Christmas Hurdle Race	Kempton Park
27th Dec	The Castleford Steeple Chase	Wetherby
27th Dec	The Coral Welsh National (Handicap Steeple Chase)	Chepstow
27th Dec	The Finale Junior Hurdle	Chepstow
28th Dec	The Northumberland Gold Cup Steeple Chase	Newcastle

The fiasco at the start of the 1993 Grand National is a fitting reminder to all who host major sporting events of how the little things matter and that nothing should be taken for granted. However, the sad loss of the National may have a silver lining. I am sure that the start of 1994's Grand National will receive unprecedented media attention. The event was a tragedy for all concerned but the racecourse has progressed enormously in recent years and whilst that was a black day for racing it should not colour the splendid achievements of the last decade.

Aintree is in the capable hands of **Charles Barnett**, who acts as the **Managing Director** and **Clerk of The Course**. The secretary is **Ian Ainsworth**. If you wish to make enquiries with reference to the Grand National Festival, please write to **Aintree Racecourse Co Ltd, Aintree, Liverpool L9 5AS. Tel: 051-523 2600.**

Travelling to the Course

The racecourse itself lies seven miles from the centre of Liverpool in the suburb of Aintree and approximately one mile from the end of the M58 and M57. Travellers coming up from London should expect a journey of some 213 miles. The M1/M6 double is the answer for these southerners, while visitors from north of Merseyside might care to use another motorway double; the M6 followed by the M58. North-bound travellers from Birmingham should use the M5 before joining the M6/M57. If you are a train traveller then the Euston line is the one to be on. From Liverpool, Lime Street take the Merseyrail to Aintree. The station is opposite the course entrance—very convenient. The No. 5 Bus from Lime Street also stops next to the track. Car drivers should note that there are over 230 acres in which to park your car or coach—follow the signs for your chosen enclosure and arrive early to see the non-race entertainment and avoid the queues! The cost of parking varies from £5 to £20 on the Saturday. If you prefer to fly, helicopters only please, please contact the course in advance. You will need written permission and then you will only be allowed to buzz in on the first two days of the National Meeting.

Major Races and Charges

The Aintree Festival lasts three days, during which racing of the highest quality is guaranteed. Each day features pattern races and champions and old favourites reappear every year, particularly in the National with many horses seeming to love the big day and being kept in reserve just for the occasion. Some come from the Cheltenham Festival, attempting to enhance or redeem reputations. During the meeting, racing takes place over three different courses—the Grand National course, the Mildmay course and the Hurdle course. Thursday features the John Hughes Memorial Race over the National fences, whetting the appetite for the big day. You also have a sight of the Grand National fences on the Friday, during the Martell Foxhunters Chase, and prospective star hurdlers appear in the Glenlivet Hurdle.

Aintree does not indulge in Annual Membership but tickets are available for the whole meeting. For 1994, the rates have yet to be confirmed and will not be available until late this year. On National Day 1993, entry to the County Enclosure cost £29, rising to £60 depending on whether you had a seat in the County Stand, Glenlivet Stand or a place on the County Stand roof. The Western, Central , Steeplechase and Paddock Enclosures, have accommodation for 10,000 persons, bookmaking and Tote facilities, and an arcade of shops: this costs between £5 and £16, depending on the day. Transfer badges may be purchased daily subject to availability. There is an alternative; a car and all occupants label which admits you to the Central, Western or Steeplechase Enclosures, was available at a cost of £20 last year. It is likely that there will be a small increase for all admission prices in 1994, but there are various discounts available for large parties if you contact the course well in advance. One sensible addition to Aintree's facilities is three starvision screens, giving you a life size view of the action throughout the day—essential for some if they are to see the racing given the large crowds which attend the meeting. It is also splendid to report Aintree's new fixture for November 1993. The seven race card, three of which will be televised will offer prize money in excess of £100,000 with The Crowther Homes Becher Chase over the National fences.

Racecourse Facilities

The course is pleased to announce the addition of many new snack bars in the country part of the course. This will enable the numerous course walkers to have a chomp should they feel peckish. Facilities for the disabled include viewing ramps in the County and Glenlivet Stands. Banks are represented in the form of the appropriately named National Westminster in the County. If you want to spend your cash then visit the many trade stalls, if you want to gamble with it then there are two betting shops; in the Paddock and Glenlivet Stand in addition to usual array of bookies and Tote outlets.

There are numerous opportunities for corporate entertainment and the course now offers 90 boxes and chalets, which are very well used as the National seems to be one of the most popular events for the corporate entertainers. A tented village can also provide accommodation for parties of between 20 and 100.

Aintree is continually improving itself and it is interesting to note that the catering contract has been awarded to racecourse specialists Letheby & Christopher Ltd. One catering opportunity is the Breakfast at Aintree. The Grand National runners parade early and this is followed by breakfast from 7.30 am to 9.30 am with lots of non-racing entertainment going on too. Suitably fuelled up, you should then take a wander around the course—an experience not to be missed at Aintree. There are many other events on the big day, not just horse racing. The restaurants at Aintree are the County Reserved, the Welcome Retreat and Rendezvous. Booking is required in both the County and Welcome Retreat and you can expect to pay between £14 and £20 per head.

Grand National Day 1994 will be a media spectacle beyond belief . I wouldn't bet against another dramatic incident. Let us hope for all those concerned it makes for positive reporting. Apart from any-

thing else, the racecourse and the race itself deserve it. You need a
bit of luck in the National!

Local Favourites

In Liverpool, the more luxurious hotels include **The Atlantic Tower
Hotel** 051-227 4444, which boasts two especially remarkable sights:
on the one hand, the docklands of the river Mersey and on the
other, a giant statue of one of Liverpool's best known sons, John
Lennon. Near to Lime Street stands what is the city's best known
hotel, the **Britannia Adelphi** 051-709 7200—good leisure and entertainment can be found within this Victorian edifice. A good place for a
pre-race celebration can be found at the **Trials Hotel** 051 227 1021—an
excellent atmosphere to savour here as your punting tribulations
are brought to the fore.

From a mind-boggling selection of more generally affordable establishments, prominent examples include **The Aachen House** 051-709
3477 and the **Penmenner House Hotel** (0326) 290370. If food is what
you're searching for then the city offers a broad selection. In
Liverpool there are a number of restaurants to sample and an
extremely popular bistro for lunch or dinner is **La Grande Bouffe**
051-236 3375. A stone's throw from The Cavern Club in Matthew
Street is **The Armadillo** 051-236 4123. There are a number of Chinese
restaurants in the city and the most popular is the extremely well
thought of **Far East** 051-709 6072. Lovers of French food might try
L'Oriel 051-236 5025, a pleasant place for late night dining.

The Lancashire coast yields some excellent golf courses; Royal
Liverpool, Royal Birkdale and Royal Lytham St. Annes. In Lytham,
The Clifton Arms (0253) 739898 is a thoughtfully modernised
Edwardian hotel. Further south, in Southport with its gorgeous sands
where Red Rum used to gallop, there are a number of good pubs
and a hotel of note is **The Prince of Wales** (0704) 536688. **The Bold
Hotel** (0704) 32578 also merits a pre-race inspection and for a budget
break, the **Ambassador Private Hotel** (0704) 543998 will almost certainly lead to a return visit.

It may well be that our golfing supremo might have wished to visit
Hoylake. If this was the case, then he might have been tempted to
stay at the **Bowler Hat Hotel,** Birkenhead 051-652 4931. Meanwhile, in
Aughton near Ormskirk, the **West Towers Hotel** is well thought of
locally as is the **Lord Daresbury Hotel** (0925) 67331, handily situated
near to Warrington.

For those who want to make a weekend of it, there are many places
to visit slightly further afield. The **Inn at Whitewell,** (02008) 222 at
Whitewell to the north of Aintree is a splendid ancient inn, whilst at
Knutsford, **The Cottons Hotel,** (0565) 50333 is well worth a look.
Staying in Cheshire, the **Hartford Hall Hotel,** (0606) 75711 at
Northwich offers 16th century charm along with 20th century com-
fort. Finally, if any more suggestions are needed, then turn to the
Haydock Park section for inspiration.

Ascot

A scot is an outstanding racecourse. In the Royal Meeting, it boasts the most vaunted of racing events in the world—woe betide those who consider it merely a garden party with racing tacked on. Although crowds for a mid week race meeting in winter will be a token offering in comparison, the racing is still first class and the atmosphere still special. A visit to a meeting in 1994—as ever—is thoroughly recommended. The management team is headed by **Captain the Hon E.N.C. Beaumont**, together with **Captain Jeremy Dreyer, Assistant Clerk of the Course**, while the **Queens Representative** is **Sir Piers Bengough**. A newly formed Marketing Department has been established which welcomes all enquiries concerning racedays and non-race days. Contact Carol Horler or Lisa Redfern for assistance. The authorities can be contacted at **Ascot Racecourse, Ascot, Berkshire. Tel: (0344) 22211.** For admission enquiries, telephone (0344) 24592. Car park details are dealt with on (0344) 20768.

Travelling to the Course

The racecourse lies approximately mid way between the M3 and the M4. Travellers from the west should use the M3, exiting at junction 3 or the M4, exiting at junction 10. The A329 is a possibility for people from the east. The traveller from the centre of London is advised to exit at junction 6 of the M4 and turn south through Windsor Great Park. The traffic for the big meetings is usually heavy so an early start is recommended. Indeed, so much so, that the train is often a sensible alternative. Although the station is a fairly stiff three furlongs uphill to the Grandstand, one is generally rewarded by a smooth trip from Waterloo station giving you plenty of time to peruse the form before the racing. Helicopters are permitted to land during major meetings through Hascombe Aviation Services: (0279) 814632.

Major Races and Charges

The course hosts some 23 race days and these range from high quality midweek jump meetings in winter to the heat of the King George VI and Queen Elizabeth Diamond Stakes, the Festival and Royal Ascot. The Royal Meeting is one of the social occasions of the year with the Royal Family parading down the centre of the course before the racing on all four days. The popularity of the event is staggering; picnics in the car park are always a feast and there is a constant popping of champagne corks before, and after the racing.

It should be emphasised that people who go racing merely for the binge are really missing out. The four days of equine excellence on offer are purely and simply the best in the racing year. Tickets to the Royal Enclosure are now unobtainable for the first three days, but Friday tickets are still available provided you follow the proper formalities; introductions by existing Members, that sort of thing. Admission to other enclosures is, of course, less demanding and less formal, and racegoers can still enjoy the pomp of the occasion. As a spectacle of elegance, the meeting really takes some beating, and as a race meeting there is no match!

Apart from the Royal Meeting which is at its busiest on Thursday, Gold Cup Day, the Queen Elizabeth II Stakes at the Festival and Diamond Day in July, there are some excellent jump meetings. These include the Victor Chandler Premier Steeplechase Final in January, the H & T Walker Gold Cup in November and the Betterware Day in December.

Whichever day you decide to go, there are definite advantages in becoming an Annual Member—special rooms and viewing areas are reserved for convenience, the Club dining room and Garden room are two examples. The Annual Membership is only £110 although it does not admit you to the Royal Meeting. The Ascot member may also purchase a guest's transferable badge which is priced at £55. The younger generation of racing enthusiasts should not mind the first rate junior membership price of £42 (16-24 year olds). Everyone is welcome at Ascot and you can book in advance for the Royal Meeting for the Grandstand and Paddock from January 1st. The 1994 prices are £22 for Tuesday, Wednesday and Friday and £24 for the Thursday. B e sure to book well in advance. Entrance to the Silver Ring is good value at £4.

Racecourse Facilites

Ascot's two principal enclosures are the Members' Enclosure and the Grandstand and Paddock. Both have good facilities and good viewing, prices vary according to the meeting: £11.50–£15 for the Members' Enclosure and £37.50–£39.00 in the Grandstand and Paddock except on feature days. Reductions of up to 25% are offered on certain days and there are a huge number of boxes at the course but—and here's the catch—there is a 35 year waiting list! However, they are often leased on a daily basis . Contact the race-course to make general enquiries with regard to dates, availability, size etc. (0344) 22211 or (0334) 876060. There are numerous rooms, bars and snack outlets in which to indulge. The food ranges from four-course, waitress served luncheons to hot snacks and sandwiches. Facilities for the disabled are good and there is a playground for under 11's and a creche for under 8's. A Barclays Bank is also open in the Grandstand, together with several shops.

There is no question that Ascot has a formidable reputation. A visit to Ascot is always a pleasure, win or lose, rain or shine. The challenge for the Executive as the millennium approaches is to ensure the status of Ascot as one if not the greatest racecourses in the world. It is a fitting tribute that Peter Scudamore decided to hang up his silks here. Racing names must surely come and go, Ascot, we hope, will always live on.

Local Favourites

There are numerous excellent hostelries in Berkshire's leafy countryside making ideal ports of call for a pre or post race chat. Somewhat alarmingly, we start our Ascot recommendations with a pub whose name does not quite match the racetrack's eminence: **The Slug and Lettuce** (0344) 883498 in Winkfield Row. There's fine bar food here and a cosy restaurant. Another good eating establishment located in Ascot is the **Thatched Tavern** (0344) 20874—a great atmosphere here as well.

Back in Winkfield Row, one finds **The Olde Hatchet** which is both handy and friendly and the small restaurant is well worth considering. Another pub with a restaurant is **The White Hart**—the bar snacks here are good. Farther west, and in Waltham St. Lawrence, **The Bell**, is a pub restaurant with a beautifully relaxed atmosphere, ideal for explaining the disastrous losses of the afternoons racing to one's better half!

Binfield has more than its fair share of good boozers—the **Stag and Hounds** and the **Victoria Arms** are two of several that should be sampled. Or if one happens to be heading to, or coming from, the south west perhaps you might try **The Crooked Billet** (0734) 780438 in Wokingham and there are numerous others in the surrounding villages of this pleasant part of England.

If Ascot is the Throne of racing then a similar title might befit the renowned **Waterside Inn, Bray** (0628) 20691—restaurant booking here is absolutely essential. There are many other restaurants to be tried too and one of the better ones is **The Warrener** in Littlewick Green (062882) 2803—superbly imaginative cuisine.

There are many people who will dash straight home after racing but for people wishing to stay locally, there are a number of possibilities; the **Berystede Hotel** (0344) 23311 on the Bagshot Road in Ascot, in Bagshot itself, the **Pennyhill Park Hotel** (0276) 71774 a grand country mansion which also has a commendable restaurant, **The Latymer Room** and its own nine hole golf course.

An alternative hotel which is less pricey is **The Cricketers**, also in Bagshot (0276) 73196. A little further south one arrives in Camberley. Here **The Frimley Hall Hotel** (0276) 28321 is not cheap but most comfortable.

Other places that are well worth considering include a brace of hotels in Egham, in neighbouring Surrey. Neither are particularly cheap, but both are extremely comfortable. They are **Great Fosters** (0784) 433822, an outstandingly elegant former hunting lodge with good facilities, and **The Runnymede** (0784) 436171 where a Thames-side setting adds scenic splendour—a warm favourite for racegoers. A jolly restaurant in Egham should also be noted when visiting the races or bloodstock sales; it also is in Egham and is **La Bonne Franquette** (0784) 439494. As its name implies, French cuisine is the order of the day. Maidenhead is also handy for the course and **Fredricks Hotel** (0628) 35934 is well worth a visit, (a superb restaurant here as well) as is the **Boulters Lock Hotel** on Boulters Island (0628) 21291. Continuing northwards, one finds another stylish establishment, **The Bell Inn** (0296) 630252 at Aston Clinton. Both the restaurant and hotel are outstanding—a day at Ascot, followed by an evening at the Bell would, to put it mildly, be memorable.

In Ascot itself, **The Royal Berkshire** Hotel (0344) 23322, is a superb Queen Anne mansion with excellent restaurants and is worth noting when visiting this esteemed course. Ascot is synonymous with style and if one wishes to experience the real glamour of days gone by, then a visit to the singularly magnificent **Cliveden** (06286) 68561 is in order. Former home of the Astor family, the house is now an hotel of unrivalled elegance. Another handy local favourite is **Stirrups Hotel** (0344) 882284 at Maidens Green near Bracknell, an excellent hotel and restaurant combination with prominent racing themes. A night spent in Ascot does not have to be extravagantly expensive; for affordable comfort try the **Highclere Hotel** (0344) 25220. Other ideas for the Ascot racegoer can be found in the Windsor, Sandown and Kempton sections of the book. Whatever happens at the racetrack there are numerous fine hostelries at which to celebrate or commiserate in and around Ascot—a thoroughbred racecourse.

Ayr

Sam Morshead is **Clerk of the Course** at Ayr and **Mark Kershaw** is **Manager**. They are ably assisted by **Clare Railston-Brown**. All can be contacted at **2 Whitletts Road, Ayr. Tel: (0292) 264179**. On race-days there is an off-course office at the main Eglinton Stand entrance. The management team here are as competent as any in the country and this befits Scotland's leading racecourse. A visit in 1994 is thoroughly recommended.

Travelling to the Course
The track is situated just outside Ayr and is easily accessible via the dual carriageway which by-passes the town centre. The course is actually 394 miles from London. The motorway network should see you through smoothly and the A713, the A70 and the A77 will carry you to Ayr from Glasgow on the latter stages of your journey. Whether you have travelled a long way, or from just down the road, you will appreciate the large, free car parks at the course. If the car journey sounds too much like hard work, then Glasgow Airport is only 45 minutes from Ayr while Prestwick is a mere quarter of an hour. The 800 yard airstrip in the centre of the course is only suitable for helicopters but please notify the Racecourse of your intended arrival. Trains depart from London Euston and the station at Ayr is a mile from the course where a bus will complete your journey.

Major Races and Charges
The management have been successful in attracting good commercial sponsorship at Scotland's premier racecourse and these include a number if Scotland's leading companies. There are several races to look out for, including the Stakis Scottish National in April, the Tennents Scottish Classic in July and the popular Western Meeting in September which features the Ladbroke Ayr Gold Cup. This three day meeting provides excellent racing and provides the ideal excuse for a jaunt to the superb Ayrshire coast. Pleasing news is that there is now a boxing day fixture—an ideal starter to any hogmanay celebrations later in the week.

The daily subscription rates, like most major racecourses, vary from meeting to meeting and are not that cheap. Daily Membership in 1993 in the Club Enclosure was priced from £12-£15, while entrance to the Grandstand and Paddock cost between £6 and £8. The admission fee also entitles the visitor to a complimentary racecard. If you happen to be a racing enthusiast of pensionable years or unemployed then you are welcomed to the racecourse at half price. A three day badge is available for the Western Meeting at a price of £36 for the Club, and £20 for the Grandstand. Generous reductions are available for parties of ten or more.

If you wish to become an Annual Member, a double badge together with a complimentary parking pass in the Western House Car Park will cost £145. A joining fee of £100 is also required. Reciprocal meetings can be enjoyed at Haydock Park, Newcastle, Newton Abbot and Goodwood.

23

Racecourse Facilities

The on-course catering facilities are comprehensive and they are managed by Gold Cup Hospitality who can be contacted at the racecourse or tel: (0292) 264179. The facilities range from a full tented village to the Western House which caters for parties of 60 to 200 and the Eglinton Rooms which can hold up to 400 guests. Other private rooms are also available for smaller parties and private boxes are available for daily hire in the New Craigie Stand. There are various restaurants and snack bars at Ayr including the Club Restaurant in Western House, a champagne and seafood bar in Members and fish and chips in the Carrick Stand.

The racecourse is a very complete track and there is a supervised play area for children who may not wish to watch their fathers frittering away their pocket money. Facilities for the disabled include viewing ramps and lavatories in all enclosures and ground floor bars. There are additional betting shops in the Paddock and Carrick/Craigie rings. Ayr is a fine racecourse it boasts competitive racing and some spectacular betting events, all in all an excellent racecourse.

Local Favourites

There are all manner of guest houses in and around Ayr and the local tourist board will help with any enquiries. People wishing for hotel accommodation also have a good choice when visiting West Scotland and Ayr racecourse.

The Turnberry Hotel (0655) 31000 is an extremely stylish place to stay with an array of leisure facilities, including two world-famous golf courses; the Ailsa and the Arran. Ayr itself is a busy market town which overlooks the Firth of Clyde. The coast line reveals some charming sandy beaches and attractive fishing villages. The town has many restaurants, bars and hotels but three hotels which stand out particularly are the Pickwick (0292) 260111–a converted Victorian mansion house with charming bedrooms, The Caledonian (0292) 269331 and The North Park Hotel (0292) 42336. The Ladyburn Hotel (06554) 585 at Maybole lies within easy reach of Ayr and also many of the renowned local golf courses. More golf is available in Prestwick and, as you might imagine, the town is also well placed for the nearby airport of the same name. Fairways Hotel (0292) 70396 is an excellent and convenient guesthouse. But if it's racing you are after, an ideal place to stay near the racecourse is The Carlton Toby (0292) 76811 on the Ayr road. The bedrooms are comfortable and the bars and restaurant should also be visited. Further north still, one arrives at yet another golfing delight, Troon. Two more hotels to note are The Marine Highland (0292) 314444 which overlooks the golf course and the Isle of Arran. This is a well equipped and comfortable hotel with a superb Bistro. Secondly, visit Piersland House (0292) 314747. Another, albeit modern, place to stay is the Hospitality Inn (0294) 74272 in Irvine. The bedrooms are as inviting as the restaurant The Mirage–a really imaginative menu is to be found here. A short way from Irvine in the Montgreenan Estate, near Kilwinning, lies the Montgreenan Mansion House (0294) 57733, former home of Lord Glasgow. Two miles from the village of Stewarton, amid the valleys and countryside, is the splendid Chapeltoun House Hotel (0560) 82696–quite tremendous. Our final thought is situated someway south of Ayr, Knockinaam Lodge (077681) 471 an outstanding hotel with a first class restaurant, a real favourite.

The roles of **Manager** and **Secretary** are held by **Mr. P.W. Ockleston** whilst the **Clerk of the Course** is Mr. B.R. Davies. Contact can be made with these officials by writing sto **The Racecourse Office, Chorlton Hall, Malpas, Cheshire, SY14 7ET.** Tel: (0948) 860438 Fax: (0948) 860842.

Travelling to the Course

The course is located in the Bryn y Pys estate near Bangor-on-Dee on the Welsh border and not, as some people may believe, on the north-west coast of Wales. Chester is some 15 miles to the north and Shrewsbury some 25 miles south. London is a full 150 miles away. The major routes to the course are the A525 from Stoke and the M6. The A41 to Wolverhampton, and the M54 and A51 north towards Chester, can be used to link with the M56 network of the north-west. The course itself lies on the A525, but to reach the course it is necessary to turn off the by-pass, drive through the village and onto the B5069 for Overton-On-Dee. There are also a number of minor routes, the B5130 for instance, which can be taken in preference to the 'A' roads if this is your particular wish. One thing is certain, the border countryside is quite splendid and there is plenty of free parking at the course. The A5 from Llangollen will assist people travelling from inland Wales. Wrexham and its rail network is four miles away and is part of the Euston line, as are nearby Chester and Shrewsbury. It is slightly irritating to learn however, that there are no buses to complete the journey to the course from the railway station. If you wish to make a speedy entry/departure then your helicopter is welcomed, though please contact the Clerk of the Course to arrange this. It is anticipated that racing here will follow the same pattern as in 1993, although this is dependent on Levy Board funds.

Major Races and Charges

One feature of the 1993 calendar was the McAlpine Day in April, other major racedays occur in October. If you do make the excellent decision to embark on a day at Bangor-on-Dee, then you will not be too shocked by the entrance prices that await you; £8 for the Paddock/Members' and £4 for the Course Enclosure. If you are intent on making regular visits to the track then you ought to consider an Annual Members badge: £65 (waiting list) is the asking price and it is worth noting that the members' car park has one of the best vantage points from which to view the racing. In addition to the days at Bangor, there are ten reciprocal meetings at some exceptional racecourses. If you are planning to take a party racing at Bangor, there are discounts available and these are 25 per cent for parties of 25 or more. You may also wish to know that there is a sponsors room and larger parties should note that marquees are available. The course authorities have pointed out that they will accept sponsorship for as little as £250 but, quite naturally, would prefer to have at least £1,000 per race. The sponsor's package includes a return of ten per cent of the sponsorship contribution in free badges and additional badges can be purchased at half price.

Racecourse Facilities

There is a restaurant in the Paddock enclosure and the caterers are Hughes of Welshpool, tel: (0938) 553366 if you wish to make bookings. In addition to this, there are snacks available at the bars, where you can munch roast beef sandwiches whilst watching the newly-installed, closed circuit television.

Children are admitted free and disabled people are not put to too much inconvenience as the whole course is entirely visible from the Paddock and the car parks. There are public telephones and betting shops in the Paddock enclosure and these are easily accessible, as is the whole course which delights in its country setting and splendid atmosphere. If you are seeking a fun day out in 1994 at one of Britain's idyllic national hunt courses, make sure that Bangor is on the short list.

Local Favourites

This is an area positively rife with hotels and hostelries of merit and one of the favourite establishments in the area is the **Boat Inn** (0978) 780143, whose delightful Deeside setting makes for beautiful floodlit evenings. The restaurant is open seven days a week in summer and this is an ideal place to go when racing at Bangor-on-Dee.

Some of the best places to stay are in Llangollen, home of the Eisteddfod festival of song and dance for racegoers who appreciate a fiesta as well as a flutter. **The Hand Hotel** (0978) 860303 affords an extremely comfortable stay, while in Bridge Street, **The Royal Hotel** (0978) 860202 enjoys a fine setting overlooking the River Dee. The restaurant here is good and the bar's ideal for a leisurely chat before racing. **Rhydonnen Ucha Rhewl** (0978) 860153 (please note the phone number to avoid having to pronounce it to directory enquiries) is modestly priced and can also offer shooting (after a bad day at Bangor!) and trout fishing. Three miles east of here, The **Bryn Howel Hotel** (0978) 860331 is another cosy place to stay. One of the most strikingly pretty spots is the Horseshoe Pass where the **Britannia Inn** (0978) 860144 is a pleasant place to relax. If you are merely looking for a restaurant with views over the waters of the Dee, then **Caesars** (0978) 860133, where an imaginative menu makes good use of fresh, local produce, is an excellent idea. If you prefer a wine bar, **Gales** (0978) 860089 is well thought of and ideal for an early lunch, though it has a few bedrooms too if required. Another good performer is the **Cross Lanes** (0978) 780555—extremely convenient and increasingly popular with the racing fraternity, it offers special racing breaks.

In Llanarmon Dyffryn Ceriog, **The West Arms** (069176) 665 is over 400 years old and remains a charming place to stay. **The Hand** (069176) 666 is also most welcoming, as is the **Golden Pheasant** in Llwynmawr. In Llanyblodwell, **The Horseshoe** (069181) 227 is particularly recommended for people who might wish to take in some fishing, good bar food and good value accommodation. Another Shropshire selection is **The Blacksmiths Arms**, Loppington, some way south but worth the trip. Closer to hand and appropriately titled, **The Stableyard Country Restaurant** (0978) 780642 is another fine local performer. **The Cross Foxes Inn** (0978) 780380 and **Buck House Hotel** (0978) 780555 are extremely handy for the racecourse for those of you who prefer not to travel too far to the races.

Bath

This beautiful track outside Bath is managed by Captain Toller who also acts as Secretary. He can be contacted at The Racecourse Office, Greenfields, Little Rissington, Cheltenham, Glos. GL54 2NA. Tel: (0451) 820517. Rodger Farrant is Clerk of the Course and can be contacted on (0291) 622260.

Travelling to the Course

In order to reach Bath racecourse several points should be noted: London is approximately 100 miles away; Bath 3 miles away and Bristol 10 miles yonder. The M4 route is quick but rather boring while the A4 is more interesting but can be fairly congested. Junction 18 off the M4 is the appropriate exit point. The course is well signposted from here, nestling amidst the villages of Kelston, Charlcombe, Swainswick and North Stoke. For travellers from the north and west the M5/M4 is the better route while the A46 is an alternative if time is not so pressing. If, however, time is of the essence and you decide to take a helicopter, then please land at the north end of the coach park. Car parking areas abound and are free although if you wish to park in the centre of the course, a charge of £4 is levied—this admits the driver only. All additional occupants will also be charged. Members are entitled to reserved parking. The railway station in Bath is on the main Paddington-South Wales line and Buses from the station go to the racecourse.

Major Races and Charges

The 1994 fixture list will follow a similar pattern to last year with 12 flat race meetings. The course's feature race remains the Somerset Stakes. Although crowds are always fairly good at Bath, the course is not surprisingly at its busiest during its week-end fixtures in June and July. The charge for a day's racing at Bath is £12 for a Daily Members badge, £8 if you prefer the Tattersalls and £3 or £1 if you have an inkling for the Silver Ring or the Course Enclosures. The Annual Members' badge is priced at £70.00 whilst a double badge can be ordered for £140. Junior Members (21 and under) are asked to part with £15 which is good value. Annual Members also enjoy ten reciprocal race meetings. One final point worth noting is that if you want to organise a larger gathering a 20% saving can be made on parties of 20 or more, but this only applies to the Tattersalls and Silver Ring enclosures.

Racecourse Facilities

There are a total of eleven private boxes available for hire and betting vouchers in 2 or 5 units can be pre-arranged in advance for guests. Should you wish to take a larger party, there are three rooms available for entertaining. Catering is organised by Letheby & Christopher, tel: (0242) 523203. These facilities are well used so you are advised to book well in advance. If you would prefer a marquee then these can be erected—please contact the racecourse office for further details. You can also make bookings for lunch in the Members' and Tattersalls Restaurant indeed, this is sometimes advisable. One final point that should be noted is that there is access to the stand roof which makes for an interesting vantage point.

If you are disabled or taking a disabled friend racing, then do contact the course and they will make life as easy as possible for you. Telephones can be found at various points on the course and there is a betting shop serving Tatts and the Silver Ring.

Local Favourites

Bath is a beautiful city with many good hotels and restaurants among its attractions. An excellent hotel is the **Priory** (0225) 331922, where the French cuisine is superb and the Georgian mansion exudes luxury. The **Lansdown Grove** (0225) 315891 is also charming and slightly less expensive!

Bargain seekers will also find solace at the **Laura Palace Hotel** (0225) 463815, **Orchard House Hotel** (0225) 466115 and **Paradise House Hotel** (0225) 317723. Very close to the Assembly Rooms is **Popjoys** (0225) 460494—former home of Beau Nash. Outside the town at Box, the **Clos Du Roy** (0225) 744447 at Box House is a Georgian mansion housing a first class French restaurant. Heading south out of town quickly brings you to the excellent **Combe Grove Manor** (0225) 834644.

The hotel and fine restaurant of **Ston Easton Park** (076121) 631 is one for the notebook—an outstanding pedigree well worth a detour if your funds are in plentiful supply. In Hinton Charterhouse, **Homewood Park** (0225) 723731 and **Green Lane House** (0225) 723631 are both good while in Hunstrete, **The Hunstrete House Hotel** (0761) 490490 boasts an outstanding restaurant in a distinguished Georgian manor house set in rolling parkland. Nearby Chelwood houses the first class **Chelwood House** (0761) 490730. **Lucknam Park** (0225) 742777 at Colerne near Bath is another Georgian manor house, quite unsurpassed in luxury and cuisine.

Less pricey, but extremely comfortable accommodation can be discovered in Limpley Stoke, at **The Cliffe** (0225) 723226 which has a tremendous restaurant. In Beanacre, **Beechfield House** (0225) 703700 is outstanding. In Melksham, **The King's Arms** (0225) 707272 is great value, and in Old Sodbury, **The Cross Hands** (0454) 313000 is the place to go. Last, but not least, the splendid **Hare and Hounds** (0666) 880233 at Westonbirt is an extremely popular spot for Cheltenham racegoers as well as visitors to Bath. In Winterbourne, **The Grange Hotel** at Northwoods (0454) 777333 is an elegant place to dine and in Dunkirk, the **Petty France** (0454) 238361 is also first rate. But people who are content with a bar snack or just a post-race pint may care to try any of the following gems. Hanton Wick offers the **Carpenter's Arms** (0761) 490202 a tremendous all rounder, good ales, excellent food, bar meals and restaurant, even some cosy bedrooms if required. **The George** at Norton St. Philip, is charming; **The Inn** at Freshford and **The Red Lion** at Woolverton are appealing, and returning to Hinton Charterhouse, **The Stag** has style. **The Royal Oak**, Winsford, has a delightful country setting, and nearby in Ford, **The White Hart** (0249) 782113 is a welcome pub with a pleasant restaurant and some bedrooms. Another splendid White Hart lies in the charming village of Castle Combe. Our final selection is the **Manor House** (0249) 782206—romance is in the air here and racegoers with a conscience should consider it a firm favourite for their less enthusiastic partners!

The authorities to contact at this excellent track are headed by John Cleverly, who acts as **Manager** and **Clerk of the Course, Mrs J. Parry** is the **Secretary**, and **Mrs Sheppard** is in charge of sponsorship, marketing and other bookings. Contact them at: **The Grandstand, York Road, Beverley, HU17 8QZ. Tel (0482) 867488.**

Travelling to the Course

Beverley itself is situated to the south-east of York and north-west of the Humber estuary. The southbound traveller should make best use of the A1, the A19 and the A1079. If one is travelling from the south or east make your way via the A1(M) to the M62, exit left through North Cave (junction 38) and from there pursue the B1230. From Lincolnshire, the A15 Humber Bridge followed by the A164 is probably a good each-way bet. There are a number of routes east of Beverley, should one be venturing from that part of the country, the A1035 looks to be the obvious choice. When it comes to a train journey the best idea is to go to Beverley itself, although it may be prudent to journey via York or Doncaster and thus catch a faster train. A bus service runs from Beverley station when you reach that destination. For more speedy journeys, helicopters will come in handy. If you happen to have one available you are welcome to land it in the centre of the course. Parking for your helicopter is free, as it is for your car. There is a separate car park for Members at the course.

Major Races and Charges

The fixture list will be similar to last years with 18 days booked for the season. The first July meeting is a popular occasion—well worth attending. There are also some attractive two-day fixtures in April and May. The feature races are now worth approximately £10,000 and they include the two oldest established ones; the GRP Massey Two Year Old Trophy and the Hilary Needler Trophy.

For 1993, the daily fee was £12 for admission to the Members' Enclosure (£8 for 16-21 year olds), £7 for Tattersalls and £2.50 for the Silver Ring. Party rates are offered for all enclosures except the Club Enclosure, with groups of between 10 and 30 being offered admission to Tatts for £6 and groups of more than 30 for £5.50. Members at Beverley paid £70 for a single badge in 1993. An Associate Membership was £110 and Junior Members could purchase discounted subscriptions of £40 per annum. Under-16s are admitted free of charge provided they are accompanied. No decision has yet been taken as to whether prices will increase in 1994.

Racecourse Facilities

The main Grandstand has now been extended to form a larger Club Dining Room with a suite of three Entertaining Boxes which may be taken as one to accommodate a large party. On the second floor there is a new box suitable for parties of up to 50 in addition to the four original boxes. Prices are available on application to Mrs Sheppard at the Racecourse Office. No bookings are required for the restaurants but should you need to make any catering enquiries then Jacksons, the racecourse caterers, tel: (0482) 632361, are the chaps to contact. If you really want to push the boat out, the racecourse staff will be happy to organise the construction of a marquee.

There are three telephones at the course—vital for placing those bets should you be out of cash as there is no bank here. There are however two betting shops, in Tattersalls and the Silver Ring should you wish to lighten your purse, or hopefully add to it.

Local Favourites

Beverley is a flourishing market town surrounded by some outstanding countryside. To the north, The Wolds and the North Yorkshire Moors. To the west, the Pennines and to the east, the ragged coastline. The delightful 17th century **Beverley Arms Hotel** (0482) 869241 is an extremely comfortable inn in which to stay and a good place from which to explore.

Aside from the Beverley Arms, **The White Horse**, better known as Nellies, has a superbly traditional pub atmosphere. **The Kings Head** is also a good pub to put the racegoer in the right spirit before racing—or equally after the racing is over as the latter has some satisfactory bedrooms. Nearby, a number of welcoming hotels include **The Tickton Grange Hotel** (0401) 543666 a superb Georgian country house two miles from Beverley. Slightly further afield in Driffield one finds **The Bell Hotel** (0377) 46661, a pleasant inn in the market place—ideal for a post race bar snack or dinner in the restaurant. Alternatives to the south of Beverley include **The Rowley Manor** (0482) 848248 at Little Weighton—a splendid parkland setting with a particularly relaxing bar, ideal for studying overnight declarations in style. There is further comfort to be found with another manor, this time in Willerby, **The Willerby Manor** (0482) 652616 A mention here also for the **Grange Park Hotel** (0482) 656488, just to the south of Beverley—exceptionally well-equipped and comfortable. For seafarers, comfort and a sight of the sea can be found at **Hotel Seaforth** (0964) 532616 at nearby Hornsea. If you are lured into Hull then an excellent restaurant in which to have a bite is **Ceruttis** (0482) 28501, a harbourside spot with first rate seafood. Another harbourside setting for **The Marina Port Hotel** (0482) 225221 ideal for people with a nautical, as well as an equine, bent.

A whole host of pubs are to be found . In Brandesburton, **The Dacre Arms** appeals—note the Wensleydale Ploughmans, while in Bishop Burton, **The Altisidora** is a friendly pub with a delightful setting. The pub takes its name from the 1813 St. Leger winner. In Kirkburn, **The Queens Head** is most attractive and offers good food. In South Dalton, **The Pipe and Glass** has great character and serves good food while in Market Weighton, **The Londesborough Arms** (0430) 872214 also has bedrooms. **The Triton** in Sledmere (0377) 86644 is very popular and ideally situated for **Sledmere House**—well worth a post race inspection. Before we leave the area we should pay special mention to the **Manor House** (0482) 881645 at Walkington. The hotel is superbly relaxing and the restaurant has already made an excellent impression—one for the notebook for those of you considering a trip to Beverley races in 1994.

The course is run by **Pratt & Co.**, and the **Clerk of the Course** is **Cliff Griggs**. Their address is **11 Boltro Road, Haywards Heath, Sussex. Tel: (0444) 441111.** On racedays they can be contacted on (0273) 603580.

Travelling to the Course

The course is situated in the region of Kemptown, high up on White Hawk Hill. In order to get to this eastern suburb of Brighton one will have a 60 mile journey from the capital. The A23 and the M23 are the best roads out of London. Travellers from the north of London will find the M25 ring road to be of assistance; the A27 and the A259 sandwich the course and eventually run alongside the coast serving both east and west bound racegoers. The Brighton-London Victoria line is most efficient and there is a bus service from the station to the racecourse on race days. The Brighton / Hove buses all stop near the course too. Another point with regard to your journey which should be of help is that there is plenty of space for car parking which is provided free. Helicopters and light aircraft are not able to land here which may be an inconvenience to some.

Major Races and Charges

It is expected that racing will follow the same pattern in 1994 as last year. Eighteen fixtures are in the pipeline and the highlight of the year is the three-day August meeting.

Prices are likely to remain the same for the 1994 season when admission to the Members at Brighton cost £11 while the price for Tattersalls was £8 and £3.50 for the Silver Ring. Annual Membership was priced at £100 which included free car parking and reciprocal meetings at Epsom, Goodwood, Lingfield, Folkestone and Hickstead. If you are planning a group outing you will be entitled to a discount of 20% off parties of 20 or more.

Racecourse Facilities

Parties of between 20 and 200 can be entertained in various places around the racecourse and private boxes can cater for up to 200 guests. There are also sites for marquees which can hold 500 guests comfortably. Bookings for any of these facilities should be made through Pratt and Co. Race sponsors are offered a free box and admission tickets. The number of tickets you receive depends on the amount you give as sponsorship—the more you pay the more you get! There are also numerous bars throughout the course as well as a more formal restaurant, bookings for which can be made by telephoning (0273) 602987. Prices range between £10 and £15 and the caterers are the racecourse experts Letheby and Christopher, tel: (0273) 602987.

There are no banks on site, but there is a recently refurbished betting shop located in Tatts. Facilities for children are available at summer meetings. Sadly, nothing is done for the disabled at Brighton—they must make their own way to a vantage point.

Pratt & Co now handle four of the racecourses in Southern England; Fontwell, Folkestone, Brighton and Plumpton and as administrators they do a splendid job. I am also pleased to say that sponsorship and marketing opportunities are now available at each of the above venues. This will surely prove a popular option for many south coast based companies, particularly if economic confidence begins to return in 1994.

Local Favourites

Perhaps it's the sea air, which makes so many organisations choose Brighton for their annual conference. Whether you are a company man or a single woman the following hotels should be of interest. **The Old Ship** (0273) 29001 is well known for catering for business or pleasure, an intimate elegance coupled with a central location makes it an obvious choice. Other centrally located hotels include **Topps** (0273) 729334 where the welcome is friendly, the prices reasonable and the restaurant **Bottoms** is recommended. Away from the hurly burly of the sea front, one finds another comfortable hotel, **The Courtlands** (0273) 731055. A modern hotel particularly well liked for conferences and business is **The Bedford Hotel** (0273) 29744, which is able to take advantage of the facilities of another splendid sea front hotel, **The Brighton Metropole** (0273) 775432—note the splendid restaurant, **Starlit Room**. Another good value hotel which boasts a tremendous restaurant is **The Twenty One** (0273) 686450. Perhaps the most renowned of all the Brighton hotels is **The Grand** (0273) 21188. Grand!

The waters of Brighton stretch round the coast and meet with Hove. Here a number of good hotels can be found. The best is **The Dudley** (0273) 736266—an elegant and extremely well appointed hotel, whilst **The Alexandra** (0273) 202722 is a listed Regency building offering good value weekend breaks.

If you are not content with the seaside offerings in Brighton, then Eastbourne is an elegant and slightly more tranquil alternative. Good value accommodation is plentiful; examples include **The Bay Lodge Hotel** (0323) 32515 and **Hotel Mandalay** (0323) 29222. **Byrons** (0323) 20171 is an excellent restaurant making great use of some delightfully fresh produce; fish is the obvious selection. A busy pub to note for its tremendous views is The **Devil's Dyke** at Devil's Dyke on the downs above the town. For some really good food, the **Tottington Manor Hotel Restaurant** (0903) 815757 at Edburton is also worth a visit, as is the extremely comfortable **Avisford Park Hotel** (0243) 551215 at Walberton; well worth the extra journey for those who enjoy excellent food and sporting facilities. A final selection that should not be overlooked is **Amberley Castle** (0798) 831992—medieval style and 20th century comfort. We would strongly recommend a hotel of real character, **Ockenden Manor** (0444) 416111—a Travelling The Turf favourite. Brighton has a whole host of attractions for the children if mother or father wants to punt in peace. As the 1990's begin to stretch its legs let us hope that Brighton racecourse enjoys its fair share of customers.

At Carlisle, **Johnnie Fenwicke-Clennell** is the **Clerk of the Course**, **Mr T.E. Robinson** the **Managing Director** and **Mrs Ann Bliss** the **Racecourse Secretary**. The course address is **Blackwell House, Carlisle, Cumbria**. Tel: **(0228) 22973**. The Secretary's Office is at **Grandstand Office, Durdar Road, Cumbria, CA2 4TS**. Tel: **(0228) 22973**.

Travelling to the Course

Carlisle is a good 300 miles from the capital. However, it is easy to reach for racegoers from all areas of the country. The M6 is the motorway to follow, exiting at Junction 42 and then follow the signs to the course. The A69 Carlisle-Newcastle Road is the best route from the North East whilst people from areas west of Carlisle should travel on the A595 or the A596. The racecourse is 2 miles south west of the town and the No 66 bus from Carlisle will deposit you at the course. From London, Carlisle bound trains depart from Euston station or alternatively jump on a King's Cross train and change at Newcastle-Upon-Tyne. If you are making the trip by car you will find some 20 acres of grass on which to park your motor. Aviators please note that Carlisle Airport is some eight miles away. Helicopters can land on the racecourse provided prior arrangements have been made.

Major Races and Charges

The Cumberland Plate and the Carlisle Bell, two of the course's major races, are steeped in tradition and both prizes are keenly sought after by owners and trainers alike. In 1993 the daily admission charge to the Members' was £12 on Saturdays and bank holidays and £10 at all other times. Entry to Tattersalls was set at £6. Annual Membership is £75 whilst a double badge is a good buy at £115, although there is a waiting list. Eight reciprocal meetings are also laid on for the Carlisle Member. People under 21 will be glad to know that membership is priced at £50. Price structures for 1994 had not been finalised at the time of writing.

Party organisers will be pleased to hear of the following, albeit rather complicated, arrangements. Parties in excess of 10 but under 30 save £1 per badge to the Tattersalls, plus a free badge for every 10 purchased. Larger parties can save £1.50 per badge and secure two free admissions.

Racecourse Facilities

Facilities at Carlisle include the Club Restaurant (please book) and Tattersalls Cafeteria. There is also a refurbished bar and restaurant in the old Tote building—the very first Tote in operation, beating Newmarket by 15 minutes! With regard to more private facilities, three rooms are available in which 20 to 100 guests can be entertained at a cost of £80 minimum. Marquees can also be organised and there is a large hall which seats between 250–300 people.

Enquiries with regard to on-course catering should be addressed to the secretary, Mrs. Ann Bliss. Expect to pay between £5 and £12.50

for lunch. Romfords (tel: (0434) 688 864) also supply the catering for the cafeteria and snack bars and their food is of a very high standard. Children are admitted free of charge to the racecourse, if accompanied by an adult and there is a free creche provided for fixtures which take place in the school holidays. They will also be delighted to hear of the imminent opening of a new playground at the course. Facilities for disabled racegoers are most considerate at Carlisle with two viewing ramps, wash rooms and easily accessible bars. There is also a trackside car park and picnic area where a levy of £3 per car (£5 on Saturdays and bank holidays) is requested. There is a betting shop in the Paddock area but no banks are in operation on the course so make sure you have enough money to see you through the day. This friendly racecourse is well positioned between Lakeland and the Borders and those of us seeking a day's racing while touring beautiful countryside will find Carlisle a welcoming port of call.

Local Favourites
In Carlisle itself, one finds three possible candidates for a quiet and comfortable night. Firstly, the Edwardian **Crown and Mitre** (0228) 25491 in English Street near the city centre and secondly, the **Swallow Hilltop Hotel** (0228) 29255. This hotel is convenient for the A6 and may act as a good spot for business meetings. Lastly in Carlisle, visitors should note the **Cumbria Hotel** (0228) 31951 in Court Square.

North of Carlisle lies Rockcliffe where a good pub for a snack is **The Crown and Thistle**; the village guards the mouth of the River Eden and is particularly convenient for the A74. Another riverside setting is provided by **The Crosby Lodge Hotel** (0228) 573618 in Crosby-on-Eden. This hotel enjoys a pastoral setting and also has a superb restaurant. East of the city, is another outstanding place at which to stay, a rambling old inn, **The String of Horses** (0228) 70297, in Faugh. This hotel is not only renowned for excellent fresh food but also for some quite extraordinarily lavish bedrooms. Returning to the waters of the Eden and on this occasion to Warwick-on-Eden, **The Queen's Arms** (0228) 560699 is yet another inn of character. Here you will find a jolly little restaurant and some comfortable bedrooms. In Talkin, as well as a good golf course, one finds **The Hare and Hounds Inn** (0697) 73456—this is an ideal spot for an early evening stroll to work up a good appetite as the inn is surrounded by some beautiful fells.

A little farther north lies Brampton. Three thoughts here; on the one hand **Tarn End**, at Talkin Tarn (0697) 72340 is a good restaurant which also provides homely accommodation and secondly, **Farlam Hall Hotel** (0697) 746234 which is definitely the pick of the paddock, a splendid 17th century manor house in gorgeous grounds and a grand restaurant as well—a really classical performer in every way. **Edmond Castle** (0228) 70651 is another hotel well worth visiting here. One other restaurant that is strongly recommended is **Fantails** at Wetheral (0228) 60239 where excellent cooking accompanies friendly service—the perfect double. A nearby hotel to note is **The Crown** (0228) 61888, a coaching inn with first rate facilities. The surrounding hostelries and friendly people coupled with a well balanced calendar of sporting fixtures make a visit to Carlisle racecourse a priority for those who have not enjoyed the pleasure.

Cartmel offers festival racing with a fun 'shirtsleeve' atmosphere which makes a welcome contrast to some of the country's more 'stiff upper lip' racecourses. It is immensely popular and a thoroughly successful part of Britain's racing scene. In 1994 there will be a number of new faces at Cartmel with **Jonnie Fenwicke-Clennell** acting as **Clerk of the Course** and Tom Banister the **General Manager**. They can be contacted at **Cartmel Racecourse, Nr. Grange-over-Sands, Cumbria**, or at **Coniston Hall, Coniston Cold, Gargrave, BD23 4WB. Tel: (05395) 36340.**

Travelling to the Course

The road to the course meanders through the hills of the Lake District. The most direct routes into the area from the north and south are via the M6, exiting at junction 36 for the A590. From the north east, the A69 a is good bet whereas the A590 will assist east-bound racegoers. A word of warning, leave plenty of time if travelling by car, especially on bank holidays. The British Rail Euston line which stops at Cark in Cartmel and Grange Over Sands is your best bet if you prefer to use public transport. Parking facilities are separated into two categories: cars parked in the Paddock Parks are charged £5 but there is restricted space in here while the Course Area is free. Coaches are restricted to the latter area. Helicopters can land here too but only by prior arrangement with the Clerk.

Major Races and Charges

Cartmel racecourse has a most attractive natural setting. Until the early 1960's, racing was held here only once a year, on Spring Bank Holiday Monday. Since then it has been increased to five days with the Spring Bank Holiday weekend and the August Bank Holiday providing the main and the most popular meetings. Racegoers come from all over the country to enjoy the olde worlde atmosphere of racing here. After all, what could be better than to spend five days at Cartmel in May with the two non-race days being spent in the surrounding countryside of the Lake District? If that does not appeal to you then all I can say is you shouldn't be reading this book!.

The subscription rate for Annual Membership in 1993 was £70. This gives the member two badges (a single badge costs £35) and a car pass, plus access to a special viewing area. Demand is always high for these badges and as a result the Members' Enclosure has no Daily Members. The Paddock Enclosure was priced at £8 and the Course, £3.00, while accompanied children under 16 are admitted free. A 20 per cent discount is given to parties of 10 or more. There are also reduced entrance charges in all areas for senior citizens. There are continued improvements elsewhere at the track, 12 boxes have been built and a back stairway enables Members to gain easier access to their own vantage point. Despite the changes, the Manager's ultimate policy is to foster the pleasant atmosphere and character of the racecourse.

Racecourse Facilities

The race meeting however, brings more than horses to this rural setting. A traditional fun fair is in attendance and marquees can be provided for parties on request. Picnickers are positively encouraged here too although there is a catering marquee in the Paddock. Enquiries with regards to on-course catering should be directed to Romfords, The Boundary, Langley, Haydon Bridge, Northumberland, tel: (0434) 84315. Disabled racegoers have their own viewing area at Cartmel. Other public facilities include telephones (for those all important bets) and a betting shop in the Paddock.

Local Favourites

Not surprisingly, there is no shortage of hotels in this part of the world and a little guidance cannot go amiss. In Cartmel itself, **Aynsome Manor** (05395) 36653 is a super old manor house which makes a good base while **The King's Arms** holds an imposing position in the square. In Cartmel Fell, one finds the absolutely outstanding **Mason's Arms** (04488) 486, always a friendly crowd and some excellent cooking—watch the foreign beers though, they bring on nasty hangovers when mixed with our own blue blooded brews—just as well it also has bedrooms! In Heversham, **The Blue Bell** (05395) 62018 offers excellent value bar lunches and some accommodation. A little further west in Lowick Green, **The Farmer's Arms** (022986) 376 is a pub with similar facilities and an excellent dining room as well.

Two packs of **Hounds** and a couple of **Hares,** one at Bowland Bridge and another at Levens, both have good value bar food. **The Swan** (05395) 31681 at Newby Bridge comes with an enviable reputation and is less than five miles from the racecourse. Two other pleasant establishments with accommodation include the **Queen's Head** (05394) 32174, Troutbeck, north of Windermere which also yields **The Mortal Man** (05394) 33193 with its particularly friendly welcome and first class cooking. Bowness-on-Windermere offers two appealing restaurants: the **Gilpin Lodge** (09662) 2295 which has a beautiful situation two miles out of the town—bedrooms here are first class, and **Jackson's Bistro** (09662) 6264—you must try this, it really is delightful. In Windermere, there are some spectacular establishments: **Rogers** (09662) 4954 is a relaxing French restaurant—well worth trying. At the **Miller Howe** (09662) 2536 first class cuisine, breathtaking views and some really special accommodation make this a favourite in the most challenging of fields. Another good runner is the **Langdale Chase** (05394) 32201. There is a cottage available there and this makes it an ideal spot for a party of friends taking in a long weekend. Further good hotels can be found in and around Underbarrow overlooking the Lyth Valley. In Crook, **The Wild Boar** (09662) 5225 is a comfortable place to stay. Another absolute pearl of an hotel is to be found in Grasmere; **Michael's Nook** (09665) 496 is delightfully cosy and conjures up exceptional cooking. Grasmere also offers **The White Moss House** Hotel (09665) 295—another gem. A similarly favourable critique can be made of the **Wordsworth Hotel** (09665) 592. Cumbria has a whole host of outstanding hotels and what better excuse could one have for visiting than Cartmel Races?

The Managing Director, Secretary and Clerk of the Course for flat racing at Catterick is John Sanderson, a well known figure in both British and international racing circles. The winter jumping programme is looked after by Charles Enderby. The address for all correspondence is The Racecourse, Catterick, Richmond, North Yorkshire. Tel: (0748) 811478, fax:(0748) 811082.

Travelling to the Course

Catterick is very convenient for the north and southbound traveller; the A1 is the route to follow and Catterick lies a short distance from the junction of the A66 (Scotch Corner) on the east side of the Great North Road. Travellers from York should take the A59 west until they reach the A1 and then drive north. From another nearby racecourse town—Thirsk (south-east), the A170 and the A61 lead to the A1. By rail the nearest station is at Darlington which is on the line from London's Kings Cross. With regard to parking there are two options. The reserved car park costs £2 a car, though on ground adjacent to the racecourse there is free parking for both cars and coaches.

Major Races and Charges

The course has a full calendar of 26 days with at least one meeting in every month of the year. A number of distinguished trainers have yards nearby and consequently, many a good nag has been sent up here in the past. Smaller country courses offer outstanding value for money in terms of sponsorship and promotion, often attracting as much media coverage as the big tracks. As we have already mentioned, Catterick is well situated and eager to attract commercial support. With Leeds, Bradford, York, Newcastle, Teeside and Manchester fairly close by, it is surprising that more local businessmen have not taken the opportunity to utilise Catterick as a medium for publicity. A quick glance at the Catterick fixture list will indicate that the course holds a good mixture of jump and flat racing with Wednesdays and Saturdays the two most popular days. With the North Yorkshire Moors so close by, Catterick is an ideal place to escape to when a major gamble has gone astray. Alternatively, the Dales and Fells offer an outstanding number of small hotels and pubs in which to celebrate that first victory as owner,punter,trainer, jockey or even sponsor.

If you should wish to support Catterick racecourse by becoming an Annual Member, then in 1993 a joint husband and wife badge was good value at £114, while a single badge was £67. Juniors between the ages of 16 and 21 years were asked £33—excellent value. By comparison, £10 was asked for joining the Members' for a single meeting. The Tattersalls was slightly better value at £6, while the Course Enclosure was priced at £2. All children under 16 are admitted free when accompanied by an adult. There are also two car parks, one is free, the other is £2 a day, or £26 for an annual pass. If people want to organise parties then Catterick is quite definitely a place to do it. There is a £1.50 reduction for Tattersalls if as few as 10 people get together and one free pass for every tenth person. The course also offers reciprocal racedays, as well as cricket at Headingley.

Racecourse Facilities

The facilities at the racecourse are on the up and although there are no boxes at the course hopefully their addition will not be too long in coming. There are two private rooms which have space for between 30 and 60 guests to sit down or 80 people to enjoy a more simple buffet and these can be hired at very reasonable rates. There are several bars available for liquid sustenance between races to suit everyone. There is a self service restaurant adjacent to the track and a dining room situated in the Paddock. The Club was recently refurbished and 1993 has seen the opening of a new bar and betting shop in the Tattersalls enclosure.

There are a number of experienced personalities involved with the running of the course and I wouldn't mind making a small wager that facilities will continue to improve here dramatically in the 1990's. If you enjoy your racing in either the height of summer or the depths of winter, don't forget that, in racing parlance, Catterick is an improving type. Catterick has fondly christened itself 'the course with character'—I have no doubt that in this instance the character will show through extremely well.

Local Favourites

In this area, Middleham stands out as prime racing country with some excellent local establishments. Most notably, the **Millers House Hotel** (0969) 22630 in Middleham which offers quality accommodation and a restaurant of note. Special racing breaks are also on offer here. **The Bridge Inn** (0325) 350106 in Stapleton is not residential, but has a good pub restaurant. **The Black Swan** (0969) 22221 in Middleham is another must for all race-goers, but beware the journey—through deepest Wensleydale sheeps eyes, rather than cats eyes light your way. Another training area is Richmond and here **The Castle Tavern** (0748) 823187 should be noted, fine ales and some good home cooking. In East Layton nearby **The Fox Hall Inn** (0325) 718262 is a good value place to stay and the restaurant is also worth a visit. **The George** at Piercebridge is a good pub, as is the convenient **Farmers Arms** but you must remember these are only a small selection of some 400 public houses to be found in North Yorkshire. Moulton also reveals a really excellent port of call. **The Black Bull Inn** (0325) 377289 has particularly good fish and for loved ones, the carefully restored Brighton Belle Pullman Car is ideal for gruesome twosomes. In fact, if you are in the dog house this establishment is a great place to visit. A short journey south reveals Northalerton and yet more good accommodation in the form of **Porch House** (0609) 779831.

Scotch Corner also provides a pleasing hotel which is handy for a number of courses, **The Scotch Corner Hotel** (0748) 850900 is the location in question. A particularly well thought of alternative is **The Vintage Hotel** (0748) 824424. Both hotels are only minutes away from the A1. Much of this area is somewhat remote but that is part of its charm. What could be better than a day in the country of North Yorkshire and an evening aside the fire in one of its many friendly hostelries.

There are few sporting occasions which offer more anticipation and excitement than the National Hunt Festival. There are few, if any, racecourses that are so expertly run. Much of this credit must go to the racecourse Managing Director, Edward Gillespie. His fantastic enthusiasm and dedication are a credit to any industry and despite many potentially ruinous incidents the meeting and indeed the entire fixture always seems to improve. Let us hope for the good of the course that he never loses this enthusiasm and let us hope for the good of the industry that more racecourses are run with the same umpf and imagination. In 1994, as with any year I recommend a visit to this jewel of British Sporting arenas

Edward Gillespie and Major Philip Arkwright, Clerk of the Course, can be contacted at Cheltenham Racecourse, Prestbury Park, Cheltenham, Gl50 4SH. Tel: (0242) 513014. For advanced bookings for the Festival, ring (0242) 226226.

Travelling to the Course
If you are planning to visit these gorgeous Gloucestershire gallops then you are advised to take the train. The main line service leaves Paddington and arrives at Cheltenham Lansdown where a bus is available to take you to the racecourse. However, many people naturally prefer the independence of the motor car. London is 95 miles away and the course is a mile from Cheltenham's busy town centre. Traffic from the A40 is advised to turn right at the lights near Andoversford which is sign- posted for Stow-on-the-Wold and aim for Winchcombe. People who prefer the motorway will note the M4 and the M5 routes, the former should be exited at junction 15 and the latter at junction 4 in order to make the best ground towards Prestbury Park. If you are coming from the north then there are now big improvements to your route, allowing you to by-pass Evesham. Whichever direction you approach from, you will find AA signs to guide you to the racecourse. If people wish to travel by helicopter, inform the course in advance and you will be welcomed. There is parking for 14,000 cars—all free except during the Festival, when the charge is £5.

Major Races and Charges
Rates of admission vary depending on the day, but for the 1993/4 season prices will vary from £12.00 to £35.00 for the Members' Enclosure and £10.00 to £15.00 for the Tattersalls Enclosure. For the Foster's Enclosure, entrance is £3.00 to £5.00. A 20% discount is offered to parties in Tattersalls and Foster's Enclosures at Cheltenham. Because of the huge crowds at the festival you are advised, when travelling by car, to arrive early and to listen to the traffic reports on the Festival radio (1584 khz). Above all, be patient!

The National Hunt Festival with its massive crowds reflects the interest in this superb sporting meeting—gems in the crown include the Tote Cheltenham Gold Cup, the Queen Mother Champion Chase and the Smurfit Champion Hurdle. Cheltenham offers a feast of racing in an excellent atmosphere and amidst a perfect setting. Other meetings to note include the Mackeson Gold Cup in November, and in December the Arlington Bula Hurdle and the Triple Print Gold Cup. It should however be noted that the smaller meetings still provide good sport but without the crush.

Annual Membership should definitely be considered here. £125 is the asking price plus a £90 enrolment fee for new Members. Seniors (over 65 years) and Juniors (under 25 years) are charged a £65 and £75 entrance fee respectively. Membership lasts for the season (Oct.–May). Members' privileges include priority booking of seats for the National Hunt Festival and in 1994, there will be no ballot for the Festival unlike recent years. Priority bookings can be made from the first meeting of the season at the course, or in writing a few days afterwards. You are strongly advised to book in advance.

Racecourse Facilities

The course is always superbly well turned out. Facilities include over 100 boxes which are let on an annual basis. However, these can be obtained for a day at a cost of £250-£500 (except during the National Hunt Festival) accommodating between 12 and 24 persons. Several rooms are also available for private parties numbering between 40 and 200 people. There are sites for marquees if required and the ever expanding metropolis of the tented village at the Festival is a pleasure to be a part of. For people who prefer their own catering, stick to the car parks and organise your own picnics—thoroughly recommended if the weather happens to be good—tho' this can be a bit of a long shot. There is a good restaurant, The Gold Cup Restaurant for which booking is advised; tel: (0242) 523203. Other restaurants include the Mandarin and Sea Pigeon, plus a carvery and of course, Barry Copes' excellent seafood bar. The fish and chips in Tatts is a recommended outsider. A new addition to the stable is the L'Escargot Bar behind Tatts. This I imagine, is named after the great chaser rather than the well known French dish. All in all, there are over 90 food outlets during the Festival so you shouldn't go hungry. There is sometimes a tented village at the larger meetings and The Guinness Village at the festival is a pleasure to be a part of. At smaller meetings there is less choice but the crowds are far smaller and the racecourse is a real pleasure to visit.

Although children are admitted free (except for the Festival) there are no special facilities for them but I understand they are on the agenda for the course enclosure. Disabled racegoers are well looked after with special areas overlooking the parade ring and on the lawn in the Club. There are three betting areas for off track betting and overall one must say that Cheltenham is a most complete racecourse. There is no doubt that Cheltenham has like all racecourses been effected by the recession but it has soldiered on and continues to improve. It is an example to all in the industry and with Irish winners a plenty at last years festival there will be many eyes a smiling in anticipation of success at Prestbury Park.

Local Favourites

Cheltenham never stages a bad day's racing, though sometimes the weather is extraordinarily bitter. However, this is a natural hazard of the winter game and certainly at Cheltenham one has the blessing of some really first class accommodation and drinking haunts in which to shelter before, or after (preferably both) a day at the races.

Cheltenham itself owes its growth to the discovery of a mineral spring in 1715. Today, the Pittville Pump Room dispenses the only drinkable alkaline water in Britain which may make a pleasant change from the numerous bottles of whisky, champagne and of course Guinness. The best known hotels in town are **The Queen's** (0242) 514724, scene of many a fine Irish celebration after racing, and **The Cheltenham Park Hotel** (0242) 222021 which is actually two miles out of Cheltenham, set in nine acres of gorgeous grounds. There are numerous other small hotels and guest houses too, a quick phone call to the local tourist authority is always a good idea. A charming Georgian hotel is **Prestbury House** (0242) 529533. Some ideas for dinner after racing include **Redmond's** (0242) 672017 at Malvern View. This is an outstanding restaurant and there are also six appealing rooms—definitely a warm favourite. **Le Champignon Sauvage** (0242) 573449. is excellent too. Neither establishment is cheap but both provide excellent excuses for a post-race celebration of major proportions. Less expensive dining and an appealing Chinese restaurant can be found at the **Mayflower** (0242) 522426. So many people now make a pilgrimage to Cheltenham that we will endeavour to comment on as many large hotels as possible. In the town itself, **The Golden Valley Thistle Hotel** (0242) 232691 is modern but most comfortable. A Victorian building houses **The Wyastone Hotel** (0242) 516654, cheaper than average but still of a good standard. It cannot be emphasised strongly enough to book well in advance if you wish to stay in close proximity to the racecourse. Some people stay as far away as Bath, Stratford or Hereford while others commute daily to the Festival. Naturally, it is easier to find accommodation outside the March extravaganza but plans should not be made at the last minute if you can possibly avoid it.

It should also be emphasised that although opulence and extravagance are not an uncommon feature of this neck of the woods, cost conscious visitors are by no means forgotten and two excellent establishments are **Lypiatt House** (0242) 224994 and **Allards Guesthouse** (0242) 862498.

There are also some super restaurants in the better hotels clustered around Cheltenham. In Shurdington, **The Greenway** (0242) 862352 has a lovely rural setting and is a really first class hotel in which to stay. Elsewhere., in nearby Southam The **Hotel de la Bere** (0242) 37771 is convenient for the racecourse and there are good leisure facilities here while in Bishops Cleeve, **The Cleeveway House** (0242) 672585 is a striking Cotswold building with an outstanding restaurant and some very reasonable accommodation too. For the more frugal, the neighbouring **Old Manor House** (0242) 674127 will satisfy most requirements. Upton St. Leonards brings us **Hatton Court** (0452) 617412, an elegant hotel in Cotswold stone with good views over the Severn Valley.

One option when racing at Cheltenham is to head off into the nearby Cotswolds. The Cotswolds are an ideal dumping ground in which to discard one's non-racing partners—a wealth of country houses, galleries and antique shops should keep them quiet. Some places to catch an hour or twos kip are any one of three hotels located in Broadway. **The Lygon Arms** (0386) 852255 exudes charm and style and the Great Hall which acts as the restaurant is superb— expect a fairly large bill though. **The Dormy House** (0386) 852711 is another excellent hotel/restaurant double. The **Broadway Hotel** (0386) 852401 is a beautiful Tudor hotel, complete with minstrels gallery, and nearby **Collin House** (0386) 858354 is excellent -a good each way selection without a doubt. Another favourite here is the **Hunters Lodge** (0386) 853247—a charming restaurant. A perfect example of a Cotswold manor is the **Buckland Manor** (0386) 852626 in Buckland—once again luxurious rooms accompany an outstanding restaurant. In Upper Slaughter another elegant building, **The Lords of the Manor** (0451) 20243 can be found; superbly comfortable and a fine place for breakfast. Moreton-in-Marsh, riddled with antique shops, is also the home of **The Manor House Hotel** (0608) 50501 another for your shortlist.

Although many people are able to take in all three days of the Festival, some have to make do with a quick visit. Places to stop afterwards include a number of quaint villages which inevitably yield a fair selection of boozers. In Colesbourne, **The Colesbourne Inn** is a good stop off point for a pre-race breakfast. **The Green Dragon** near Cowley is a super place for bar food. Filling bar snacks and some accommodation are also good at the popular **Mill Inn** (0242) 89204 in Withington, a town which also houses the charming **Halewell Close** (0242) 89238. A pleasant Whitbread house in Painswick is **The Royal Oak**, a good idea if you're heading for Tetbury. There are a number of worthy hotels to consider in this area. In Tetbury itself one finds **The Snooty Fox Hotel** (0666) 52436 which is a welcoming coaching inn and **The Close** (0666) 52272 in Tetbury is also extremely promising. A little way outside the town one finds one of the areas most outstanding hotels and restaurants, **Calcot Manor** (0666) 89355—really tremendous.

Further afield in Westonbirt, **The Hare and Hounds** (0666) 88233 is popular with Cheltenham racegoers. People bolting up the M5 may pause for thought as well as a swift one at Twyning where the **Village Inn** is a pleasant village pub. Travellers on the A46 should note **The Mount** at Stanton—more good value food and a fine collection of racing prints.

There are a number of other very fine hotels to consider. Some of the best include the outstanding **Corse Lawn House Hotel**, Corse Lawn (0452) 78479. This is tremendously well run but inevitably packed for Cheltenham—its restaurant is also excellent and well worth booking months in advance. Further away in Blockley, near Moreton-in-Marsh, **Lower Brook House** (0386) 700286 is a delightful Cotswold inn. Cirencester offers two inns of note; **The Fleece Hotel** (0285) 68507 and the 14th Century **King's Head** (0285) 3322. **Stratton House Hotel** (0285) 61761 on the Gloucester Road also has pre-race appeal. Crossing the county to the Forest of Dean and Coleford, try **The Speech House** (0594) 22607—intimately pleasing.

Outside Cirencester in Ewen, one finds the **Wild Duck Inn** (0285) 77364 a fine old inn. Another nearby roost in a welcoming market place hotel, **The Bull** (0285) 712535 can be found in Fairford. **The Hyperion House Hotel** (0285) 712349 is also a pleasant stayer, it is named, as you might expect, after the Derby winner, not so appropriate for Cheltenham, but most certainly a tremendous stayer just the same.

Returning to the Cotswolds, that lovely part of England—differing ideas for a recommended Cheltenham stayer include; **The Lower Slaughter Manor** Lower Slaughter (0451) 20456, **The Old Farmhouse Hotel** (0451) 30232 in Lower Swell and in Moreton-in-Marsh, **The Redesdale Arms** (0608) 50308. In Stonehouse, B (0453) 825155 is a fine manor house while **Wyck Hill House Hotel** (0451) 31936 in the busy Stow-on-the-Wold also fits into the manorial category—incidentally, the restaurant here is extremely good. A compliment should also be paid to the ever popular **Rose Tree** (0451) 20635 in Bourton-on-the-Water. Continuing our Cotswold tour, the Chipping Campden area is well worth a visit—preferably a long one. The superb **Cotswold House Hotel** (0386) 840330 is a beautiful Regency building where your stay will be both comfortable and relaxing and **Greenstocks** (0386) 840330 is a restaurant which guarantees the hungry race-goer a truly delicious meal. For the lover of Italian food, **Caminetto** (0386) 840330 is a local favourite, whilst just outside Chipping Campden, **Charingworth Manor** (0386) 78555 at Charingworth is a hotel where no expense is spared in making the guests stay a memorable one.

Less vaunted, but more reasonably priced post-race stabling can be secured in a number of the pubs that riddle the villages of Gloucestershire. In North Nibley, the **Black Horse** (0453) 46841 is recommended—a friendly, beamed pub with some bedrooms available if you want to make a weekend of it. Blockley offers **The Crown** (0386) 700245 with an excellent array of real ales, bedrooms and good bar food. Some fair bar snacks can be tried in the **Slug and Lettuce** in Cirencester. **The New Inn** (0453) 3659 in Waterley Bottom is also highly recommended. In North Cerney **The Bathurst Arms** (028583) 281 offers good bed and breakfast besides being a welcoming and popular pub. In Naunton, **The Black Horse** (04515) 378 is also charming: excellent bar food and some accommodation here. The same can be said of **The George** (0242) 35751 in Winchcombe—a converted Whitbread establishment. People returning to London have a plethora of places to discover. If you wish to break the journey consider Eynsham—here one finds a whole clutch of boozers, the best of which is **Newlands** (0865) 881486 which also boasts a first class restaurant.

Yet more pleasant village pubs abound many offering some accommodation if you enjoy pubs rather than hotels: In Fossebridge, **The Fossebridge** (028572) 721 is popular and in Ford, **The Plough** (038673) 215 has two bedrooms and is a lively local.

There are literally hundreds of hostelries in which to reflect on the outcome of the race, and two not to be missed are **The Shutter** in Gotlington and **The Apple Tree** in Woodmancote—local favourites for a first class racecourse.

Chepstow

R odger Farrant is the **Manager** and **Clerk of the Course** and he is
assisted by **G C Francis** who is the **Secretary**. All enquiries should
be made to **Chepstow Racecourse, Chepstow, Gwent, NP6 5YH. Tel:
(0291) 622260.**

Travelling to the Course

Since the opening of the Severn Bridge in 1966, Chepstow is easily
accessible from the east and London via the M4. If the road is clear
(it often isn't) Piercefield Park is only two minutes drive from the
Bridge. The M4 motorway provides a swift route to the course and
if the racegoer is making his journey from the north then the M5
which joins the M4 at junction 22 is the route to take. The same
junction should be used for travellers from the south of England.
Once at the course you will be delighted to hear that all parking is
free and there is lots of it! Chepstow has a rail station and the racecourse is a mile's canter from the town centre. Bristol Parkway station is only a 15-minute drive away and this might be a good bet if
you are travelling from London's Paddington station. There is a bus
service (Chepstow to Monmouth) which will deposit you outside
the course. If a helicopter is more your style then you may land in
the middle of the track, opposite the stands. As yet light aircraft are
not allowed.

Major Races and Charges

Chepstow racecourse usually hosts a total of 23 days racing: 13 meetings over the jumps and ten on the flat course. Chepstow meetings
are generally one day occasions with the Easter Monday and
Tuesday meeting the only two day fixture. The year's racing begins
in January and there are at least two meetings per month throughout the year. The course is perhaps best noted for its National Hunt
racing, but we should also emphasise the beauty of the setting and
the local countryside—an opportunity to visit Chepstow at any time
of year, especially when the spirit is somewhat waning, should
always be taken. Feature events include; the Coral Welsh National,
the Philip Cornes Hurdle, the Rehearsal Chase and the Tote Silver
Trophy.

Chepstow Membership in 1993 cost £108. This included an amazing
twenty five away days at 14 other courses including Ascot,
Salisbury, Taunton, Exeter, Newton Abbot, Wincanton, Goodwood,
Bangor, Windsor, Wolverhampton, Uttoxeter, Ludlow, Newbury and
Plumpton—an impressive list. The membership badge is not transfer-

able but if a second member's badge is applied for, then this can be transferred. A total of 48 days racing for £108 can't be bad value! The Chepstow Member has full use of the Club Stand facilities and is entitled to free car parking. The daily membership charge was £11 on weekdays and £13 at weekends in 1993. The Tattersalls charge was £8 and £9 respectively. The Silver Ring and Centre Course prices were £4 each. It is important to note that prices for the Coral Welsh National are inevitably higher and that the two cheaper enclosures are only open on the following days; Easter Monday and Tuesday, the Whitsun May Bank Holiday and August Bank Holiday. If you are organising a party then a reduction of £1 per person will be made for parties of 25 or more booked seven days in advance for the Tattersalls or Members Enclosure. The organiser will receive a free ticket which seems like a good incentive. Another generous stimulus relates to pensioners with a £2 entrance charge to the course on public holidays, and £4 to Tattersalls on other days.

Racecourse Facilities

Chepstow is set in 370 acres of parkland and nestles in the slopes of the Wye Valley. Its facilities include 39 boxes, and 9 hospitality suites which can be hired on racedays. £2 million has been spent on the provision of new private boxes and hospitality suites, these cater for 25 to 200 people. If a company wants to arrange a bigger function, then marquees can be arranged. The racecourse has three exhibition halls of varying sizes as well as the more exclusive Piercefield Suite. The caterers Letheby & Christopher have varying menus on offer. Enquiries with regard to catering should be made to them on (0242) 523203 (racedays (0291) 625189. The Paddock to the rear of the Grandstand is large and provides the racegoer with a good pre-race vantage point. Chepstow's betting facilities include the Tote building and betting shop but facilities for children are limited. The course also provides a reserved viewing area for wheelchair-racegoers. Telephones are available but as yet there are no banking facilities on the course: another small omission at an otherwise improving and excellent circuit. One for the notebook in 1994.

Local Favourites

Although not quite on the Welsh side of the border, a quite exceptional hotel to be found in Avon is **The Thornbury Castle** (0454) 418511. It is an expensive establishment but has much charm and history as well as comforts that make it all the more appealing. The hotel is an outstanding Tudor castle with marvellous bedrooms and a restaurant and wine list to match. People who wish to stay more locally should consider Chepstow itself. Here, the **Castle View Hotel**

(0291) 620349 overlooks the Castle (who would believe it!). The inn's ivy clad exterior hides some comfortable bedrooms and both the food and the welcome are good—ideal for lunch before racing. **The George Hotel** (0291) 625365 adjoins the 16th century gate and town walls. This is another good spot for a pint and a snack. Chepstow is well situated for visitors to the Wye Valley, the Forest of Dean and the splendid Tintern Abbey. It also offers a range of other activities—one of which is golf. The best place to stay if you're a golfer as well as a racing enthusiast is the **St. Pierre Hotel** (0291) 625261—the hotel also offers a whole string of other leisure facilities and some good value weekend breaks can also be arranged—the ideal place for a short breakaway. Finally, in Chepstow, **Beckfords** (0291) 626547 is a restaurant to shortlist.

The Welsh border country is well known for its beauty—the Wye and the Usk are two delightful stretches of river. There are numerous possibilities. Some particularly good ideas include a visit to Crickhowell, a night at Gliffaes (0874) 730371, a friendly hotel, or a visit to The Bear Hotel (0873) 810408—note also some splendid markets and antique shops to be found in the area. Other thoughts include The Crown at Whitebrook (0600) 860254—a popular place to stay, while the delightfully historic town of Monmouth reveals the Kings Head Hotel (0600) 712177 a splendid half-timbered inn. Be sure to consider The Village Green Restaurant (0600) 860119 on your way to Monmouth—there are also some good value rooms available here. In Clearwell, a country inn with bedrooms and restaurant as well as friendly bars is the **Wyndham Arms** (0594) 33666. The **Clearwell Castle** (0594) 32320 is another popular suggestion; this 18th century edifice is an amazing place to stay especially for four poster lovers. A well located inn for the Forest of Dean is Speech House, **Coleford** (0594) 822607—some more splendid four-posters for the more romantic racegoer.

Chester

Chester is one of the most appealing racecourses in Britain. This delightful course is managed by **Mr Ray Walls** and **Clerk of the Course** is **Capt. C B Toller**. Both, however, are ably assisted by **Eric Lightfoot**. Contact them at: **The Racecourse Chester, Cheshire, CH1 2LY. Tel: (0244) 323170.**

Travelling to the Course
The racecourse actually lies to the south east of the town. The M6/M56 motorway will adequately serve racegoers from the north and south of the country and Junction 14 is the recommended exit point. Eastbound travellers will find the M62/M6/M56 the clearest route into Chester while A roads abound in the area if you prefer not to use the motorways. The course itself is well signposted by AA and RAC signs as well as the occasional bobby. There is a new signpost system in operation directing traffic from the M6 onto the Chester By-Pass, thus avoiding the busy City Centre. On arrival at the track, cars and coaches can be parked in the centre of the course and the respective prices are £1 and £2.50.

The Euston line goes directly to Chester General (the station, not the hospital) and there is a bus service from the station to the course on racedays. In this intensely busy age some people elect to travel by helicopter and there is a landing pad available should you wish to buzz in.

Major Races and Charges
The pattern of racing this year is likely to follow that of 1993. The principal event is the May Festival Meeting and the feature races include, The Chester Vase, the Dee Stakes, The Shadwell Stud Cheshire Oaks and The Chester Cup. Indeed, this mini-festival is a true delight for racing enthusiasts. Annual Membership at Chester cost £100 in 1993 and included free car parking and free entrance for a member's day at Bangor-on-Dee, Carlisle, Doncaster and Uttoxeter. Another advantage for the Annual Member is the provision of a special marquee for the May meeting. This gives a more refined area in which to go about one's business—a really first class idea. A three-day badge for the May meeting cost £45 and the daily rate for Tuesday and Thursday was £17. On Cup Day, the entrance was £22. Daily Junior badges for racegoers (aged 17 and under) cost £3. Reserved seats for the 3 days cost an additional £15. Tattersalls charges were £9 and £11 for Cup day; the Dee Stands cost £4 per day. There was also a charge of £1 for spectators on the open course. Coaches and mini buses can be parked on course for £2.50 but booking is essential. For the remaining meetings, daily badges cost £12 in the County Stand, £7 in Tatts and the Paddock, and £4 in the Dee Stands.

Racecourse Facilities
Visitors to the County Stand can view the magnificent panorama of the Roodee, the wide sweep of the River Dee and the Welsh Hills beyond. Children are admitted free to all enclosures except the Members but there are no special facilities for them due to the restricted space. Disabled people have a small reserved stand, wash

facilities and a new private box facility by the winning post with C.C.T.V. There are extra betting shops in Tattersalls and the Dee Stands and cash can be topped up by the Nat West Bank in the County stand—a bit of a bore if you've blown your loot and remain stranded in Tatts! Chester is an outstanding racecourse in every way and its popularity grows year after year. Anew extension to the County Stand will be available from may 1994 and includes special owners and trainers accommodation plus eight new boxes. When racing is having as hard a time as any industry, Chester racecourse is an example to one and all and a credit to the industry.

Local Favourites

A splendid place to stay is **The Chester Grosvenor** (0224) 324024 the restaurant is particularly well thought of. For unadulterated luxury perhaps the surrounding countryside comes up with the answer for at Worleston, near Nantwich, there stands **Rookery Hall** (0270) 626866, an outstanding hotel with restaurant and cellar that can only be described as superb. **Broxton Hall** (0829) 782321 also comes highly recommended. Back in Chester, there is an abundance of guest houses and small hotels so the racegoer on a more limited budget should not worry. Names worth mentioning here are **The Chester Court** (0244) 320779, **Green Gables** (0244) 372243 and The **White Lion** (0928) 722949. Not the cheapest, but still an outstanding favourite, is **Crabwall Manor** (0244) 851666 two miles outside Chester.

Venturing some way north of Chester to the South Wirral and Puddington, one finds the **Craxton Wood Hotel** (051) 339 4717 with a small but selective and very stylish restaurant. People looking for a little luxury when visiting the city should consider one of several hotels. In St Johns Street, **Blossoms** (0244) 323186 is close to the city centre and its many amenities include a good restaurant and two friendly bars. **The Malt Shoppe** and **The Snooty Fox** are both well worth considering. A little farther afield, but still convenient for the city is a splendid country house hotel, **The Mollington Banastre Hotel** (0244) 851471. There are excellent facilities available here—together with two restaurants—and its own village pub. In Rowton lies another fine country house—**The Rowton Hall Hotel** (0244) 33562—the service here is good and if you don't want to be in the middle of Chester this may well be the answer. South of the city lies the excellent value and secluded **Pheasant Inn** (0829) 70434. A relative newcomer to the Chester field, is the **Chester International Hotel** (0244) 322330. Meanwhile, the **Wild Boar Inn** (0829) 260309 at Beeston has modern facilities and a pleasing setting. If it is unashamed luxury that you are after, look no further than **Llyndir Hall Hotel and Restaurant** (0244) 571648.

In the countryside, there are some fine pubs to note; **The Bickerton Poacher** in Bickerton is an exceptionally busy pub but is good fun too. **The Cock O'Barton** at Barton is quieter. In Taporley, **The Swan** (0829) 32411 is a worthy Greenall's pub with a restaurant and some bedrooms if you require them. More of the same can be found in Sutton, north west of Chester at **Sutton Hall** (02605) 53211. Finally, a very special hotel can be found at Mold, some twelve miles from Chester. Here, a warm welcome awaits you at **Soughton Hall** (0352) 207, a stunning hotel in Italianate style with a fine a la carte restaurant. Finally, **Frogg Manor** (0829) 722629 is as chracterful and welcoming as any. With outstanding hotels and a first class racecourse a visit to Chester in 1994 simply has to be organised!

In more than two hundred years, the Town Moor has witnessed war, suffered peace-time traumas, enjoyed all the thrill of the sport and has basked in the acclaim during the Golden Age of British racing. Recent years have been less generous to this historic track. However, the staging of Britain's first ever Sunday racemeeting in July 1992 was a significant feature in what we will hope will be a re-emergence as a genuine Grade 1 Classic venue. Indeed, User Friendly's victory in the St Leger was a tremendous boost to the great race itself. The main Grandstand was refurbished in 1989 and 1990 saw the opening of the St. Leger Grandstand. The Clock Tower Stand (second enclosure) has also been re-developed.

The racecourse also has a dynamic new leadership, **John Sanderson, Clerk of the Course** for flat racing and **Major Moore** for **National Hunt.** Information can be obtained by writing to them at **The Grandstand, Leger Way, Doncaster. DN2 6BB. Tel:(0302) 320066.**

Travelling to the Course
Doncaster is in South Yorkshire, some 180 miles from Battersea Power Station and one mile from the centre of Doncaster itself. The course is within easy access of motorways and there is a dual carriageway to the course carparks. The A1 and the M1/M18 are good routes from the south and the course is well signposted from both motorways. In fact, new signs now direct racegoers from all motorway approaches. If you are coming from the west then use the A57 and M18 and from the east the M18 and M180. Let the train take the strain from Kings Cross and your journey time will be 85 minutes with a bus from the town to complete the final leg of the journey. Buses from Doncaster (Nos. 55, 170 and 171) will drop you 300 metres from the gates—perfect! Helicopters are permitted to land at Doncaster but only by special arrangement so if this is your desired mode of transport then please check with the General Manager first. Car parking is easy here with space for 3,000 cars—all free. There is also a reserved area for Members.

Major Races and Charges
The season at Doncaster consists of 26 days racing—19 flat and 7 over the sticks. Principal meetings are the St. Leger Festival in September and the William Hill Lincoln in March, The Racing Post Trophy in October and the William Hill November Handicap. Doncaster has the honour of opening and closing the flat season—a worthy privilege.

Rates of admission for 1993 varied from meeting to meeting and day to day. There was a standard charge of £14 for the Members Enclosure and £8.00 for the Tattersalls but these were higher on more prestigious race days. £3.00 is the standard charge for the Clock Tower Enclosure and again this rises on principal days. For example, charges for St Leger day are £24 £14 and £5 respectively. Annual Membership at Doncaster costs £140. Included in this are eleven reciprocal meetings at nine racecourses varying from Newbury through to Chester and entrance to Yorkshire Cricket

Club matches on 11 days. This has to be good value. Dual Membership, husband and wife, are offered a double badge for £195 and Junior's Badges were £60 in 1993. Party discounts are also available and you should contact the racecourse for full details if you are planning a large outing.

Racecourse Facilities

Boxes, and there are a total of 70 now, are let on an annual basis only but a tented village exists for the St. Leger meeting. There are numerous bars as well as the sponsors' rooms; the Classic Suite, the Royal Box and three restaurants; Ladies Restaurant, the Club Annexe and Members' Restaurant. If you wish to be assured of a seat it is worth while booking a table on major race days. The caterers are Metro and can be contacted on (0302) 349740. Picnickers will be sad to hear that they are not welcome but the Gainsborough Restaurant in the Grandstand and the Lonsdale in the Club are available for luncheon and there are the usual number of snack bars around the track.

In 1993 the racecourse has developed its own in-house corporate and private entertainment department. Despite the recession, sponsorship has grown considerably and with the all inclusive package offered the course provides excellent value racing. Despite the recent problems it is hoped that this strong management can develop 'Britain's User Friendly racecourse' into a racecourse that remains as friendly as ever but is used by many more ever more frequently.

Local Favourites

The most historic of Yorkshire racecourses is to be found at Doncaster—perhaps not the most attractive of towns but an excellent racecourse nonetheless. In Doncaster, **The Grand St. Leger** (0302) 364111 is extremely comfortable and its restaurant has an imaginative menu. **The Doncaster Moat House** (0302) 310331 is also very appealing. A little south of the town, in Bawtry, stands **The Crown Hotel** (0302) 710341, a pleasant inn in a quiet market square. **The Regent Hotel** (0302) 364180 and the **Mount Pleasant** (0302) 868696 are shortlisted by people in the know, and the **Rockingham Arms** (0302) 360980 also has a good reputation. Two other hotels to consider are **The Danum Swallow Hotel** (0302) 342261 in the town centre—more good bars here which are ideal meeting spots and the bedrooms are also of a fairly high standard and the **Earl of Doncaster** (0302) 61371, a mere half mile from the racecourse. On a less lavish front, the **Almel Hotel** (0302) 365230 is an excellent option.

For people who may want a little more comfort and style there are two hotels that are warmly recommended north of Doncaster. In Wentbridge, **The Wentbridge House Hotel** (0977) 620444 has a pleasant location in the parkland scenery of the Went Valley. A similar distance north of Doncaster, one finds the **Monk Fryston Hall Hotel** (0977) 682369 in the West Riding village of the same name. Pubs to note nearby include the excellent Inn at Cadeby—very busy and good food. Another thought is the **Green Tree** at Hatfield Woodhouse. Dinnington, to the south of Doncaster, offers the **Dinnington Hall Hotel** (0909) 569661—a beautiful Georgian building set in three acres of grounds.

Edinburgh

The authorities at Edinburgh include **Sam Morshead**, who is **Clerk of the Course** here and **Mark Kershaw** who is the **Manager**. All enquiries should be made to **Ayr Racecourse, 2 Whitletts Road, Ayr, KA8 0JE. Tel: 0292 264179.** On racedays the team can be contacted on 031- 665 2859. This is a celebrated duo who also hold the reins at Scotland's premier racecourse, Ayr.

Travelling to the Course
The racecourse stands proudly around the historic golf course of Musselburgh links which in turn lies on the Firth of Forth, overlooking the River Esk. Its situation, eight miles west of Scotland's capital city, is some 350 miles north of its English counterpart. The major routes to be considered are the M8 and the City by-pass from the west and the A1 and A198 from the east. The A7, A68 and A702 should be used for people coming from the south. The Musselburgh By-Pass (A1) is now in operation and traffic to and from the racecourse is much improved as a result.

Edinburgh's main railway station, Waverley, is on that excellent Intercity 225 line from Kings Cross which, following electrification is little more than three and a half hours away. The nearest station to the course is Musselburgh East and on racedays buses from here will take you to the course. A special bus also makes trips from Waverley Station to the course on racedays. If you decide to drive you will be pleased to hear there is an excellent choice of areas in which to park your car and these are all free. Coaches are also welcome. If you are an aviator and happen to be passing in your helicopter, approach the course from the north and land in an area adjacent to the car park.

Major Races and Charges
There are two enclosures, the Members which in 1993 cost £11 for a day badge and Tattersalls where a fee of £6 is charged for entry unless you happen to be an O.A.P. or unemployed—in either of these cases there is a £3 levy. £90 was charged for a years membership in 1992 with £60 being asked for an additional badge. Membership includes reserved parking and reciprocal meetings at Perth, Kelso, and Newton Abbot. Racing should keep to the same pattern as 1992 with twelve days of flat racing and eight days over the jumps—the latter running from December to February.

Racecourse Facilities
Sponsors rooms are available for hire at Edinburgh, catering for numbers of 20-80 where you can entertain in style. Local companies can sponsor fences and hurdles as well as the races themselves. On a larger scale, companies are being encouraged to sponsor the course; flat, hurdle or steeplechase, for a three year period. These are ambitious plans—but with the Fosters Oval now completed it makes me wonder whether this would not be a good way forward for British racecourses, provided they can attract sponsors in these still difficult times. Marquees are also available to hire and the management hope to have a number of private boxes built in the near future.

There are a number of snack bars throughout the course and two restaurants; the Tote Club and The Paddock. Lunch will set you back about £13.50 and £8.50 for just the main course. If you are keen to know more with regard to the racecourse catering, your initial contact should be George Steel on (0292) 264179.

If you wish to take children and they are under 16, they are admitted free but there are no additional facilities for them. As you would expect, there are public telephones, and viewing ramps, loos and some bars for the disabled racegoers. No banking facilities are available, but if you have a particular fancy then Ladbrokes run a quite superb on-course shop. A pleasant racecourse well worth a visit when looking for a few winners.

Local Favourites

Outside Edinburgh, a simply outstanding hotel should be visited if at all possible. It has the class of a Derby winner and a history and character as rich as the Grand National—**Greywalls** (0620) 842144. Overlooking Muirfield, this superb hotel and restaurant is thoroughly recommended. Gullane also reveals an excellent restaurant **La Potiniere** (0620) 843214—it's small, cosy, refined and enormously popular; you really must plan ahead and book if you want a table here, but its well worth it. Golfing enthusiasts will vouch for the fact that guesthouses of ambience abound—**The Golfers Inn** (0620) 843259 is but one example. South of Gullane in Gifford, **The Tweeddale Arms** (0620) 81240 makes a good base—ideal for exploring the North Lothian coast. Remaining outside the city, one finds Howgate and **The Old Howgate Inn** (0968) 74244, a splendid pub for food as is **The Horseshoes Inn** at Eddleston a little south of Howgate. Nearby the **Cringletie House Hotel** (0721) 3233 is an extremely welcoming hotel—comfortable too. The restaurant is also very good. Indeed, if you are reluctant to stay in the busy city, then this hotel is a super idea. Returning north to Penicuick, one finds another fine pub with a separate restaurant, **Habbies Howe** (0968) 76969 and some bedrooms. In North Berwick, one finds another excellent establishment, **Hardings** (0620) 844737.

There is a whole host of restaurants that gather thoughtfully outside Edinburgh. Pride of place goes to the **Champanay Inn** (0506) 834532 in Linlithgow where steaks are said to be among the finest in Britain. The **Lauriston Farm Restaurant** 031-312 7071 is another where a slight detour will reap tasty dividends. A restaurant within a hotel can be found in Uphall:- **Houstoun House** (0506) 853831 is a charming place in which to stay with a delightful restaurant. Finally, mention should be made of the **Cramond Inn** 031-336 2035, Cramond, a pleasant place to spend an evening.

In Edinburgh itself there is much to do other than visit pubs—hotels and restaurants are equally good. **The Caledonian Hotel** 031-225 2433 is extraordinarily grand, superbly comfortable and **The Pompadour** restaurant is really something to cherish. **The George Hotel** 031-225 1251 is first class and once again the restaurant should be noted. Less traditional is the **Sheraton Grand Hotel** 031-229 9131 which stands opposite The Usher Hall.

Epsom

Major Michael Webster is the Clerk of the Course at Epsom, Andrew Cooper is the Manager with Jo Dillon handling the administration. Enquiries should be addressed to United Racecourses, The Grandstand Epsom Downs, Surrey, KT18 5LQ. Tel: (0372) 726311.

Travelling to the Course

Epsom itself stands on the Surrey Downs of the same name. The mode of transportation depends significantly on the meeting. Derby Day is enormously busy—even helicopters hover in line. However, on other days traffic is less congested. The racecourse is fairly close to the centre of London and people heading from that direction should pursue the A3 south, exiting at the Tolworth junction. Traffic from the west is advised to join the M25 and exit at Junction 8 or 9 for the course—the M25, if it is flowing freely, also serves people from the east and the south of the country. The A217 is the best route to observe in order to complete your northbound journey. An excellent idea for transportation is to take the train. Lines from the London stations of Waterloo, Charing Cross and Victoria stretch to Epsom. The Downs can be reached from Victoria alone, while Tattenham Corner visitors should take trains from either London Bridge or Charing Cross. Fear not if you travel to Epsom by train, buses will take you to the course itself. However, passengers to Tattenham Corner station can enjoy a pleasant walk across the Downs before racing. Many people have picnics here and this seems as ideal a place as any to indulge in your nose bag. Other places in which to have a pre-race snack are the car parks, of which there are many. There are charges but these vary according to your particular setting. Finally, If you are lucky enough to organise a helicopter trip, then the Downs welcome you—its quite a sight I assure you.

Major Races and Charges

There are a whole range of charges for the various enclosures. Derby Day is unsurprisingly expensive. In 1993, £50 was the asking price for a Members Badge while Oaks Day was priced at £22. It should be emphasised that admission to the Club Enclosure is limited to Annual Members who may introduce, by way of a voucher, two guests. Reserved seats are in the Anglesey Stand, necessitating a £40 pay out. Tattersalls was better value £20, £13 on Oaks Day and if you just want to be there on the big day then the Paddock and the Lonsdale Enclosures are £10 (£5 on Oaks day). Finally, the more relaxed Tattenham and Walton Enclosures which are only used during Derby and Oaks Weeks are priced at between £3 and £7. Two problems here though, you can't see the horses in the Paddock and there are a lot of other people desperately trying to reach the rails. However, it's an excellent atmosphere that's well worth being a part of. In order to get a comprehensive listing of the various charges contact the racecourse. Annual Membership in 1993 was priced at £120. A Junior Membership badge was priced at £45. The principal advantage to this membership is that it gives you, and two guests, admission to the Members Enclosure for the Derby—a real bonus. Prices in 1994 are likely to be held at 1993 levels—tremendous to report.

Racecourse Facilities

As with many of the year's principal sporting events, there is a tented village for company promotions. It is situated away from the Grandstand, alongside Epsom's splendid paddock. The pavilions are ideal for private and corporate entertainment. Each Pavilion offers full dining and Tote facilities and closed circuit television. Please contact the racecourse for all the details. People seeking to be closer to the action should perhaps try the Classic Stand. The private enclosure located near the furlong post, close to the Grandstand is a tremendous place to enjoy the most magnificent of racing days. Contact the Ever Ready Derby Hospitality Office on (071) 821 6222. Finally, the racecourse has a number of rooms and private boxes available.. Please ring the racecourse for full details.

There is a restaurant in the Members Enclosure and you should book. A less busy alternative can be found in the Grandstand. The numerous snack bars serve sandwiches but these are fairly expensive so be prepared. Disabled facilities have been radically improved at Epsom with ramps, lifts and toilets now provided. A bank can be found behind the Grandstand during Derby week should you blow all your cash early on in the Tote or Corol betting facilities. Lastly to note, is that children under 16 are admitted free to all enclosures except the Members on Derby Day.

The pedigree of the Derby speaks for itself and it is the challenge of the distinguished racing and business brains at United Racecourses to ensure its development in future years. My own view is that the whole meeting needs to be fundamentally rethought. In fact, with competition from around the world getting stronger, the whole meeting needs to be reviewed continually.

Some of the recent improvements include an increase in entertainment in all enclosures before and during racing; from jousting tournaments to steel bands. The introduction of giant screens opposite the Grandstand are welcome and, to my mind essential for the paying racegoer. The fact that horses went down via Tattenham Corner enabled the entire crowd a more generous pre-race view. Coupled with this, the new entry system and record prize money of over £750,000.

The fact that attendances on Derby Day increased by 20% is a tribute to all involved. Evening meetings have also been successful, with crowds in excess of 8,000. The mind boggles as to what the figure will be when the Derby is held on a Sunday!

Local Favourites

People who are staying in this area (rather than in the capital) should note **The Burford Bridge Hotel** (0306) 884561, in Burford Bridge near Dorking—a welcoming hotel beside the A24 and well sited for Epsom Downs. **The White Horse Hotel**, (0306) 881138 also has great character, though less class. Both these are ideal for the tourist as they date back centuries. Epsom itself contains the **Epsom Arms Hotel** (0372) 740643, a good value and relaxing hotel. In Banstead, a convenient yet unpretentious stayer is **Heathside** (0737) 353355. Further south in Rusper, an hotel for people who enjoy a little peace and quiet, **Ghyll Manor** (0293) 871571 is a delightfully comfortable old manor house. Turning back towards the racecourse again, the busy town of Reigate is home to the excellent **Cranleigh Hotel** (0737) 223417. **The Whyte Harte** (0883) 743231 in Bletchingly is also a fine place to stay while **The Bell** in Godstone is ideal for a steak and a drink.

There are numerous pubs to be found in the area—some near, some far. **The Olde Swan** in Thames Ditton is most obliging as is the **Lincoln Arms** in Weybridge. More Arms can be found in Ewell where **Glyns** is reported to be well worth a visit (note some filling bar food here). In Kenley one finds a further coat—**The Wattenden Arms**, on this occasion, an extremely popular pub with some distinguished bar food available. Further afield in Warlingham, **The White Lion** is a charming place to discover.

If you're contemplating dinner, **Les Alouettes** (0372) 464882 in Esher should be tried out. Other thoughts for this extremely civilised post-racing occupation include a local favourite, **Partners Brasserie**, (081) 644 7743 at Sutton. This is really outstanding and thoroughly recommended:- the place to go if you are expecting a good result in the Derby. In Surbiton, **Chez Max** (081) 399 2365 is also good—a small restaurant with an ambitious menu. An alternative nearby is to be found in Chipstead; here **Dene Farm** (0737) 552661 is not cheap but offers a really first-class menu, friendly service and a distinguished wine list. Finally, in Hersham **The Dining Room** (0932) 231686 is reported to be excellent, where a friendly atmosphere accompanies bold English cooking

The **Kings Arms** (0306) 711224 in Ockley should be noted; the well priced menu is extremely appealing. Another pleasant pub to inspect near here is the **Punch Bowl** which has a lovely setting and serves some simple bar snacks as well as having a good dining room. Two other pubs to note while in this area of Surrey include another part of the kings anatomy, on this occasion **The Kings Head**, to be found in Holmbury St. Mary, a really good atmosphere here as well as a separate restaurant. In Shere, **The White Horse** is also popular—rightly so, it is charming and offers some excellent home-made food. People who are fond of eating and enjoy the ambience of a good restaurant should try the **Onslow Arms** (0483) 222447 in West Clandon—a classic of its type. Lovers of the ex-P.M. can go overboard and try **Thatchers Hotel** (04865) 4291. The Derby attracts all sorts of people. Gypsies promise you luck but you will still lose your shirt. The Derby is one of the most colourful events of the year and if you want to end it in style visit the village of Nutfield. The hotel here is situated in the former local priory. **Nutfield Priory** (0737) 822066, the perfect place to count your winnings or lick your wounds after a day at the Derby.

Finally, if your appetite has not been whetted by any of these suggestions, (unlikely!) then turn to the Kempton Park and Sandown recommendations where you will see more places to satisfy the Surrey race-goer.

If you are planning a visit to England's delightful West Country then stop off at the recently refurbished Exeter Racecourse. This pleasant track is in the capable hands of Mr R.H. Merton as Manager and Clerk Of The Course and Mr B. Soper as Manager and Secretary. The address is, Devon & Exeter Steeplechase Ltd, Exeter Racecourse, Kennford, Nr. Exeter, EX6 7XS. Tel: (0392) 832599, fax: (0392) 833454. Enquiries concerning membership should be addressed to Mrs J A Soper. Cherry Hi, Rectory Road, Ogwell, Newton Abbot, Devon. Tel: (0626) 61843.

Travelling to the Course

When travelling to the course it may be as well to stick to the motorways to ensure a speedy route—the M5 merges with the M4 and the M6. The course is some 190 miles from London and seven miles south-west of Exeter. The A38 is the best route to take after having exhausted the motorway network. Haldon lies a mere stone's throw away from this A road. The A30 will guide westbound travellers; the M5 can also be put to some use here. The A38 which wiggles from Plymouth will also serve those who live west of the course. On arrival at the racecourse there is ample car parking to be found. Essentially this is free, although a £2 charge for a special position on the rails. The nearest train station is at Exeter, St. Davids, which can be comfortably reached from Paddington. The nearest major bus station is also in Exeter, but the Exeter—Plymouth line stops outside Haldon.

Major Races and Charges

The National Hunt programme at Exeter features fifteen meetings with the main race to note being Gold Cup Day in early November—a listed race. However, racing spans the year here and lovers of the Devon sun should note the splendid two-day meeting in early August. Lovers of winter sport should sample the New Year's Day fixture, which is the course's most popular day and seldom affected by seasonal weather. In fact 1993 was a glorious day—a marvellous start to the year. In order to become an Annual Member the sum of £75 is charged for a single badge. This also includes some 23 reciprocal days, although Exeter Members certainly have to do some travelling to enjoy them! 1994 daily rates will be £9 for the Members and Tattersalls and a really good value £4 for the Course Enclosure. Party discounts are available for the Members and Tattersalls—please apply to the course for further details.

Racecourse Facilities

The course has five boxes in the new Tote building which can hold up to 16 people each, while the old one has been converted to accommodate two function rooms for large parties. Booking details are available from the Clerk or Secretary with prices from £200 (+VAT). There is also a carvery restaurant at the top of the Members Stand with prices around £11 per head. More elaborate catering can also be arranged through The Brend Catering Division tel (0392) 59268 and there are facilities for marquees if you wish to have a really good party.

The only drawback to what must be considered to be one of Britain's favourite holiday courses is the lack of facilities for children, although they are admitted free to the racecourse if accompanied by an adult. In their defence, however, the racecourse executive are faced with a less than user freindly course layout which makes special facilities impractical. They have given the matter much thought which is I suppose half the battle. Telephones at the racecourse are located in Tattersalls and the betting shop is also to be found here, whilst for the disabled there is a special viewing platform and toilet facilities.

Local Favourites

East of the course lies Exeter and here, the **Royal Clarence** (0392) 58464 is the pick of the bunch, with the **White Hart,** (0392) 79897 also well thought of. Cheaper accommodation, but still of a high standard can also be found here; **Park View Hotel** (0392) 71772 and **Trees Mini Hotel** (0392) 59531 are sure to fit the bill. Lovers of good food and the seaside should seek out the **Victoria Hotel,** Sidmouth (0395) 512651. One thought for golfing enthusiasts and holiday makers alike is the **Thurlestone Hotel** (0548) 560382 in Thurlestone. A number of these places are much quieter in the off season and are therefore that much more appealing, so book up now and take a well earned break. A particularly good sporting break hotel is **The Manor House** (0647) 40355 at Moretonhampstead. This is a stylish place to stay, as is **Woodhayes** (0404) 822237 in the rather unfortunately named village of Whimple. Both the restaurant and accommodation here are first class. **The Old Mill** (0392) 59480 in Ide is a cosy and stylish restaurant with good fish. In Doddiscombsleigh, one pub that really should be noted is the hugely welcoming, but somewhat unlikely, **Nobody Inn** (0647) 52394, with good value bedrooms if you like pub accommodation. The bar food here is also good. In close proximity, **The Huntsman** is a grand alternative. A tremendous pub for a visit after racing is **The Coaching Inn,** Chudleigh, great character and food. Another place to eat is **The Thatch** in Halden, an interesting Portuguese slant here. In North Bovey, **The Ring of Bells** (0647) 40375 is a well known real ale pub—accommodation here is also good value. For those who wish to spread their sightseeing net slightly wider, the **Royal Beacon Hotel** (0395) 264886 at Exemouth provides a splendid and comfortable base.

Heading further into Dartmoor there are some really first class hotels. In Chagford, The **Gidleigh Park Hotel** (0647) 432367 is isolated but beautiful and has a first class restaurant; **The Great Tree Hotel** (0647) 432491 is also extremely tranquil while **The Mill End** (0647) 432282 has yet another delightfully quiet setting in the Teign Valley. Head too for the excellent value **Bly House Hotel** (0647) 432404. Some twenty miles from Exeter is Ashburton, which houses the **Holne Chase Hotel** (03643) 471, a lovely country house hotel where fishing is available. Finally, the neighbouring course of Newton Abbot could come up with some fine runners, to turn to this section for more suggestions.

Fakenham

Now this is a racecourse which is well worth a visit—not the greatest course, but tremendous fun. The man at the helm at Fakenham is **Pat Firth** who acts as **Clerk of the Course, Manager** and **Secretary**. All enquiries should be addressed to **The Racecourse, Fakenham, Norfolk, NR21 7NY. Tel: Fakenham (0328) 862388.**

Travelling to the Course

Fakenham is situated just off the A148 and the town is by-passed to the north making your journey somewhat less tricky. Although the course is well signposted from all directions, London is only 125 miles away, King's Lynn 22 miles and Norwich 26 miles. The going can be heavy since one cannot rely on the services of the motorway network but roads in the area are being improved. From the north, the A1 and A17 combine to make the most direct route. From the south use the A1065, from the west the A148 and from the east the A1067. Parking facilities at the course are thankfully very good. The main railway station is some 22 miles away at King's Lynn (departing Liverpool Street and Kings Cross). However, what the area lacks in the way of public transport it makes up for in terms of private facilities. Helicopters may land in the centre of the course.

Major Races and Charges

Despite being a six-meeting country course, Fakenham has some fairly worthwhile prizes and is well sponsored by local and national firms. Racing highlights are the Prince of Wales Cup, the Queen's Cup, and Robert Hoare Hunter Chases and the Renoak Event Caterers Handicap Hurdle. Easter Monday and Spring Bank Holiday Monday are the major days racing and much recommended. The later meeting must be re-scheduled to an evening meeting in the third week of May. This is a direct result of the withdrawal of full Levy Board funding which underlies the vulnerability of even the most potentially busy of days.

The cost of entering various enclosures in 1993 was £10 for the Members' on bank holidays and £8 on other days. Similarly, Tattersalls prices varied between £7 and £4 on the different days. The Silver Ring costs £3.50 on bank holidays and £4 on other days. But please note that Tattersalls and the Silver Ring are combined as one enclosure except on bank holidays. If you're local or just keen on Fakenham then you should buy a £45 annual double badge—a worthwhile saving and with only six days on offer it's hardly going to ruin your social or sporting diary. Annual single badges can be ordered for £30 and a year's membership includes a reciprocal day at Huntingdon, Market Rasen, Yarmouth and Southwell plus one car park badge. Daily Badge holders must pay £4 or £5 (bank holidays) to park in the Members'.

Racecourse Facilities

If you're thinking of organising a party to go to Fakenham a 30 per cent discount is available for groups of 30 or more who book in advance, 20 per cent for groups of 20 to 29, and 10 per cent for groups of 10 to 19. If you want to make a real day and night of it, marquees can be hired and all the various trimmings laid on. The Paddock Buffet Restaurant serves good food and there is no need to book. The new caterers at the course are Renoak Event Caterers who can be contacted on (0328) 864918.

Facilities for the disabled are good here and include their own viewing stand and reserved parking. Children are welcome at Fakenham and are admitted free if under 16 and accompanied by an adult. There is a Tote betting shop close to the paddock but no bank to replenish your wallet should you be unsuccessful. All in all, Fakenham is a small, rural and friendly racecourse, well run, well supported and recommended to all those who relish travelling the turf.

Local Favourites

Where better to dream of tomorrow's winners than in the serenely peaceful village of Great Snoring? Here, the secluded and personal **Old Rectory** (0328) 820597 is an impressive manor house dating back to 1500. If you are looking for an outstanding place to stay and eat, then you really must visit **Grimston and Congham Hall** (0485) 600250—a delightful country house. Closer to the course, restaurants of note include **The Tollbridge** (0362) 84359 at Guist. **The Fakenham Wine Bar** (0328) 862032 is also a particularly popular haunt. And now for a few inspired selections; **Yetmans Restaurant** in Holt (0263) 713320) is reputed to be very good and we are also informed that **Lenwade House Hotel** in Lenwade (0603 872288) and **Grady's Country House Hotel** in Swaffham (0760 23355) are delightful. Last, but most definitely not least, the quaintly named Barney houses the highly recommended **Old Brick Kilns** (0328) 878305.

If you decide that a little sea air is in order then the **Jolly Sailors** (0485) 210314 at Brancaster Staithe may be somewhere to visit after racing—a pleasant bar and a fine English menu in the restaurant. A little way from the coast, two locations should be considered. Firstly, in Burnham Market, **Fishes** (0328) 738588 where some superb fish can be enjoyed in an informal atmosphere, and secondly, in Burnham Thorpe, the **Admiral Nelson**—an original pub.

The Crown (0328) 710209 is a pleasant inn; a restaurant and some accommodation are also available here. Moving into Blakeney, **The Manor Hotel** (0263) 740376 has a marvellous quayside setting and the whole atmosphere is most pleasing. Two pubs to note are the **Kings Arms** and **The White Horse** where excellent bar food is available—ideal for a weekend visit after racing. Some way off in Weybourne there are two excellent establishments; **The Swiss Restaurant** (026370) 220—a super restaurant in a thatched cottage setting and secondly, **The Maltings Hotel** (026370) 731 near the seamost appealing. Two final places to consider are **The Old Bakehouse** (0328) 820454 in Little Walsingham which offers accommodation, food and a characterful bar and **The Buckinghamshire Arms** (0263) 732133 in Blickling which is also well worth a visit. I am looking forward to my next visit already—one for the diary in 1994.

The **Clerk of The Course** is **Cliff Griggs** and he can be contacted at **Pratt & Co., 11 Boltro Road, Haywards Heath, Sussex, RH16 1BP.** Tel: **(0444) 441111,** or alternatively via **Folkestone Racecourse, Hythe, Kent. Tel: (0303) 266407.**

Travelling to the Course

Located 4 miles west of Folkestone, Kent's only track is a mere 65 miles from London. Road users from London should leave the M20 at junction 11 and take the A20 towards Lympne, Newingreen and Sellinge. There are AA road signs once you are off the M20. The racecourse is only about one mile from the motorway. From Canterbury, the best route is the B2068, the historic roman 'Stone Street', picking up the AA signs as you go over junction 11. Train users are well catered for—special raceday services depart Charing Cross and Waterloo East (3 minutes later) to BR Westenhanger. The station adjoins the course and is about 100 metres from the main entrance, (tel: 071 928 5100) for details. There is no bus service. Those with helicopters should call the course the day before the meeting to make landing arrangements. Whatever your mode of transport, you will find ample free parking, although if you are planning a picnic you will be expected to pay £3 for your car and £3 for each occupant.

Major Races and Charges

The racecourse has a mixed calendar with about 20 fixtures, the most popular invariably being the aptly named Garden of England Day, which traditionally takes place in early September and is well worth a visit, and also the United Hunts, the May jump meeting.

For the 1993 season, Annual Membership was priced at £120 (or £110 if paid before year end). One of the particular benefits of your membership is that it includes five reciprocal meetings at other tracks; Fontwell, Goodwood, Brighton and two days at Hickstead. This means that punters can enjoy a taste of flat racing and chasing and hurdling as well as show jumping, ideal for lovers of all manner of equestrian pursuits. Daily rates in 1993 were priced at £10 for the Members', £8.50 for Tattersalls and £3 for the Course Enclosure. For people wishing to organise a party of 20 or more, you will receive a discount of 20 per cent per person. This should be organised through the racecourse management in advance of the meeting. Children under 16 are admitted free to all enclosures if accompanied by an adult, except the Members' where they will be charged £2.

Racecourse Facilities

If a picnic sounds like hard work then it may be an idea to sample one of the two restaurants. Bookings should be made through the racecourse caterers, Letheby & Christopher, tel: (0273) 602987. The course has 12 splendid boxes which can seat up to 16 guests and are available to hire from £150 per day. If you are inclined to go for a real bash, then Pratt & Co will be happy to guide you.

As we discussed earlier, children are admitted free to the Members and Tattersalls, but there is no junior subscription to the course. If you wish to place an off-track punt then Tattersalls is where you will find the necessary betting facilities. There is no bank yet at this course and other facilities, including those for disabled, are limited.

There are numerous plans afoot for the continued improvement of Folkestone Racecourse. It will be interesting to see what, if any, benefit the opening of the Channel Tunnel will have on the course. 'Entente Cordiale' and all that sort of thing. I wonder if the first mixed racing, French and English, could be organised to tie in with the grand opening. It would certainly receive media attention and that could be useful.

Local Favourites

In Folkestone, **The Burlington Hotel** (0303) 255301 has much to offer. The bars are cheerful and many of the bedrooms overlook The Channel—ideal for a night stop before visiting nearby Chantilly or Longchamp. Another hotel with a watery view is **The Clifton** (0303) 851231. Reasonably priced accommodation can also be found at the **Belmonte Private Hotel** (0303) 254470. While dining at the Burlington is recommended, there are a number of other restaurants to consider: **Emilios** (0303) 255762 is a spicy and well priced Italian restaurant, **Pauls** (0303) 259697 in Bouverie Road is also a fine place to spend an evening. If you are in Hythe and are searching for a good place to stay then **The Hythe Imperial** (0303) 267441 should be the answer. This hotel is particularly comfortable and offers excellent leisure facilities including special golf packages, ideal for those of you who enjoy following the fairways as much as travelling the turf.

Dover obviously contains a host of more modest guesthouses where the welcome is guaranteed to be greater than the bill. Potential gems include **Beulah House** (0304) 824615, **Number One** (0304) 202007 and **Walletts Court Manor** (0304) 852424 which is really outstanding. In Wingham, **The Red Lion** (0227) 720217 offers a good restaurant and some satisfactory, well priced bedrooms.

One of the most appealing things about Kent is the many pubs one can find. In the delightfully named Petts Bottom, **The Duck** (0227) 830354 has a pleasant restaurant and is a really welcoming pub. Chilham, a most attractive little village, offers **The White Horse**, an old coaching inn and **The Woolpack** (0227) 730208 where some good accommodation is offered, making it an ideal base for preparing one's excursion to the racecourse. If you can't relax in this village you may as well call it a day! The star of the show, in terms of intimate dining, is to be found in Wye, **The Wife of Bath** (0233) 812540. Finally, **Eastwell Manor** (0233) 635751, situated in the gorgeous Eastwell Park, Ashford, is a delightful place and has a first class dining room, a front runner in any field.

There is no more pleasant a course for a day's National Hunt racing than Fontwell Park where Cliff Griggs is the Clerk of the
Course. He can be contacted at Pratt & Co, 11 Boltro Road, Haywards
Heath, Sussex, PH16 1BP. Tel: (0444) 441111. On racedays, tel: (0243)
543335.

Travelling to the Course

Sadly, no major short-cuts have been discovered to this somewhat
outlying course. However, there is a new road system outside the
racecourse which helps traffic considerably. The racecourse is situated on the Fontwell Road which lies close to the junction of the A27
and the A29, midway between Arundel and Chichester some six
miles away. London is 60 miles farther and the M23 is a motorway
to choose after which one must seek the services of the A29. The
M23 adjoins the M25—that frustratingly one paced track. The A24 is
the best selection to make if one is keen to pursue a trunk road. The
trains into this county run from Victoria and the nearest station is at
Barnham. There are free buses from the station to the course on
race days so this may be an alternative mode of transport.
Unfortunately, you may not land your helicopter here so the motor
is probably the best bet, especially as there is ample car parking
available which is provided free.

Major Races and Charges

The racecourse staged fifteen National Hunt fixtures in 1993 and fixtures for 1994 are expected to follow a similar pattern. The most
popular annual event is usually the Spring Bank Holiday meeting.
There are many Monday and Tuesday meetings at Fontwell Park
and it may be a good idea to relax for a few days in West Sussex
and take in one such meeting.

Entrance to the racecourse in 1993 was priced at £11 for daily admission to the Members', £8 for the Tattersalls and £3.50 for the Silver
Ring. The management have advised us that these prices are unlikely to rise in 1994. There is a very popular picnic car park in the
Silver Ring if you want to make a real day out of it. The charge here
is £3.50 per car plus £3.50 per person. The Annual Members badge
which includes 4 reciprocal meetings was priced at £90 in 1993, plus
£10 for a superior parking place. If you are thinking of organising a
party to go to Fontwell races then the first point of interest is the 20
per cent discount available on parties of 20 or more.

Racecourse Facilities

There are 15 private boxes at the course which can each cater for
up to 14 guests. There are also two large rooms for 70-90 people and
these limits can obviously be increased if a buffet is required. The
racecourse management are happy to assist in organising parties.

There is a Club restaurant at Fontwell and bookings can be made
through Letheby & Christopher, tel: (0273) 602987. The opening of
the new Kerman Stand in May 1991 has added greatly to Fontwell's
facilities with new bars, Tote credit and additional boxes for enter-

taining. Snack bars can also be found throughout the enclosures and there is an off-course betting area in the Paddock area although no banks. Children under 16 are admitted free to all enclosures except the Club. There are lavatories for disabled people positioned in the Silver Ring Enclosure and Tattersalls. If you are blessed with a clear crisp windless day's racing at Fontwell and a couple of fancied flutters oblige you will be pretty close to heaven. Even if they don't you can still anticipate a fine day's racing.

Local Favourites

Where better to begin our gastronomic wander around this most pleasant of English counties than in Storrington where we find **Manleys** (0903) 742331—a very distinguished restaurant. It is extremely popular and bookings for both lunch and dinner are strongly advised. Also in Storrington, one can find a really beautifully situated hotel, **Abingworth Hall** (0798) 813636. There is a warm welcome here and the food and wine list are also first class. However, perhaps even more delightful is the outstanding **Little Thakeham** (0903) 744416 with its Lutyens exterior and gardens designed by Gertrude Jekyll. The hotel and the restaurant are both outstanding.

Another extremely peaceful and relaxing hotel and restaurant double is the **Roundabout Hotel** (0798) 33838 in West Chiltington. The name really does give the wrong idea; not only is the service good, but the prices are reasonable too. If one chooses to visit Arundel, perhaps to view the Castle or to browse through some of the delightful antique shops that line the streets, a particularly relaxing establishment is **The Norfolk Arms** (0903) 882101—a coaching inn for over 200 years and still welcoming today. There are numerous pubs in Arundel but one to note is **The Swan** (0903) 882314. In addition to bar snacks and a pleasant welcome there is some accommodation here too. A really excellent choice is **Bailiffscourt** (0903) 723511—lost it's form for a couple of seasons but is now better than ever.

Not everyone will be able to slumber in Sussex, but any visit should certainly be combined with one of the many splendid pubs that adorn the county. **The Fox Goes Free** at Charlton is a convenient diversion and **The White Hart** at South Harting is especially handy for Goodwood and Fontwell visitors. Nearby in Fittleworth, **The Swan** (0798) 82429 is a lovely old inn. Farther afield, **The Black Horse** (0798) 42424 in Byworth is also worth a visit—a comprehensive range of bar snacks and a really cosy restaurant, ideal for a quiet evening after racing. In Petworth, there are a number of places to note. **The Angel** (0798) 42153 in Angel Street offers good value food in a pleasant medieval inn—the bedrooms also have appeal. **The Red Lion** also welcomes; good food and friendly atmosphere combine extremely well, the pub also offers a wine bar. In Pulborough, **The Chequers Hotel** (0798) 872486 is a small Queen Anne building where lunch and dinner are both well priced. More expensive, but quite superb, is nearby **Amberley Castle** (0798) 831992 near Arundel. Its outer walls predate racing itself—a fine atmosphere in which to consider the heritage of this sport.

Goodwood enjoys one of the most scenic settings in world racing. It also offers in Glorious Goodwood one of the racing and social events of the year. The racecourse is continually upgrading its facilities and as a result hosts numerous additional fixtures that are also given a five star rating, a visit to the course is thoroughly recommended.

The management team at Goodwood are headed by **Rod Fabricius**, who acts as **Clerk** and **General Manager** and **John Thompson** who is Goodwood's **Operations Manager**. They can be contacted at Goodwood Racecourse Ltd, **Goodwood House, Chichester, West Sussex**. **Tel: (0243) 774107** on non-race days and **(0243) 774838** on race days.

Travelling to the Course
The racecourse is a 66 mile journey from London. Chichester, the nearest large town, is some five miles away. Chichester railway station is on the Victoria line and there is an efficient bus service from the station to the course on race days. If you do travel by car from London the journey time is likely to be an hour and a half. The A29 or the A3 doubled up with the A27 should produce a satisfactory result. The M27, which bypasses Chichester, also serves racegoers from the east and west and has recently been improved. Goodwood has ample parking and this is provided free or at £2 (£5 for the July Festival) depending on how far you are prepared to walk. Light aircraft can land at Goodwood Airfield, two miles from the course, helicopters or taxis can be taken to the course from there. Goodwood racecourse provides a prospectus with some of the best information available so do telephone in advance so you can make your own individual arrangements.

Major Races and Charges
Major races to note are the Schweppes Golden Mile at the Glorious Goodwood meeting, the William Hill Cup, the Goodwood Cup, the Vodac Stewards Cup, the Richmond Stakes and the jewel of the year, the outstanding Sussex Stakes.

The annual membership subscription at Goodwood is £120, admitting the member to the Richmond Enclosure on all Goodwood racedays in the year. The cost however, does not include parking which is an extra £32 per annum. Twenty-one Reciprocal events are arranged at fourteen other venues. At the July meeting, daily badges are not on sale to the general public but Members may purchase them at £30 each. Entry to the Gordon Enclosure for this meeting costs £15; alternatively, entry to the Public enclosure costs £5. Parking for the July Meeting is £5 (£2 normally). At all other meetings, day badges for the Members are obtainable at £14, with £9 being the price for the Gordon Enclosure and £4 for the Public Enclosure. Members are advised to make reservations for seats for the July meeting. Junior Membership (5-21) can be purchased for £63. Parties of 20 or more are entitled to discounts in all enclosures except The Richmond Enclosure.

Racecourse Facilities

Tailored packages are available for all your entertainment requirements. Please contact Miss Christine Farren who looks after the marketing, for further details. There are many facilities at Goodwood to suit all tastes and budgets. Enquiries with regard to the catering should be made to Payne & Gunter, tel: (0243) 775350. They do a fine job at providing all the ingredients for a good day's racing. The ever expanding tented village and the superb racing makes for massive crowds at the July fixture, so be warned. Try and arrive at the racecourse in plenty of time, Goodwood always provides a number of worthwhile additional attractions before racing commences.

The third Duke of Richmond organised the first Goodwood Race Meeting in 1801. It was a friendly competition between himself and brother army officers. The event was such a success that in the following year the public was admitted. Thereafter the fame of the location and quality of racing has been so widely acclaimed that racing here has gone from strength to unbridled strength. But Goodwood is also an occasion in the sporting calendar to savour and has been referred to as 'a garden party with racing tacked on'.

Top racing it is too! Goodwood organises various events during the summer meetings which include barbeques, jazz and steel bands, over 65s' Days and Family Days—all of which are highly commendable, and highly recommended. Other especially laudable points about the course are the excellent children's playground, the lifts and stands for the disabled and numerous betting facilities. There is a Gordon Enclosure creche facility at July/August meetings.

Goodwood has a tremendous setting on the South Downs and certainly the major re-building programmes of recent years have improved the Course. There are sadly, few classic sporting arenas in Britain when compared with our competitors around the world. This may be a result of underfunding or poor management or other less tangible reasons. One thing is clear however, Goodwood is constantly being improved and when coupled with the sport available it makes one of the most glorious amphitheatres in racing.

A fellow lover of Britain was recently heard lamenting the demise of certain British industries to various international competitors. 'What,' he asked, 'do we have that maintains international respect?' I thought, worried and then relaxed. 'Our sporting events!' I exclaimed. Wimbledon, the Open, Royal Ascot—genuinely world class events. Goodwood may not have the same internatinal impact but surely no foreign visitors could fail to be impressed. With Britain hopefully coming out of recession in 1994 the Government will be well advised to nurture these events of national and international prestige. They are a vital confidence booster at home and abroad.

Local Favourites

There are all manner of good reasons for visiting Goodwood, not least because it is surrounded by some first rate hotels, but make sure you book early as the crowds are enormous. The Goodwood Park Hotel (0243) 775537 is a charming hotel with some delightful rooms, a pleasant restaurant and a friendly welcome that make for a thoroughly worthwhile place to stay. Lovers of golf should make a point of booking here. A visit to nearby Goodwood House should also be fitted in if at all possible. The Royal Norfolk Hotel (0243) 826222 in Bognor Regis offers special Goodwood weekly rates. Bognor was incidentally given the addition of Regis after George V recuperated there in 1929. If it was good enough for him, its good enough for me.

Goodwood is situated between Midhurst and Chichester. Both towns have a lot to offer. Near Midhurst, the **Park House Hotel** (0730) 812880 is a great favourite whilst **The Spread Eagle** (0730) 816911 is a first class 18th Century inn. The accommodation is most comfortable; lunch and dinner in the restaurant are good. The **Coal Hole** buffet bar opens at lunch for cold meals and seafood. Get there early and you'll still make the first. There are a number of excellent pubs in and near to Midhurst and the civilized **Angel** (0730) 812421 offers good value bedrooms. Midhurst really is ideal for lovers of the post race pub crawl. Restaurants are also in abundance—**Mida** (0730) 813284 is particularly well liked. **Maxines** (0730) 816271 is also well thought of. West of Midhurst is Pulborough, home of the **Chequers Hotel** (0798) 872248, an ideal base for some energetic exploration of the countryside, as is the majestic **Amberley Castle** (0798) 831992 which simply oozes history and class. A genuine favourite in any field.

Travelling south on the A286 en route to Chichester, one finds the **Horse and Groom** in Singleton, a pleasant pub. However, in Chichester a number of other delights exist, **Clinchs** (0243) 789915 in Guildford Street has a small number of rooms so do book well in advance. Elsewhere in the town is **Comme ca** (0243) 788724. **Thompsons** (0243) 528832 is also well fancied and goes from strength to strength. Meanwhile, lovers of Thai food should sample the **River Kwai** (0243) 773294 in Tangmere. The **Dolphin and Anchor Hotel** (0243) 785121 is a satisfactory place to spend the night. The streets of Chichester are often extremely busy, there are some excellent shops, ideal if you don't wish to attend every day of Glorious Goodwood. At night, the streets have an excellent atmosphere and the Cathedral and the Festival Theatre (0243) 781312 are worth a visit. Further west one arrives in Bosham, a delightful village which houses **The Millstream Hotel** (0243) 573234, an attractive small hotel which is a convenient place to stay, especially if you like the coast. In Chilgrove, **The White Horse Inn** (0243) 59219 is excellent—a superb pub and also a fine restaurant not to be missed, the wine list here is breathtaking. In case you take the wrong road out of Chichester and find yourself heading east, do not despair, but head instead for Rustington, where the **Kenmore Guesthouse** (0903) 784634 will ease the most furrowed brow. Finally, in Langrish, near Petersfield, **Langrish House** (0730) 66941 is a little farther afield but is particularly enjoyable.

If, by chance, you anticipate owning or backing a winner, we strongly recommend that you book a table in **Morels** (0428) 651462 in Haslemere, an outstanding French restaurant. Two pleasant pubs can be located by people trekking northwards. In Lickfold, **The Lickfold Inn** is a fine Tudor establishment which offers some good value bar snacks. Meanwhile in Elsted, **The Three Horseshoes** is well recommended. The pub lies just off the B2141 between Chichester and Petersfield. The beauty of this area is that it has an all-round, pleasant appeal. If you have any spare time—do try and get off the main roads and explore the villages you will inevitably find a quiet pub or inn in which to relax. For people seeking more liquid refreshment, visit the Chilsdown vineyard. Near Chichester, the Fishbourne Roman Palace is worth a peep while the Weald and Downland Open Air Museum is also something to note. We are grateful to the Goodwood team for suggesting the following places to try: **The Fox** Goes Free, in Charlton, **The Hurdlemakers** in East Dene, and **The Trundle Inn** in West Dene. These are recommendations from the horse's mouth so to speak and should definitely be carefully considered when assessing the form. **Avisford Park** (0243) 551215, comes with a strong recommendation from the racecourse executive.

If you have any energy left and the summer sun still shines, one place you should not miss near Plumpton is Glyndebourne (0273) 812321—the location of the Glyndebourne Festival (May to mid-August). If you can tie in racing with an evening's opera the contrast will be enormous, but the appeal no less great. **Horsted Place** (0825) 75581 provides a luxurious base, depending, of course, on the state of the following day's betting fund! Golfers will find this hotel particularly appealing. The thought of a day or more at Goodwood fills the heart with joy a night or two at Horsted Place is icing on a tremendous cake.

The people in charge at Hamilton are **Clerk of the Course, Jonnie Fenwicke-Clennel** and **Chief Executive Hazel Dudgeon.** They can be contacted at **Hamilton Park Racecourse, Bothwell Road, Hamilton, Lanarkshire, Ml3 0DY. Tel: (0698) 283806.**

Travelling to the Course

The course is situated 10 miles south of Glasgow, in Hamilton, and the track is accessible from Glasgow via the M74, Junction 5 or from Edinburgh via the M8, Junction 6 and the A723, which runs near the course from east to west. The A776 from East Kilbride may prove an alternative route for eastbound travellers. For punters from the south, the A74 and the M74, Junction 4 is an advisable route from Carlisle. Glasgow Central is the city's principal station and trains from London can be caught at Euston; there is a connecting line to Hamilton West which is the course's local station. Other public transport possibilities are the buses from Glasgow which pass the gates of the course. People with light aircraft and helicopters are not able to land at the course itself but please note, a shuttle service between Heathrow and Glasgow as well as other major cities, could be of some use if you need to make a big plunge and avoid paying tax!

Major Races and Charges

In 1994 there are likely to be 17 days of flat racing at Hamilton Park with plenty of action between March and September. Evening meetings are well worth considering here—ideal for unwinding after a hard day's work in Glasgow. The most popular meeting remains the Saints & Sinners Charity Meeting held in June. I imagine a number of both can be found at such events.

The Annual Membership rates are as follows: a single badge will cost £100 and a double badge (lady and gent) will cost £150. A more fleeting relationship with Hamilton will cost £12 for a Members badge or £7 for the Paddock with a reduced rate if you are a student, pensioner or unwaged (another thoughtful idea from the Hamilton executives). The reduced rate for 1994 is £4. In addition to this concession there is a reduction for couples which is priced at £20 for the club and £10 for the Paddock. So if you are on your own make sure you chat up another single in the car park!

Racecourse Facilities

There are various points that should be noted when considering your trip to Hamilton Park. If you are planning a day out for more than 20 people you will receive a discount and this applies to all enclosures. Full details can be obtained from the Secretary but it may be of help to know that there are private boxes of various sizes and a sponsor's room. Marquees are also available. The new caterers at Hamilton are the well known racecourse catering company Letheby & Christopher and they can be contacted on (0698) 422070. There are various restaurants—Club dining room, snack bars and the string of drinks bars but, as one might expect, these are fairly busy areas.

The course is compact and the atmosphere is excellent. Those of you with children under 16 will be pleased to hear about their free admission and the playground. There are some facilities for disabled racegoers which include a snack bar but be warned, there are no banking facilities so if you intend to make use of the on course betting shops bring your stake money with you.

There have been some major developments at Hamilton Park in recent years which include the extension of the Grandstand to accommodate additional boxes. There are new steppings in front of the Hamilton Park. Local people should note that the facilities can be used for all manner of conferences and receptions throughout the year. Hamilton Park may not be one of Britain's foremost racecourses but with a situation near to Glasgow the racecourse is extremely popular and to be a part of the throng when your fancy is coming through the field is a happy feeling indeed.

Local Favourites

For the businessman, **The Holiday Inn** 041-226 5577 in Argyle Street offers pleasant cocktail bars and a wealth of leisure facilities. **The Hospitality Inn** 041-332 3311 is another high-rise hotel but is well run and comfortable while **The Stakis Grosvenor** 041-339 8811 is a most impressive hotel with a delightful situation opposite the Botanical Gardens. **The Terrace Restaurant** is also well worth visiting. Glasgow offers a variety of attractions and an exquisite Victorian hotel in which to stay is **One Devonshire Gardens** 041-3392001, home of a renowned restaurant.

Glasgow has become a veritable mecca for lovers of fine cuisine with **Rogano's** 041-248 4055 one of its most celebrated. **The Buttery** 041-221 8188 in Argyle Street, is convenient for the Holiday Inn and an excellent spot for lunch or dinner. Upstairs is expensive and correspondingly elegant while downstairs has a more relaxed air with slightly lower prices! A Cantonese restaurant with an extensive menu can be found in Sauciehall Street—it's called **Long Fung** 041-332 1240. **The Amber Restaurant** 041-339 6121 also provides Chinese cuisine of an award-winning standard. Just around the corner, **The Ubiquitous Chip** 041-334 5007 is also fancied but the favourite in a quite competitive field is still **The Colonial** 041-552 1923.

To the west of Glasgow stands **Gleddoch House** (047554) 711, a distinguished hotel and restaurant. Built on the banks of the Clyde this impressive hotel is particularly charming and golfers will be delighted to hear that there is a nearby course. Golf courses, like pubs, are never far away in Glasgow and its surrounds.

Returning south of the Clyde is another busy town, East Kilbride. Two superbly Scottish names to note are **The Stuart** (03552) 21161 and secondly, **The Bruce** (03552) 29771. Both are modern, friendly and relatively convenient for the racecourse. **The Westpoint Hotel** (03552) 36300 is ideal for those who may be on business or who prefer hotels with extensive leisure facilities. Within a mile of the racecourse is the **Silvertrees Hotel** (0698) 852311. It is family run and well regarded by the local racing fraternity. One for the notebook in 1994.

Haydock Park is the best all round racecourse in the North of England. P.W.F. Arkwright and F. Smith act as Clerk and Secretary respectively and can be contacted at **Haydock Park Racecourse, Newton-le-Willows, Merseyside**, or on **(0942) 725963**. The appointment of a General Manager will add strength to the team and it is hoped that Haydock maintains its reputation as one of Britain's best tracks under the new management.

Travelling to the Course
Access to the course is off the A49 close to Ashton. The course is superbly served by motorways and the M6 and the M62 converge close by. However, with traffic building up during the hour before racing, it is advisable to avoid junction 23 of the M26, especially during the summer, as the police tend to direct all traffic down the A580 to the eastern end of the racecourse. Because of the one-way system inside the racecourse, it is impossible to reach A, B and C Car Parks, the O & T Car Park and disabled parking from this gate. There is an overflow car park for those who do enter from this gate but it is beyond the stands. In order to ensure entry through the western gate, M6 traffic from the north can leave at junction 24 and turn left, then right at the lights—the racecourse is a mile farther, on the left. If, after all this, the car sounds like too much effort then catch the Euston train to Warrington Bank Quay or take the local link to Newton-le-Willows, or catch the 320 bus from Liverpool which will deposit you at the gates. More speedy access can be obtained by using the landing strip or helipad.

Major Races and Charges
The fixture list planned for 1994 is likely to remain similar to that of 1993 when 28 days racing were held. The course's most popular event is the fixture held on the first Saturday in July as part of a three day fixture—a highlight of an excellent calendar of Flat and National Hunt racing.

Admission prices in 1994 are expected as follows; For the County Enclosure, you will pay £13.00. Prices for Tattersalls will be £7 and the Newton Enclosure £3. Haydock's Park Suite (viewing restaurant) will cost you £23 and a badge must be purchased in advance to confirm your booking. You will however receive a free racecard. Pensioners are admitted to Tattersalls and the Newton Enclosure at half price. If you are a regular here then an Annual Badge for the County Stand offers a definite saving: in 1993 a single badge for the year was priced at £140 and £50 for Juniors (under 21). This is outstanding value and includes a special car pass and 12 reciprocal days racing at 12 different courses. The racecourse also offers discounts in Tattersalls and Newton Enclosures if you are considering organising a party of 25 or more.

The facilities at Haydock Park are excellent—they include 32 boxes and eight sponsors rooms. The boxes are sited on three floors of the Tommy Whittle Stand, and can accommodate up to 20 people. All boxes are let on a long term basis but a waiting list is maintained as several are made available for sub-let every race day. For larger parties the Luncheon Rooms can be linked together. The Park Suite in the new Grandstand runs the whole length of the top floor and is capable of seating 450 people but can be sectioned off to accommodate parties. CCTV and Tote facilities are also provided. If you wish to use this restaurant, bookings for a table start three months prior to each race day. A more fun way of catering for a larger party may be to organise a marquee—the racecourse is happy to help here. The Lancaster restaurant in the County Enclosure offers a la carte and tables can be booked in advance by telephoning the Catering Office (ext. 214). Other points to note when ι ppraising the racecourse are that admission for accompanied children under 16 is free and there are very good facilities for disabled people in all rings. There are two betting shops but Barclays Bank who used to attend meetings are no longer present so bring plenty of cash if you happen to have a 'fancy'. Haydock Park is a first class racecourse and we wish the new management team well in 1994.

Local Favourites

In Lower Peover, **The Bells of Peover** (0565) 722269 has a delightful setting and as well as super bar food the restaurant is recommended. North of the Bells, in Plumley two pubs can be noted, firstly, **The Smoker** (0565) 722338 which also has an adjoining restaurant as well as serving excellent bar food and secondly, **The Golden Pheasant**— another fine real ale pit stop with bedrooms as well. In Mobberley, **The Bird In Hand** (0565) 873149 is one of the growing band of good food pubs. Other pubs in the area include the extremely welcoming **Fiddle ith Bag** at Burtonwood. **The Pickering Arms** at Thelwell is an attractive and friendly village local while in Risley, **The Noggin** is another popular food pub. However, perhaps the most convenient pub for the racecourse is the **Bay Horse** or even the relaxing County Inn. An enticing alternative is the **Bulls Head** (0942) 671621 in Newton-le-Willows where the food, beer and atmosphere are good and if you wish to make a really early start—bedrooms can be organised. Another likely place for the early bird is the **Post House** at Newton-le-Willows (0942) 717878 for it stands in parkland fringing the Haydock Park racecourse. For those expectant racegoers travelling from Liverpool on the A580, a **Travelodge** provides a convenient stopover. There is also the **Thistle Hotel** (0942) 272000 which lies near to the course—a good place for post race celebrations and ideal if you're going to the National too.

In Manchester, a former Victorian warehouse—the distinguished **Britannia Hotel** 061-228 2288 is found. From the foyer to the bedrooms, the hotel is excellent. Another suggestion is a far more modern edifice **The Hotel Piccadilly** 061-236 8414. This is a real favourite for business meetings and the pleasant sofas and pastel shades— what a perfect ambience for discussing Haydocks runners. Another polished hotel is the **Portland Thistle** Hotel 061-228 3400, an elegant establishment which also boasts an extremely good leisure centre. Manchester boasts an outstanding array of cosmopolitan cooking. **Yang Sing** 061-236 2200 in Princess Street is an excellent Chinese restaurant. **Blinkers** 061-228 2563 is an appropriately named French restaurant while near the airport **Moss Nook** 061-437 4778 is the most established restaurant in the area

Britain, like France has a multitude of charming rustic racecourses and with so much of England being taken up by sprawling urbanisation it is a real pleasure to escape to the country. The shire of Hereford contains many such green fields and within its acres a welcoming picturesque racecourse, Hereford. The team in charge at Hereford are **Clerk Of The Course** and **Secretary, John Williams** and **Manager** of the course **Charles Dawson** who can be contacted at **The Racecourse, Roman Road, Hereford HR4 9QU** or **Shepherds Meadow, Eaton Bishop, Hereford. HR2 9UA.** If the immediate attention of the aforementioned is required tel: **(0981) 250436.**

Travelling to the Course
Hereford Racecourse is clearly signposted and there are good roads on the northern outskirts of the city. Indeed, the whole area is bordered by several major roads from the Midlands, South Wales and the South West. From the north, the racecourse can be reached via the A49 from Leominster and the A4110. The main southern approach roads are the A49 and the A495. The A438 through Hereford itself passes close to the racecourse and there's also an approach on the A4103 from Worcester. London is approximately 123 miles away and if you are travelling to Hereford by train then Paddington station is the one from which to make your departure. The station is a mile from the course and a taxi will be required from there unless you wish to take a short stroll. Should you be fairly busy and/or well off then subject to prior arrangement helicopters are welcome. If you decide to take the motor two large free car parks await you, one of which is a picnic style car park with a complete view of all the racing. Please note however, that the entrance for the Course Enclosure is off the A49, whilst the Tattersalls entrance can be found off the A4103.

Major Races and Charges
The racecourse will hold 15 National Hunt Meetings in 1994. The bank holiday fixture in April is the most popular and there is also a splendid alternative to the Grand National. As the Clerk of the Course points out, most of the racing here is bread and butter stuff but there are often large fields and racing is competitive. The course has also been granted a further Bank Holiday fixture on Whit Monday making a total of three such events. Admission to the Members Enclosure was £10 in 1993 and £8 for Tattersalls. The Silver Ring cost £3. There is no Annual Membership here. Discounts are available for Tattersalls for larger groups and you should contact the racecourse for further details.

Racecourse Facilities
Boxes are available to hire on a daily basis and differ in size catering for up to 40 guests. There is a larger room which will take up to 150 guests or marquees can be erected if you wish for an even bigger party. There is also a restaurant in the Course Enclosure where there is no need to book. Various packages are on offer here from the caterers, Hughes of Welshpool (0432) 353135. The usual snack bars are dotted around the course for those who only need a quick bite.

If you wish to take your children racing and they are under 16 they are admitted free. Disabled racegoers will be pleased to note that access is easy from Tattersalls as well as a special viewing area. There is also a betting shop located in the Tattersalls.

Hereford is one of those delightful out of the way county towns where the pace of life is slightly slower. The horses may also be of lesser speed than those of Ascot or Cheltenham but racing is still competitive here and should you wish for a peaceful day out, there are few finer courses at which to spend the day.

Local Favourites

For those who wish to really soak up the racecourse atmosphere, a five minute walk from the aforementioned track brings one to the doorstep of the **Starting Gate Inn** which is attached to the extremely convenient and functional **Travel Inn** (0432) 274853. **The Green Dragon** (0432) 272506 and **The Hereford Moat House** (0432) 354301, dating from 1850, are also safe bets (always a dangerous claim to make). The beauty of a visit to Hereford also lies in the sprawling countryside which surrounds it, the Malvern Hills for example. Pubs to try here include the splendid **Butchers Arms** (0432) 560281 at Woolhope, a half-timbered building which offers good bar food, a restaurant and some accommodation. Nearby, in Fownhope, **The Green Man** (0432) 860243 is a popular local fancy with excellent food and good pub accommodation. The incongruously named **Bunch of Carrots** (0432) 870237 has an attractive setting and is only 3 miles from the racecourse. Ledbury has a host of places to visit. The timbered **Feathers** (0531) 5266 is appealing. **The Hope End** (0531) 3613, at Hope End, is also peaceful with a fine restaurant. Another Ledbury thought is **Ye Olde Talbot** (0531) 2963 which has a beautiful exterior as well as a friendly interior. Northwest of Ledbury in Bishops Frome, you come across **The Green Dragon** (0885) 490607 whose good beer, filling bar food and traditional atmosphere make for a perfect post-race rendezvous.

The county of Herefordshire, characterised by brown and white faced cows, is stunning with the countryside approaching the Welsh border of particular note. In this direction, **The Lord Nelson** (0981) 22208 at Bishopstone has a good restaurant and bar food. In Eardisland, the **White Swan** is a good stop-off point for people travelling north, while at Whitney-on-Wye, **The Rhydspence** (0497) 3262 offers superb bar meals and some accommodation—a must for a long weekend if booked well in advance. Venturing back towards England, one finds **The Broad Oak**, Eastway, an excellent place for a post-race supper. Where else? At Sellack, try **The Lough Pool** (no rooms here though). Our trip comes full circle at delightful Ross-on-Wye where some outstanding hotels can be found. **The Chase** (0989) 763161 is a charmingly, personal Victorian hotel and **The Pengethley** (0989) 87211, a little outside the town, is also a marvellous hotel with a super restaurant. In nearby Walford, **The Walford House Hotel** (0989) 63829 offers great hospitality and accommodation. Finally, **The Royal** (0989) 65105, provides another excuse for visiting this gorgeous area in the unlikely event that Hereford Racecourse is not attraction enough.

Clerk of the Course, Secretary and Manager at this delightful course are all roles admirably carried out by one **Charles Enderby**. He may be contacted at **The Racecourse Office, The Riding, Hexham, Northumberland. Tel: (0434) 606881.**

Travelling to the Course

Hexham lies 20 miles from Newcastle, 40 miles from Carlisle and some 300 miles from the bustle of Trafalgar Square. The course itself is a mile south of the market town of Hexham, sandwiched between the B6305 and the B6306. The road that runs between Newcastle and Carlisle, the A69, is convenient for joining either of these two minor roads. The new Newcastle western by-pass is now open and this should speed up your journey considerably if you are using the A1. If you are northbound on the A1 and have a little extra time in which to make your journey, leave the A1 at its junction with the A68 and follow the road through the Durham Hills—stunning. The M6 and the A69 are the most direct routes for those travelling from Carlisle and the west of the country, although the A686 through the Gilderdale Forest is an appealing alternative. There are bus and train stations in Hexham. Newcastle is on the main 225 Kings Cross—Edinburgh route and the journey time is swift. A connecting train can be caught from Newcastle to Hexham. There is a free bus from the train station to the racecourse on race days which is particularly handy. The majority of racegoers however, seem to drive to the course where there are acres of free parking and Members have a reserved area. There is also plenty of room in this rustic, charming, peaceful setting to land your noisy helicopter should you so wish, but please notify the course prior to your arrival.

Major Races and Charges

The major race is the Heart of all England Hunters' Steeplechase, run in late April is Hexham's busiest day but throughout the season some good chasing and hurdling is on offer. The rates for the various enclosures in 1993 were as follows: £9 for Members and £6 for Tattersalls and this includes a free racecard. If you wish to enrol as an Annual Member, the price will be £55 for a single, £90 for a double, and £20 for a junior (16-21) badge. This includes free racecards and car parking as well as eleven reciprocal meetings at nearby Carlisle, Newcastle, Perth, Catterick, Bangor and Haydock. For people wishing to organise parties, there is a 20 per cent reduction for groups of 15 or more in both enclosures. These prices will remain fixed for the 1994 season which is good to report.

Racecourse Facilities

The racecourse has a new sponsor's suite, bookable by appointment, with splendid views over the course, together with the usual boxes and bars. There are the usual Tote betting facilities and a handy bar offering hot snacks and soup as well as spirits. This overlooks the parade ring. (The spirits are particularly welcome when the east wind hits hard). There are two restaurants here; the Bramble Tudor and Racecourse where you can expect to pay between £5 and £10.

Prices and specifications for catering can be found out from the excellent local caterers; Romfords, tel: (043484) 8864. If you are taking a child or disabled friend racing you will be pleased to know that the former is allowed in free, whilst the latter is invited to make use of a raised mound for better viewing. There is a car park from which disabled drivers may watch racing; entry next to owners/trainers gate. This is one of the most scenic of England's National Hunt racecourses—cherish a visit, it epitomises all that is good in the sport.

Local Favourites

The market town of Hexham provides a charming and relatively tranquil contrast to the bright lights of its near neighbour Newcastle. Close by, in Chollerford, **The George Hotel** (0434) 81611 is particularly relaxing and is an ideal place to rest your weary head. Alternatively, one could pop in for a drink—a quiet, cosy bar is always worth a visit don't you think? Other places in which to discuss the card include a delightful country house hotel in Alston, **The Lovelady Shield** (0434) 381203. Alston is the highest market town in England and enjoys a supremely rustic setting.

In Blanchland, **The Lord Crewe Arms** (0434) 675251 is hidden in the heart of the countryside. In addition to an extremely welcoming hotel some good value weekend breaks can be arranged. Speaking of good combinations, one might look to Corbridge—another pleasant and picturesque town. **The Black Bull** is a popular meetin spot and **The Ramblers Country House** (0434) 632424—a fine idea for dinner. Comfortable, down to earth accommodation is available in Corbridge at **Low Barns** (0434) 632408. Back to Hexham itself, **The Beaumont Hotel** (0434) 602331 overlooks the Abbey grounds and is perhaps the most convenient place to stay. On the main street, **The County** (0434) 602030 is an amicable pre-race hotel where the bars are a popular rendezvous. More conveniently placed for the racecourse, outside the town itself, lies **The Dipton Mill**, a splendidly rustic pub which should be visited if time allows. The Fox and Hounds at Whitley Chapel is also unassuming, welcoming and good value.

In Wall, **The Hadrian Hotel** (0434) 81232 is ideally placed for exploring the nearby Wall of the same name. The countryside here is exceptionally beautiful and full of historic interest. Another watery haunt lies at Warden where **The Boat** is a super country pub. Another delight can be found north east of Hexham in the village of Great Whittington—**The Queens Head** has a pleasant village setting and very good bar food and a newly opened restaurant. Another thought is the excellent **Bishopfield**, at Allendale (0434) 683248—extremely comfortable accommodation in a converted Georgian Farmhouse.

High up, with spectacular views overlooking the moorland, just off the A68 is The **Manor House** (0207) 55268 at Carterway Heads which serves some excellent pub food and now has some accommodation. Finally, on the road out of Hexham towards Slaley, you will find the **Black House** (0434) 604744 where the atmosphere is friendly yet sophisticated and the food first class. An ideal place to end your day after a visit to one of Britain's most enchanting racecourses.

The Clerk of the Course, Hugo Bevan and the new Manager, Mr Richard Thomas, can be contacted at the Racecourse Office, Brampton, Huntingdon, Cambridgeshire. PE18 8NN. Tel: (0480) 454610/453373

Travelling to the Course

The course is situated just outside the village of Brampton, two and a half miles from the town of Huntingdon. It is conveniently positioned for travellers from the south (London is 60 miles away) and also from the north of the country as it is a mile to the east of the A1, just off the A604 (the extension of the M11). The nearest railway station is just outside Huntingdon, two miles away. It's on the main 125 line and it is really a very short journey from Kings Cross. There is no direct bus service from the station to the racecourse but there is a bus to Brampton which is one and a quarter miles from Huntingdon and taxis are easy to find.

Major Races and Charges

They only race over the sticks at Huntingdon, but a full 15 day fixture list is on offer. The meetings are all one day affairs, the most popular tending to be Easter Monday and Boxing Day which always guarantee large and merry crowds. Highlights of the year include the Sidney Banks Memorial Hurdle and the Peterborough Chase. This listed race carries a prize of £25,000 It is a much sought after prize and often produces excellent fields.

Huntingdon has free parking for cars and coaches. However, if a picnic is the order of the day then £1 is charged for parking adjacent to the rails. Membership is reasonably priced—the charge for double membership was £110 in 1993 whereas a single badge cost £70. Junior Membership for the 16-24 age group is available at £45. There was an £11 charge for a daily members badge whilst the entrance charge for Tatts was £8 and the cost for the popular Course Enclosure, £4. The management offers a 20 per cent discount for parties of 20 or more in Tattersalls.

Racecourse Facilities

Various boxes on the course provide for parties of all sizes, with prices ranging from £250 to £650 plus VAT. The Centenary Room can accommodate up to 35 in each of its two rooms. Both have their own bar and private viewing. The Waterloo Room will hold up to 100 racegoers. The most encouraging point here is that the boxes are taken by companies from all over the country and not merely local concerns. Marquees can also be arranged for larger parties of 50 or more.

The racegoer is able to lunch in either the Members or Tattersalls restaurants. Booking is advisable for the former. The caterers are Letheby & Christopher and they can be contacted on (0638) 662750. The course has a selection of snacks available from the bars which are scattered through the Grandstand and in the Course Enclosure. The course management allows children under 14 to be admitted free. There are public telephones on the course but there is no bank which makes life frustrating if you spot a likely winner and you've blown all your cash! The courses off-track betting shop is, however, a retreat for the hardened punter who wants to keep in touch with racing around the country and escape the outrageous odds that some bookmakers lay when taking money for races elsewhere. This is a friendly unpretentious racetrack which offers competitive racing.

Local Favourites

The town's foremost hotel is **The Old Bridge** (0480) 52681, a popular meeting place where one can happily enjoy a drink, a quiet lunch, a more comprehensive dinner in the fine restaurant or if you have travelled some distance, a room for the night. You should be well satisfied on all counts. An alternative suggestion is **The George** (0480) 432444, another popular bar with satisfactory accommodation.

South of Huntingdon is St Neots and here, a comfortable bed can be found at the **Old Falcon Hotel** (0480) 72749. Slightly farther towards Bedford is the moderately priced **Church Guesthouse** (0234) 870234 which is also excellent. In Fen Drayton, **The Three Tuns** (0954) 30242 is another pleasant drinking establishment—very popular with people in the know throughout Cambridgeshire. In Arrington, The **Hardwicke Arms** (0223) 207243 is a really super little pub and some excellent rooms can also be taken advantage of here. Another nearby hall which doubles as an hotel has a particularly appropriate name, **Slepe Hall** (0480) 63122 (pronounced as in a long snooze!) in St. Ives. Needingworth is very close to St. Ives and here, the **Pike and Eel** (0480) 63336 is exceptionally cosy, offering comfortable accommodation and views of the River Ouse with boats mooring in front of the inn. A good pub restaurant is sheltered within **The Pheasant** (0801) 4241 at Keyston; if you prefer a bar snack then once again you will not be disappointed. People who are unable to sample these various offerings and need to journey home up the A1 then a pint at **The Bell** (0733) 241066 at Stilton may be an idea while further north at Wansford, a pint at **The Haycock** (0780) 782223 is a must. Lest you get the wrong impression, these establishments are not your average boozers, both are splendid hotels with excellent restaurants as well as comfortable bars. People who are making their merry way south should perhaps try one of three pubs near to the A1. Firstly the **Leeds Arms** (0480) 87283 at Eltisley which is a particularly welcoming establishment offering some accommodation if needs be; **The Eight Bells** in the pleasant village of Abbotsley is also worth a stop and finally, **The White Horse** (0480) 74453 at Eaton Socon is a part 13th Century inn with a pleasant restaurant, good atmosphere and also some bedrooms. The perfect place to celebrate having plundered the good old bookies of Huntingdonshire.

77

This friendly course is exceptionally well administered by **Richard Landale** who is the **Manager** and **Secretary** and is the person to contact for further information at the following address; **Sale & Partners, 18/20 Glendale Road, Wooler, Northumberland, NE71 6DW. Tel: (0668) 81611.** The Clerk Of The Course is Jonnie Fenwick-Clennell.

Travelling to the Course
Kelso is easy to find and the course lies to the north of the town itself, off the A6089 and the A699. The journey from London is 320 miles. The A1(M) is the best route to take and the A697 or the A698 are both spectacular routes through the Borders and Northumberland. From the West take the M6 to junction 44, from whence the A7 and the A698 are the best roads to choose. From Edinburgh the A68 and the A698 is the combination to follow. Both the Edinburgh and Newcastle by-passes have now been completed and these have greatly eased travel from both north and south to Kelso.

There are other options for your journey, but the car has to be the best bet. The nearest railway station is in Berwick, 22 miles away on the Kings Cross line out of London. There are no buses to the course from the station, but the racecourse can arrange transportation. Aviators are also diverted to nearby Winfield but helicopters are now welcomed. It seems fairly obvious then, that some form of motor transportation is in order and there is, after all, the incentive of free parking. What's more, there is no reserved area for Members—first come, first served! Special disabled parking can also be arranged in advance.

Major Races and Charges
Good prizes equal good horses (subject of course, to the weather) and some reasonable horses should be seen for these races. The Kelso Exectutive are also goos at finding commercial support and all but one race was sponsored in 1993. The biggest day in the autumn is The Mason Day which last year featured the first £10,000 race and in 1993 featured an impressive £15,000 chase. In the spring, the Hennessy Day is a good meeting, featuring a valuable juvenile hurdle. Prize money will in fact, exceed £300,000 over the 12 day's racing.

Admission prices are in line with most country courses; £10 is the price for admission to the Member's (midweek) £12 on Saturdays, £6 for the Tattersalls Enclosure or £3 if you happen to be an O.A.P. Annual Membership which includes a private bar/viewing room and 15 reciprocal days costs £100 for a double badge, £60 for a single and £40 for O.A.P.'s. Generous discounts of up to 50% are available to pre-booked parties.

Racecourse Facilities
As far as Corporate Hospitality is concerned, Kelso offers the Dukes Room (50 people), the Hamilton and Tweedie rooms (70 people), the Berrymoss Box (12 people), the Doody Room (20 people) and three viewing boxes (capacity 35 each). Please apply to the Secretary; prices start from £100. Marquees can be erected and will hold up to 850

guests. The catering is provided by two local firms and a very high standard of home cooked delicious food is available at tremendous value—breakfast £2.50; lunch £7.50.

The course is well stocked with the standard items expected of a racecourse—children under 16 are admitted free and for the very young there is a creche. Although there is no bank, the Secretary will usually cash cheques and there is a betting shop in the Tattersalls, together with a new Tote building in which to spend your money! There are W.Cs and viewing ramps for the disabled. More unusually there is a golf course in the middle of the course, and a Sunday market throughout the year.

In 1993, Kelso held the first free day's racing (a small charge is levied for transfers to the Member's Enclosure.) The backer, The Board of Scottish Borders Enterprise hope that, as in Ireland, first time racegoers will be attracted to the sport and return regularly. The day will also offer a trade fair. Kelso is not the greatest racecourse in the country but it is one of the best run and many others could learn from the management here.

Local Favourites
We choose to start our journey at a real favourite; **Sunlaws House Hotel** (0573) 450331. A hotel of distinction, you will find Sunlaws just south of Kelso at Roxburgh. The hotel is beautifully furnished and the restaurant first rate, it's not overly expensive and a joy at which to stay. Further north, in Kelso itself, one finds the **Ednam House Hotel** (0573) 224168. The Tweedside setting has obvious appeal for anglers, but the hotel is also most convenient for the racecourse. There are welcoming bars here which are also very relaxing. Another place to visit is the **Queens Head Hotel** (0573) 224636—the bar snacks here are excellent, as indeed they are at **The Cross Keys Hotel** (0573) 223303, in Kelso's town square.

Rain or shine, Melrose is a charming border town and **Burts Hotel** (0896) 822285 is one to note. **Dunfermline House** (0896) 822148 is a splendid guesthouse close to Melrose Abbey. **The George and Abbotsford Hotel** (0896) 822308 is also worth more than a little consideration. A little further south, in St. Boswells, two hotels should also be noted. Firstly, the most hospitable **Buccleuch Arms** (0835) 22243 and secondly, **The Dryburgh Abbey** (0835) 22261—some tremendous Scottish fare as well as the ideal de-icer—a roaring open fire!

Well warmed up, you may decide to brave the elements and visit Gattonside. Here, the **Hoebridge Inn** (0896) 823082 is appealing. Trekking north towards the soaken uplands, one arrives in Lauder. Here, the **Black Bull** (0578) 2208 is a pleasant, modernised Georgian coaching inn. Eddleston offers the excellent **Horse Shoe Inn** (0721) 3225. Again a fair distance from Kelso, one finds Ettrickbridge. Here, the **Ettrickshaws Hotel** (0750) 52229 is well worth the journey; good value hospitality and some extremely imaginative set menus. In Selkirk, one place to sample is the **Queen's Head**, another welcoming place to have a drink. The **Phillipburn House Hotel** (0750) 20747 is also a pleasant place in which to stay. The **Tillmouth Park Hotel** (0890) 882255 boasts nine miles of salmon fishing on the river Tweed and is both cosy and hospitable, an idyllic choice for the lover of country sports.

Kempton is without doubt one of the best run racecourses in the country. It considers every aspect of the sport and ensures that the professionals in the game as well as the paying casual visitor and annual member are well looked after. It may not have the status of Epsom or Sandown but it is a glowing tribute to the management of United Racecourses and to all who enjoy the sport.

The management team is headed by **Major Michael Webster**, who is also **Clerk of the Course. Andrew Cooper** is **Manager** and the **Club Secretary** is **Carol Milburn-Lee**. They can be contacted at **Kempton Park Racecourse, Staines sRoad East, Sunbury-On-Thames, Middlesex, TW16 5AQ. Tel: (0932) 782292.** The Boxes and Suites are looked after by Lucy Kane.

Travelling to the Course
The racecourse is situated some 15 miles from central London and is well served by the motorway links. The M25 and the M3 make the trip in from the country especially good. For the popular evening meetings however, one should consider the rush hour build-up. The A316 and the A308 will take you over the Thames to within a stone's throw of the racecourse. The A308 via Hampton Court is the best road from the South. For train travellers, there is an excellent service direct to the course from Waterloo. There is also a bus stop outside the racecourse gates and buses can be taken from Staines and Kingston. The main car park lies adjacent to the grandstand and costs £2, while free parking can be found in the Silver Ring car park and in the centre of the course. If you wish to arrive by helicopter, that's fine, but light aircraft are not welcomed. Helicopters are requested to land between the dovecote and the lake—but phone in advance and notify the course.

Major Races and Charges
Kempton provides some superb racing throughout the year and the highlight is, without doubt, The Bank Holiday Festival, including the King George VI Steeplechase on Boxing Day. The post-Christmas euphoria always makes for a jovial atmosphere. The absence of Desert Orchid is a great loss to the racecourse and racing in general, but the world rolls on and you can guarantee even without Dessie the King George will provide a memorable spectacle. June features the Gala Evening with bands, barbecues, a fun fair and fireworks. Purists may argue that this is far from what racing is really all about, but Kempton is booming, the racing is of a very competitive standard and if you go along I will bet you a fiver straight you'll have a

great time.

There will be a total of twenty three meetings here in 1994, with fourteen on the flat and nine over the jumps. An excellent selection of races can be seen and the rates for Daily Membership last year were as follows; on premium days, a charge of £13 was levied, which rose to £20 for the King George. Juniors (16-21) are given a 25 per cent discount. Entrance to Tattersalls in 1993 was priced at £9 (£13 on Boxing day) while the Silver Ring would cost you £4 (£5 on Boxing Day). Children are admitted free. Annual Membership in 1993 was £160 which included a free car park label. Reciprocal arrangements are made with Goodwood, Taunton, Lingfield and Devon & Exeter. There is also the opportunity to purchase one voucher for the Member's Enclosure at Epsom on any race day except Derby Day. A special rate is offered to parties of 20 or more.

Racegoers keener on the jumps are offered an interesting Dual Membership at Kempton and Sandown Park, giving 20 days' jumping and a car park label for £100 or so. Check with the racecourse that this is still available—but it does sound like a good idea. In fact, I am surprised a similar arrangement is not in order for the flat racing fraternity. Indeed this arrangement will surely be developed by the racecourse management in their efforts to increase the gates at Epsom.

Racecourse Facilities

The facilities at Kempton are excellent and boxes, suites and conference areas can all be organised. The 21 private boxes are let annually, but they do become available on some days. 16 of these have balconies overlooking the racecourse and its very attractive grounds. The boxes can seat 12 people for lunch or about 20 for a less formal buffet. Each box has close circuit television, private bar facilities and a number of other perks. Prices for these rooms range from £550 to £650, the location being the decisive factor. The course generally know whether boxes are free 2-3 weeks in advance. This may not leave much time to organise a party, but for those who do not need to plan too far in advance it is a first class idea. Lunch is available from around £20 and you can choose between sit down lunches, fork buffets and a seafood buffet. The various areas to enquire about are the excellent Lanzarote Room, The Paddock and Thames Suites, the Wayward Lad and Hampton Suites and the Manor Room. Lucy Kane will give details to companies or private individuals who wish to make the most of these areas. If you wish to have lunch before racing, book with the racecourse caterers, Ring & Brymer, on (0932) 786199. Lunch will cost you somewhere in the region of £27.50. More modest refreshments and nourishment can be found in numerous snack bars, the Tattersalls Bar, the Wine Rack and the Grooms Restaurant. Finally, one may enjoy a picnic in the course enclosure car parks, should this be your form of nourishment.

Facilities for children include a playground in the centre of the course and a creche. Good amenities for disabled people including a viewing ramp can also be found. In short, Kempton Park is a well run and friendly racecourse; we wish it well and unreservedly recommend it to racing's professionals and to the more casual racegoer.

Local Favourites

Racing at either Sandown or Kempton offers a great variety of enticing possibilities for culinary refreshment. Those journeying back to the Capital should also find that many of the following suggestions make convenient and relaxing stop-offs.

In Esher, **Good Earth** (0372) 462489 offers a good Chinese menu. In East Molesey, one finds an extremely popular French restaurant, **Le Chien Qui Fume** 081-979 7150.

There are a number of pubs in Hampton Court to sample and opposite the Palace itself, the **Hampton Court Brasserie** 081-979 7891 is an extremely popular post race haunt. People who prefer Italian cooking might wish to visit Cheam—here **Al San Vincenzo** 081-661 9763 is first class.

Pubs conveniently placed for Sandown include **The Albert Arms** and **The Cricketers**. Alternatively for Kempton try the **Kings Head** in Shepperton, or the **Three Horseshoes** in Laleham.

If you are staying in the area, then there are a number of possibilities to consider. In Weybridge, the **Oatlands Park Hotel** (0932) 847242 is an ever improving favourite. A well appointed alternative is **The Ship Thistle Hotel** (0932) 848364, while **Casa Romana** (0932) 843470 is an exciting Italian affair. Alternatively, another place for your post-race nose bag is to be found in Woking, at the reasonably priced **Wheatsheaf** (04837) 73047. Leisure lovers and golfers should note the outstanding country house hotel, **Selsdon Park** 081-657 8811 in Sanderstead, a thoroughly delightful establishment.

Before returning to London we might consider three options in Cobham. **The Woodlands Park Hotel** (037 284) 3933, **Il Giardino** (0932) 863973 a very favourable Italian restaurant, or if one just wants a post-race pint, **The Cricketers** in Cobham. In Ripley, south west of Cobham, another restaurant beckons, **Michaels** (0483) 224777—outstanding French cuisine on this occasion. Finally, the **Hilton National** (0932) 64471 at Cobham is a large, well run concern from the internationaly acclaimed stable of the same name.

There are a whole mass of outstanding restaurants in London, some cheap and cheerful, others cheerful until the bill comes! Outside the capital however, a number of establishments might be thought of. In Richmond, one finds all manner of good eating places and pubs, and a good hotel as well, **The Richmond Gate** 081-940 9998 which is a worthwhile port of call. The outstanding restaurant here is **Nondini** 081-940 5236. In Egham one should note several establishments. **The Eclipse** is an ideal place for a drink (should be nearer Sandown, I suppose), **La Bonne Franquette** (0784) 39494 is a good restaurant to note, while **Great Fosters** (0784) 433822 is an interesting building which houses a good hotel—obviously better value than London offerings. **The Runymede** (0784) 436171 is more modern but is a popular visiting spot for the many who travel this way. In Staines, **The Swan** is a fine public house as is **The Harrow** in Compton, south of Guildford—note the racing prints here. In Sunbury-on-Thames, **The Castle** (09327) 83647 is a superb French restaurant and Shepperton is also handy for the racecourse where **The Warren Lodge** (0932) 242972 is a good place to stay; it's terrace overlooks the Thames. The Anchor Hotel (0932) 221618 is another worthy candidate—pleasant bars and bedrooms and not too pricey. One of the largest hotels in the area is the **Shepperton Moat House** (0932) 241404, less intimate than some by virtue of its size, but a worthy recommendation just the same. **The Thames Court** (0932) 221957 in Surbiton is another spot to note, this restaurant offers French cuisine while the bar has a variety of sandwiches and cold meats—excellent. Surbiton also offers the **Warwick Guesthouse** 081-399 5837 for excellent value accommodation.

Racegoers who enjoy cricket should seek out **The Swan** in Claygate in summer as it doubles as the local cricket pavilion—excellent bar food as well.

If you are coming back through London, the following tips should cover most options. In Wimbledon there are a variety of pubs on the Common, all great fun. If you want to celebrate in style and don't wish to return to the better known West London eating haunts try **Harveys** 081-672 0114 in Wandsworth—it's not cheap and you must book in advance, but it is outstanding and well worth it. A number of wine bars on Bellevue Road, also in Wandsworth, are good for a post race drink and nosebag for people journeying back into London. One pub to mention is the **Alma** on Old York Road—a good local boozer with excellent pub food and a landlord who'll find you a winner in any field. The restaurant here is good value. There are a number of restaurants all along the road, ranging from Mexican to Italian to the typical French bistro. There is even an excellent fish and chip restaurant. Whatever your choice, we wish you well while racing at Kempton.

The **Secretary** and **Manager** of Leicester Racecourse is **Mr D.C. Henson**, while the **Clerk of the Course** is **Captain N.E.S. Lees**. They can both be contacted at **The Racecourse, Oadby, Leicester, LE2 4AL. Tel: (0533) 716515.**

Travelling to the Course

Leicester racecourse is situated in Oadby, two miles south east of Leicester on the A6 Market Harborough Road. Both the M1, exit junction 21, and the M69 are major roads which might prove useful in reaching the track. From the west and Birmingham (40 miles away) take the M6 exiting at junction 2 and follow the M69 to the M1. Try and use the B5418 and avoid Leicester's one-way system at all costs. Southbound travellers will find the A46 and the M1 the best routes while the A6 and the M1 are possibilities for the north-bound racegoer. People making the journey from Newmarket might wish to use the A47 turn off before Leicester, through Evington and onwards to the racecourse. The Southern District Distributor Road links the M1 (junction 21) with the A6 at the entrance to the course. Trains run from St. Pancras to Leicester and the journey takes approximately an hour and a half. A bus service runs from the station to the racecourse on race days and there is a regular service from Leicester City to the track. The ample car parking facilities are provided free of charge here and if you have a helicopter, you will be pleased to learn you can land it in the centre of the course.

Major Races and Charges

Leicester enjoys a full year of flat and National Hunt racing. There are no Annual Members at the track but at the last time of asking Daily Members at Leicester paid £11 for a badge, while Tattersalls visitors paid £8.00 and those in the Silver Ring were asked to pay £4.00; all three rates come with a free card and parking. Discounts are offered on parties of 20 or more booked in advance. This applies to Tattersalls only.

Racecourse Facilities

For companies or individuals who wish to entertain there is a hospitality complex above the Belvoir Bar in the Club Enclosure where there are boxes which can accommodate 12-14 for a sit down meal or 20 for a buffet. Moving back to the Members, there are two private rooms; The Fernie and Barleythorpe, both of which can be hired on a daily basis. One holds 20 to 30 people, the up to 50 guests. Marquees can be erected in the paddock area if required. The caterers, Drewetts, can be contacted on (0788) 544171 and will be able to assist with menus. There is a restaurant located in Tattersalls though there is no necessity to book a table and racegoers can also picnic within the Silver Ring Car Park. There are no special facilities for children, but there are viewing stands in the Members for disabled people. Public telephones are situated in all the enclosures and there is a Ladbrokes Betting Shop in Tattersalls but there are no banks at the racecourse. Leicester is a well situated racecourse and is well worth a visit—one to bear in mind when scanning the 1994 racing calendar!

Local Favourites

If you wish to stay in the city then the suggestion is that you plump for one of the two large hotels. Both hotels stand close to the city centre: they are firstly the **Holiday Inn** (0533) 531161 which is particularly modern but has swimming pools and that sort of thing to make up for the situation. Less modern, Victorian actually, is **The Grand** (0533) 555599—note here a particularly good coffee shop and some welcoming bars. Among the vast number of guesthouses and B&B's in the area, **Leigh Court** (0886) 32275 and the **Scotia Hotel** (0533) 704294 stand out from the crowd.

In Rothley, **The Rothley Court** (0533) 374141 is an idyllic manor house with a super setting and an excellent restaurant. In Quorn itself **The Quorn Country Hotel** (0509) 415050 blends together a combination of traditional hospitality and modern amenities. There are a number of appealing pubs to be found in and around Charnwood and one of them is **The Carrington Arms** (0664) 840228, Ashby Folville—good bar food here. A longer trip for a hotel of merit is the **Johnscliffe Hotel** in Newtown Linford (0530) 242228. South of the city in Whetstone, **The Old Vicarage** (0533) 771195 is a pleasant restaurant as is the **Glen Parva Manor Restaurant** (0533) 774604 at Glen Parva, close to Leicester. **The Three Swans** (0858) 466644 at Market Harborough is another comfortable and highly recommended establishment. In Old Dalby, **The Crown Inn** (0664) 823134 dates from the 17th century and is a lovely place for a pint and a fireside chat; there's also a fairly handy restaurant. A hotel of note is the **Harboro Hotel** (0664) 60121. The restaurant here is also worth a visit. Alternative accommodation can be found in the **The George** (0664) 62112, an extremely comfortable and well looked-after inn which is strongly recommended. **The Rose and Crown** in Hose is a popular pub with tremendous character and some good food. In Braunston, as opposed to Branston, **The Old Plough** (0572) 722714 is also welcoming while on the way to Oakham, **The Noel Arms** at Langham is also recommended—a good restaurant here (0572) 722931. Two supremely popular pubs are **The Bell** at East Langton (085884) 567 and **The Berwicke Arms,** Hallaton, (085889) 217, both renowned for really first-rate food.

First class is a description one should also apply to the area's leading hotel, **Hambleton Hall** (0572) 756991. The grounds lead down to Rutland Water and the bedrooms are superb. The highlight of the house is the restaurant—outstanding. Less grand, but no less welcoming accommodation can be found in Oakham's market place—**The George**, a good place for a drink as is the **Neville Arms**, Medbourne and **The Marquis Of Exeter** at Lydington (0572) 822477. The adjoining hotel has a good restaurant and accommodation. Another worthy addition to the well stocked Oakham stable is the **Whipper-In Hotel** (0572) 756971, the bedrooms here have great individual charm and the restaurant is excellent.

Lingfield Park

The Clerk of the Course is Mr. Geoff Stickels and he can be contacted at Racecourse Road, Lingfield, Surrey, RH7 6PQ. Tel: (0342) 834800. Fax (0342) 836201. The Managing Director here is Mr Tony Sunley.

Travelling to the Course

Lingfield is easily accessible from London which is only 21 miles away. The M25 and the A22 are the best routes to follow from the Capital. The racecourse itself is on the B2029. The A22 is the best route for northbound travellers, exiting for the course at Newchapel. Westbound travellers should take the A264 while those heading east should pursue the M25 and the A22, exiting at junction 6. On arrival, there is a choice of car parks with parking for 7,000 cars. The public car park is free.

The Members in the centre of the course is more convenient but a charge of £2 is levied if space is reserved in advance. If you don't want to take the car then a train from Victoria or London Bridge to Lingfield Station is a convenient option and what is more, a short walk will see you to the racecourse gates. For more local requirements, the 429 bus from East Grinstead to Godstone will take you via the track. If speed is of the essence then helicopters are free to land in the centre of the course provided you make the arrangements in advance.

Major Races and Charges

There are a staggering 71 meetings, offering both flat and jump racing on the grass track and all weather course. These include some really worthwhile evening racing. and in addition, there are 26 harness racemeetings. The most popular is the excellent Derby trial meeting in May, featuring the Derby Trial, and the Champagne Ruinart Oaks Trial. The Silver Trophy Meeting is also popular. The rates for entrance to Lingfield in 1993 were as follows; £12 for the Members if Turf Racing. and £7 for Tattersalls. Children under 16, who are accompanied by an adult, are admitted free. Prices rise to £15 and £8 for Members and Tatts respectively on Derby trial day. Discounts are available for groups of 20 or more. If you wish to join the course as an Annual Member, then in 1994 you will be charged £150 which included some reciprocal dates. Included in annual memberships is a car parking pass. Members also enjoy a fine view of the racing from their private room which overlooks the winning post.

Racecourse Facilities

Lingfield Park is an excellent and popular place at which to entertain as the facilities are good. Boxes for 12-350 guests are available. Private boxes all have racecourse videos as does the Eclipse Suite. For people who want a far bigger function, the Garden Room in the Marley Stand can accommodate from 50 to 500 guests. There are three restaurants—the Derby Restaurant in the Members, Silks in the Grandstand where booking is preferred and the Trackside Cavery. You could also try the All That Jazz brasserie/cocktail bar. Both the Members and Grandstand Enclosures have betting shops as well as

Tote facilities. There is a play area for children and a creche for 3 to 7 year olds. There are special viewing areas and lavatories for disabled people as well as car parks and it is good to see the course making an effort here. As yet, there is no bank at the track—so come prepared if you like a flutter. The Ladbrokes betting shop is located in Tattersalls. All weather racing is already beginning to show its merits in keeping the industry moving. With harness racing as well this is surely one of the busiest courses in Britain. We wish is well as it continues to expand its attractions and offerings in 1994.

Local Favourites

Lingfield Park is surrounded by good hostelries. Sampling a different one after each meeting of the year would not be impossible although the bank account might feel a little strain. One notable example is the **Castle Inn** (0892) 870247 in the delightful village of Chiddingstone. Other suggestions in the locality include **The Crown** (0892) 864742 at Groombridge—a pleasantly situated old inn with some fine ales and a restaurant if needs be. The **White Horse Inn** at Holtye, on the A264, is also a firm favourite, as is the **Royal Oak** at Dormansland—ideal for a pint or two. There are two mill restaurants in Edenbridge. **Honours Mill** (0732) 866757 is a handy place to enjoy good food and wine, and the same can be said of **Haxted Mill** (0732) 862914—be sure to book at both establishments. Another good restaurant to consider is **The Old Lodge** at Limpsfield (088371) 2996. This establishment is not cheap but it is extremely well thought of, also note **La Bonne Auberge** (0342) 892318 in South Godstone where superb French cooking can be enjoyed in elegant surroundings.

If you are keen to stay nearby, then several ideas spring to mind. Firstly, **The Copthorne** (0342) 714971 in the village of Copthorne has much appeal, (good restaurant and leisure facilities), while in Tonbridge, **The Rose and Crown** (0732) 357966 in Tonbridge High Street is also most hospitable. To the south, in Royal Tunbridge Wells, **The Royal Wells Inn** (0892) 511188 is excellent value and a super place to stay—the restaurant is also worth a visit. On Mount Ephraim, **The Spa Hotel** (0892) 20331 boasts outstanding facilities and a commendable restaurant. **Cheevers** (0892) 545524 is also extremely good: English cooking here. One should also consider **Thackerays House** (0892) 511921, which not only boasts an outstanding menu but also has a divine wine list. What better place to end up after a successful day's sport? Well, perhaps one, **Gravetye Manor** (0342) 810567, an outstanding hotel and restaurant double. Other less grand, but worthy recommendations in East Grinstead include the **Felbridge Hotel** (0342) 326992, the **Woodbury Hotel** (0342) 313657, and the **Cranfield Lodge Hotel** (0342) 321251, which are all well worth a visit. In a similar vein, nearby Hartfield offers **Bolebrook Watermill** (0892) 770425—exceptional value and very charming. Lingfield offers numerous racedays a visit would seem essential in the 1993 calendar—even if it's just to see all weather racing for the first time.

Ludlow

The roles of **Clerk, Manager and Secretary** are all carried out by Bob Davies who can be contacted at **Shepherds Meadow, Eaton Bishop Hereford HR2 9UA. Tel: (0981) 250052. Fax (0981) 250192.** Alternatively, on racedays telephone: (058477) 221.

Travelling to the Course

The racecourse is situated in the beautiful Shropshire countryside yet the course is easily accessed from major routes. The track is situated some two miles to the north-west of Ludlow. The favoured routes into the area are the A49 via Shrewsbury from the north or through Hereford from the south. Racegoers from areas west of Ludlow should follow the A4113. Travellers from the east of the country should aim to reach the A44 from Worcester and then make the best use of the A49. Anyone wishing to by-pass the town should use the Ludlow By-Pass. There are both rail and bus stations in Ludlow and the Midland Red runs from Hereford to Shrewsbury on the A49. The railway station is small but the line can be joined from Newport which in turn is on a direct route from Paddington or from Euston, via Shrewsbury. Finally, there is ample free parking should you decide to drive. Cars can be parked alongside the course in the spring and autumn although this is restricted during the winter months. Helicopters can also land at Ludlow providing you ask permission first.

Major Races and Charges

The racecourse stages B meetings, all of which are National Hunt and the principal of which is the Charity Meeting in April. Major races other than the Banks Brewery Day include the Forbra Gold Cup in March and the Prince & Princess of Wales Handicap Chase in November. All of the fixtures, bar one on May Bank Holiday, take place during the week—no doubt to the delight of the local farming community. However, for the ordinary mortal do not be put off mid-week racing.

Annual Membership in 1993 was priced at £65 with ten reciprocal meetings including Newton Abbot, Wolverhampton, Taunton, Uttoxeter and Bangor. Juniors (under 21s) are entitled to a reduced rate which in 1993 was £32.50. Daily admission charges were £12 for the Member's, £8 for Tatts and £3 for the Course Ring. These prices are unlikely to rise in 1994 and it is full marks yet again to the management for keeping the entrance charges down.

Racecourse Facilities

The new Member's building; The Clive Pavillion has recently been completed and now provides bar and restaurant facilities for annual members, owners and trainers. Non raceday functions for up to 500 people can also be accommodated. There are two spacious rooms available for entertaining parties of between 25 and 35 with prices averaging out at £30 per person (including admission, racecard and lunch). The course caterers are Hughes of Welshpool who can be contacted on (0938) 553366. Hughes also deal with all functions on non race days. Marquees can also be arranged at the racecourse if you are planning a large party. In addition to the new restaurant, snacks are available from Tattersalls and Members. A £90,000 refurbishment of the Tattersalls stand and bars is being undertaken this autumn which is to be completed by November 1993. Although children are welcome here there are no special facilities for them. The disabled racegoer is provided with a viewing ramp and ground floor toilet facilities. Tote credit facilities are available in the Member's with a racecourse betting office now being run by a local firm. If you are a punter with a fancy at another course, then the Licensed Betting Office, located in Tatts, allows you to punt on that cert. Ludlow is to be applauded for its commitment to provide modern facilities in all areas.

Local Favourites

A number of fine establishments can be found in Ludlow. **The Angel** (0584) 2581, located on the picturesque Broad Street, is a pleasant inn with good-value accommodation and some excellent ales. The half-timbered, 16th century **Feathers Hotel** (0584) 875261 is extremely popular and offers an outstanding restaurant. More moderately priced accommodation can be found at **No. 28** (0584) 876996 and **Chez Cecil** (0584) 872442. Two pubs to note are **The Bull** and **The Church**, both provide a great atmosphere for a pre or post-race rendezvous. Another hotel in which to well and truly spoil yourself is **Dinham Hall** (0584) 876464. The restaurant here is first class and the rooms very comfortable.

Just over the border in Wales, the **Radnorshire Arms Hotel** (0544) 267406 at Presteigne (not too far from Ludlow) is steeped in history—a favourite of Elizabeth I who lived here once. To the east of Ludlow at Abberley, along the A443, the **Elms Hotel** (0299) 896666 is most attractive—another hotel with an impressive history and much to commend it in the way of service and thoughtful extras. Travelling south to Leominster, the racegoer in search of solace will find a veritable haven of peace and hospitality at **Withenfield Guesthouse** (0568) 612011.

In the delightfully named Hopton Wafers, **The Crown Inn** (0299) 270372 is a popular pub which provides an excellent bar menu as well as a restaurant and some bedrooms. A pleasant place to stay is **The Royal Oak** (0694) 3266, Cardington, which is set in splendid isolation and has good bar snacks but even better breakfasts for racegoers. In Clun, **The Sun Inn** (0588) 4559 is a 15th century listed building which also has good-value accommodation and bar snacks. Thirteen miles south of Shrewsbury is Church Stretton, home of the excellent **Denehurst Hotel** (0694) 722699 and in nearby All Stretton you'll find the **Stretton Hall Hotel** (0694) 723224—outstanding if all you want is peace and quiet and relaxation in a traditional style. Before leaving the area consider a post-race celebration at **The Roebuck** in Brimfield, whose **Poppies** (0584) 72230 restaurant has a very good reputation. The setting is also excellent. Clearly, a visit to Ludlow is in order for every racing enthusiast, especially for those with a little time on their hands in the middle of the week—what a wonderful thought!

Major Charles Moore acts as **Clerk** and **General Manager** at this pleasant Lincolnshire course and **Gaynor Haxby** is the **Racecourse Secretary** and **Assistant Manager**. The role of **Assistant Secretary** is carried out by **Pamela John**, and **Paul Robinson** is **Head Groundsman**. All the members of this formidable team can be contacted at: **The Racecourse, Legsby Road, Market Rasen, Lincs. Tel: (0673) 843434.**

Travelling to the Course

The racecourse is situated some 12 miles north-east of the county town of Lincoln, at the eastern edge of Market Rasen off the A631. This is approximately 150 miles from London. The A1 is the closest major road to the course and this, coupled with the A46, is the best route to take if you are travelling from the south, or alternatively, the A631 if you are journeying from further north. The A46, due north of the course, in combination with the Humber Bridge ease your journey from the east and Humberside. The M18 and the M62 are convenient motorways for joining the A631, the racecourse road. Those travelling by train should note that the Lincoln—Grimsby line can be joined after a journey from Kings Cross station to Newark. The Market Rasen Station is approximately 10 minutes walk from the racecourse. Should you prefer to travel by car, on arrival you will find ample car parking which is provided free. If you are an aviator and a racing fan then Market Rasen is the place to take your helicopter. During the war the course was requisitioned and used as an anti-aircraft headquarters. Fear not, you are unlikely to be shot down and will receive a warm welcome.

Major Races and Charges

The racing pattern in 1993 was scheduled to include 17 meetings plus four point to points. The course's most popular occasions are traditionally their Easter Monday and Boxing Day meetings, the most popular races being the Grand National Trial, the Newark Storage Juvenile Hurdle and the Lincolnshire National, now held on Boxing Day. The rates in 1994 for admission will be similar to 1993 £10, (£12 on bank holidays and evenings) £7.00 and £3.50 for the Member's, Tattersalls and Silver Ring respectively. Additionally, a Jubilee Club for pensioners gives reduced admission to Tatts and the Silver Ring. If you are planning on taking a party of people, special rates are available depending on the numbers—15 or more is the usual figure. Contact the Secretary to negotiate terms. Annual Members are charged £90 for a single subscription while £155 was the asking price for a dual membership. This includes reciprocal meetings at Cheltenham amongst twelve days in total. It should also be noted that members are entitled to reduced rates on the on-site nine hole golf course—a sensible move given the rapidly increasing popularity of the sport.

Racecourse Facilities

There are facilities for all sorts of parties and they vary in number, price and location. The Club Enclosure's private boxes have been increased in number to an impressive seventeen, thirteen on annual lets and four sponsors rooms let on a daily basis. Bookings should be made through the Secretary and the price will be around £200-£300. The caterers can be contacted through the racecourse and provide a selection of meals in a choice of bars and restaurants. Alternatively, you may wish to take a picnic and there are two designated picnic areas. The charge for entrance to these was £2.00 per car and £3.50 per adult occupant in 1993.

The course has a new Owners and Trainers entrance, and a rebuilt enclosure for your children which is supervised by St. Johns Ambulance and is free of charge. If you are disabled there is a special viewing area and two newly built lavatories.

Lincolnshire remains one of England's most unspoiled counties, it may only have one racecourse nowadays but it's a goodun! If you are looking for a new racecourse to visit in 1994 Market Rasen would make a fine choice.

Local Favourites
Steeped in history, Lincoln is the ideal port of call for the non-racing type. Narrow cobbled streets are filled with antique and craft shops. An edifice of great note is the castle, and lovers of history should visit the cathedral which holds one of the original copies of the Magna Carta. An appealing place to eat is **The Wig and Mitre** (0522) 535190 on the appropriately named Steep Hill. The city is very popular with tourists and consequently a number of hotels can be found. The **Eastgate Post House** (0522) 520241 is modern but has pleasant views and a very comfortable restaurant. Much more convenient and with a city centre setting is **The White Hart Hotel** (0522) 526222. Less lavish but extremely comfortable and correspondingly cheaper accommodation can be found in **The Moor Lodge Hotel** (0522) 791366, Branston, a little way outside the city. Lincoln also offers the outstanding, particularly from a price point of view, **Disney Place Hotel** (0522) 538881 Those wishing to stay close to the racecourse should note **The Limes Hotel** (0673) 842357, Market Rasen, for good accommodation, food and service. The town also boasts a friendly and popular restaurant to consider, **Jossals** (0673) 843948. Slightly further afield but worth the trip is **Alfreds** in Louth (0507) 607431. In the opposite direction is **The Village** (0427) 788309 where the comfort and attention may make it your last stop!

Those merely looking for a pub for a pre-race pint, or post-race celebration are directed to the **Gordon Arms** which is thoroughly recommended. To the revamped **Chase** or the excellent **Red Lion**. If the celebrations prove unexpectedly boisterous, a more than comfortable bed for the night can be found at **The Waveney Guest House** (0673) 843236. Less convenient is Woodhall Spa, but this town should be visited not for racing but for some simply excellent golf. The **Golf Hotel** (0526) 53535 and the Edwardian **Dower House Hotel** (0526) 52588 are both good. Two pubs relatively near to the racecourse are **The Chicken**, splendidly isolated at Binrook with good bar food, and The **Nickerson Arms** at Rothwell, also remote but worth finding just the same. One final thought, consider a trip to Stamford and a night at **The George** (0780 55171). This really is one of our leading recommendations—a must for all lovers of fine hotels and a tremendous location in which to count your ill-gotten gains after racing at Market Rasen!

The **Clerk Of The Course** at the ever improving Newbury is **Mr RNJ Pridham** and **Major General J D G Pank CB** is **Chief Executive**. They can be contacted at **The Racecourse, Newbury, Berkshire, RG14 7NZ. Tel: (0635) 40015. Fax: (0635) 528354.** They are backed up by an excellent staff who deal with the plethora of matters that make up the busy racing year.

Travelling to the Course

Travellers from the east and London should use the M4 (junction 12) and complete their journey on the A4. Eastbound racegoers should also use the M4 (junction 13), while those from the south and north converge on the A34, causing chaos and terrible queues which must be circumvented if possible. There are plans afoot to build a by-pass on the north/south route but the completion date is 1996! One good thing—there is plenty of excellent parking once you finally do arrive! It's entirely free except in the picnic car park where there is a £4 charge on Hennessy Day and £3 on all other days.

A new and good idea for Saturday meetings is to take advantage of the British Rail London Racegoer Ticket. The cost of the ticket includes the rail fare direct from Paddington to Newbury Racecourse station and admission to the course. Telephone 071-262 6767 for further details. Finally, if anybody wishes to jet in there is a landing strip at the racecourse, soon to be moved to the centre of the track. Please contact the Secretary for details.

Major Races and Charges

With 28 days of racing, both on the flat and over the jumps the Newbury racegoer is blessed with some outstanding fixtures. Races such as The Tote Gold Trophy, the Singer & Friedlander Greenham Stakes, the Juddmonte Lockinge Stakes, the Geoffrey Freer Stakes, the Racal Vodafone Horris Hill Stakes the St Simon Stakes and the Hennessy Gold Cup, make racing at Newbury a delight. With so many top races on the Flat and over the jumps, its not surprising that the course does become very crowded.

Despite the quality of racing, Double Membership is well priced at £250 in 1994 which includes one non-transferable badge and one transferable badge. Single Members are charged £145. Junior Membership is £70 (18-25 years olds). A car park badge is also provided together with fifteen reciprocal meetings at some excellent racecourses. In 1994 daily admission to the Club Enclosure will cost between £13-£20 depending on the meeting. Tattersalls will be priced between £8-£12 and the Silver Ring, Geoffrey Freer Stand and Picnic Car Park at £4. Parties are encouraged and 20 per cent discounts are offered to groups of 12 or more except in the Member's. Seats can be reserved at a cost of £5 but bookings must be made in advance.

Racecourse Facilities

The Newbury racegoer is able to enjoy an excellent view of the racecourse from most areas. The Member's Restaurant can accommodate 220 people. In the Tattersalls Grill Room steaks are the order of the day. The all-day brunch in the Hampshire Stand is extremely popular and is a good place to pass time if one has arrived early to avoid horrific traffic congestion. If you do have any catering enquiries, telephone Ring & Brymer (0635) 521081. Facilities for larger parties (up to 500) can also be arranged. Corporate entertaining facilities are now first clas at Newbury and boxes and function rooms of various sizes can be reserved. Naturally, costs will vary drmatically but contact the racecourse and you are sure to be well taken care of. There are many other snack bars in all the enclosures and the restaurants and bars are open two hours before the first race. Children under 17 are admitted free into all enclosures. Younger punters may wish to make use of the well-equipped playground (with a qualified nurse in attendance) behind the Geoffrey Freer stand. The racecourse is also planning a creche which will no doubt prove popular, giving Mums and Dads the opportunity to study the card in peace. The idea of encouraging families to go racing is a good one and can only mean good for the tracks and therefore the sport in general.

The racecourse provides good viewing facilities together with lavatories for the disabled. Telephones are available but surprisingly no bank has yet set up shop despite repeated requests from Newbury's Management. Indeed, there have been may demands made on the Newbury Executive in recent years. By and large, they have responded in style and the racecourse is now one of the very best in the country. Some of the chararacter may have been lost but this has been replaced by an ampitheatre for racing that exudes class. There are other smaller and more thoughtful examples of Newbury's efforts too. A postcard is given to each owner on his/her admission to the course offering good luck and a congratulatory present should their horse win. This may seem trivial but owners put alot into the sport and such ;ittle touches are appreciated.

Local Favourites

Newbury racecourse is ideally situated well away from the capital but conveniently placed for folk from Hampshire, Oxfordshire, Berkshire and other ritzy shires of the South. In Newbury itself the Chequers Hotel (0635) 38000 is most convenient—while farther afield a hotel certainly worth an inspection is Elcot Park Resort (0488) 58100, a Georgian mansion set in 16 acres of parkland overlooking the Kennet Valley. The restaurant is good here and some attractive two-day breaks are available.

Slightly farther afield is Hungerford and within its compass are some first class places to visit. The Bear (0488) 682512 is probably the best place to stay. It is a 13th century inn with an excellent welcome. If you are looking for something to eat then the set lunches are recommended while the evening menu is also good. An alternative eating place to the Bear is an extremely pleasant pub the John O'Gaunt (0488) 683535—a tremendous meeting place before and after racing. There are a number of bedrooms too. Less glamorous but good value food can also be found at The Toad and Trout (0488) 682588. Marshgate Cottage (0488) 682307 also provides a more than comfortable bed for the night. Hungerford itself is riddled with antique shops and to many it may well be worth a visit on this score alone.

Another outstanding inn is located in Yattendon: The Royal Oak (0635) 201325. Once again, a splendid all-round performer—simple homely bars, a decent fire, cosy bedrooms and a really excellent restaurant. In Goring, the John Barleycorn and the Miller of Mansfield are fun pubs, ideal for a post-race celebration. Both offer simple accommodation and good bar food. The Leatherne Bottle (0491) 872667 offers a pleasant riverside setting in which to imbibe— a good restaurant as well. Across the Thames and into Streatley more lavish accommodation can be found at The Swan Diplomat (0491) 873737, an outstanding restaurant accompanies the hotel which also boasts fine leisure facilities.

Towards Wallingford, at Moulsford, lies the glorious Thameside retreat, the Beetle and Wedge (0491) 651381. A real must. In Aldworth, The Bell is a really cosy pub in which to take shelter. Heading towards the rolling Berkshire Downs and the Ilsleys, a number of pubs can be found. In East Ilsley, The Crown and Horns deserves a particular mention—not least for its excellent collection of sporting prints and racing photographs. The Stag is another decent pub, while in nearby West Ilsley The Harrow is pleasant and offers good home cooking. Finally, for the real galloping gourmets, a trip to Great Milton will yield the majestic Le Manoir aux Quat Saisons (0844) 278881. This is a restaurant with rooms of international acclaim but you will need a decent winner to meet the bill here but it is well worth it.

A pub with excellent food is The Dundas Arms (0488) 58263 at Kintbury. The restaurant has pride of place here but if you are looking for a place to stay this may be your solution, the bedrooms are located in a converted stable block. In Chieveley, The Blue Boar (0635) 248236 is handy for the M4, junction 13. In a secluded downs setting, its thatched exterior hides some splendid bar food and excellent ales. Accommodation is also available here. Another pub with an extremely popular restaurant and some comfortable bedrooms is the Five Bells at Wickham (0488) 38242. The answer has to be to take Friday off—go racing—eat a good lunch and in the evening nestle down in a quiet pub ready for racing on Saturday.

Other ideas? Well, in Stanford Dingley the Old Boot is worth a visit while the Bull here is a grand pub, a definite if you have won on the last. If you're travelling on the A4, as many people will, one place to pull over at is The Rising Sun, Woolhampton—really first class beer, good bar snacks and if you are feeling a little more peckish there is a separate restaurant. Another newcomer to the Newbury pub stakes, The White Hart (0488) 58201 near Kintbury is a great all rounder, but beware the 6X! In Kingsclere, a particularly strong racing influence in the village and a rather good pub as well is The Crown Inn (0635) 298956. Meanwhile, The Yew Tree Inn in Highclere (0635) 253360 has good food and some bedrooms. The Swan Hotel (0635) 298314 is also convenient and offers pleasant bedrooms and excellent food.

If you get round even half of the above for goodness sake don't drive home. To that end a few more excellent hotels. In Hurstbourne Tarrant, Esseborne Manor (0264) 76444 is outstanding—once again a tremendous restaurant, a warmly recommended all rounder. People heading south might wish to stay at Silchester; The Romans Hotel (0734) 700421 could be the answer—well priced and very comfortable.

Between Newbury and Ascot there are two particularly good restaurants to be found. At Burgfield visit Knights Farm (0734) 572366. Alternatively, in Shinfield one finds L'Ortolan (0734) 883783. The chef has an outstanding reputation and style, and high quality cuisine is quite categorically south odds on. Nearer to Newbury, at old Burghclere, The Dew Pond (063527) 408 is well worth considering, less expensive but very good.

Newbury is one of the South's growth areas and new hotels to add to your list include The Foley Lodge (0635) 528770 in Stockcross and the Hilton National (0635) 529000 in the town itself. The latter is owned by Ladbrokes and will inevitably be developing weekend breaks to tie in with the racing at Newbury. The Donnington Valley Hotel (0635) 551199 is also one for your short list—a thoroughly good all rounder,

Outside the town, but within a decent stones throw, one finds the Regency Park Hotel (0635) 71555 another first class candidate for a visit. For those travelling to farther flung parts and wishing to break their journey without squandering all their winnings, Reading offers the reasonably priced Thames House Hotel (0734) 507951 and Basingstoke, the equally good value and intriguingly named Mays Bounty Hotel (0256) 471300. Our final selection goes to a hotel that has been warmly recommended by one of our readers; the Hinds Head Hotel (0734) 712194 in Aldermaston. It sounds tremendous and reminds me to ask readers to let us know of any good information they might have. As all punters know, it is useful to have a little inside knowledge!

We hope you plunder a bounty or two while racing at Newbury in 1994. There are very few racecourses which offer so much and these local favourites also make up a select field.

David Parmley is **Manager** and **Clerk of the Course** and he, together with the **Racecourse Secretary, Mr. M. Hills**, can be contacted at **Newcastle Racecourse, High Gosforth Park, Newcastle-upon-Tyne, NE3 5HP. Tel: 091-236 2020. Fax 091-236 7761.**

Travelling to the Course

Those who are making the trip to Newcastle from the south of England should remember that the city can be by-passed by following the A1. The Great North Road, in turn, provides a direct route to the A6125 which can be joined at Seaton Burn. Furthermore, the completion of the Western By-Pass cuts around twenty minutes from your journey around the City. Racegoers should access the roundabout immediately outside the racecourse entrance. The journey from Newcastle's Tyneside to London's Thameside is a good 280 miles and one mode of transport to use is the newly electrified British Rail service from Kings Cross. The course is a further four miles from Newcastle's Central Station. A metro can be taken to Four Lane Ends and a bus service runs from here stopping inside The Park, close to the course entrance. Rather quicker transportation can be found by utilising the nearby airport or, if prior notice is given, you may land a helicopter. Parking facilities are good; there is a separate area for Members' convenience and all the parking is free.

Major Races and Charges

From the £20 purses of years gone by the prize values have increased somewhat. The courses leading fixture is The Plate Day when the feature race, The Northumberland Plate, is worth in excess of £50,000. Other valuable races in a busy calendar include The Fighting Fifth Hurdle.

Daily Membership, according to the most recent information supplied by the racecourse, was £12–(£14 on Plate and Fighting Fifth meetings). Better value is the Tattersalls at £8 or the Silver Ring at £3. Annual Membership was £95 for a lady and gentleman team and £60 for a single, (prices which include a car park badge and a very generous twelve reciprocal meetings.) Discount rates for parties in excess of 25 are fairly generous, £6 in the Club, £4 in Tattersalls, £2 in the Silver Ring.

Racecourse Facilities

The facilities at the course include private boxes and rooms for hire as well as the availability of space for marquees should you have something a little more adventurous in mind. The catering is carried out by that northern institution—Scottish and Newcastle Breweries 091-236 4148. There are two restaurants and prices range from £6 to £15. Numerous snack bars are available for you while you sup a little Newky Brown.

Children are admitted free, if under 15, and I am reliably informed that at certain times other attractions are arranged for them—including Punch & Judy shows. Other facilities include telephones a reserved area for disabled people's cars and Barclays Bank—handily located beside the Winners Enclosure. There is an off-track betting office in Tattersalls on the ground floor.

This racecourse has tremendous potential but due to legal wranglings with local authorities little of this has been seen. The course remains somewhat run down and this is a great pity. This racecourse has the potential to be in the top ten in Britain. It is a challenge to the whole community to prevent the racecourse from languishing in the second division.

Local Favourites

The busy city of Newcastle lies close to the racecourse, but at the same time, Scotland, the Lake District and North Yorkshire are all within easy striking distance. A simply enchanting place to stay in Longhorsley is **The Linden Hall Hotel** (0670) 516611—gorgeous rooms and a delightful setting in 300 acres of parkland. People who want a less formal atmosphere should visit **The Linden** (0670) 516611, a pub adjacent to the hotel. An alternative suggestion is **The Besom Barn** (066570) 627. **The Granby** (066570) 228 in Longframlington, further north, is also well situated and this is an ideal pub for a weekend in the country.

In Wylam, west of Newcastle, **The Laburnum House** (0661) 852185 is reputed to be excellent. Also out of town is the **Plough Inn** (0661) 853555—a pleasant establishment with a good local restaurant and Newcastle's newest country house hotel, **Horton Grange** (0661) 860686.

Two especially comfortable hotels in Newcastle are, firstly **The Holiday Inn** in Seaton Burn 091-236 5432 with good leisure facilities—ideal for business people and secondly the **Swallow Gosforth Park Hotel** 091-236 4111. This is an excellent, modern hotel where **The Branding** restaurant offers nouvelle cuisine while **The Vineyard** is a more informal restaurant in which to eat. Both are particularly convenient for the racecourse, the latter is situated next door.

Newcastle also has a variety of fabulous restaurants which should cater for all tastes. **The Fisherman's Lodge** in Jesmond Dene 091-281 3281 is a super restaurant while on the quayside **The Fishermans Wharf** 091-2321057 is again very good. Lovers of Chinese food should sample **The Ming Dynasty** 091-261 5787 or alternatively, **The King Neptune** 091-261 6657 and for lovers of Indian cuisine, the **Daraz** serves up a tasty treat to set you up for a night out in busy down town Newcastle.

Arguably Newcastle's finest restaurant is **21 Queen Street** 091- 222 0755 on Prince Wharf. Situated virtually beneath the famous Tyne Bridge, it is truly delightful with some of the finest food to be found anywhere—a definite favourite. For fathers who are seeking attractions for wife and children, look no further than the Metro Centre—it will suit all tastes.

The town of Newmarket literally breathes racing and it is blessed with two of the finest courses in Britain. The management team here is headed by Nick Lees who also acts as Clerk of the Course, as well as Chief Executive. He is ably assisted by Mr C.R Kennedy as Manager and he and his staff can be contacted at Westfield House, The Links, Newmarket, Suffolk, CB8 0TG. Tel: (0638) 663482, or at The Racecourse, Rowley Mile. Tel: (0638) 662762; the July Racecourse telephone number is (0638) 662752.

Travelling to the Course

Crowds flock to Newmarket for their many popular meetings, so an early start is recommended. Perhaps you will travel from London, a mere 60 mile sprint up the M11—exit junction 9 for the A1303 and the A1304 and thence to Newmarket. A more unpredictable, but less speedy track is the A1 and the A45. The A1 will also assist southbound visitors. The A604 and the A45 are both satisfactory routes on which to travel and racegoers on busy days should note the back exit via Exning onto the A45, thus avoiding the particularly heavy going. From Norwich and the east, the A11 is the obvious route, while from Bury St. Edmunds, the A45 can be a good route. There are numerous roadworks in the area so always allow a little extra time. There are numerous car parks on the Heath for both cars and coaches and if you wish, you may park in the Members Car Park for the princely sum of £1. If you should decide to travel by train, then the Liverpool Street line is the one to pursue. Buses meet the trains in Cambridge and ensure prompt delivery to the races. A further innovation is the introduction of a separate bus service to the course from Newmarket town centre. The CAA have given their permission for use of the July landing strip when there is racing on the July course. The only stipulation is that craft must not land, or take-off over the racecourse buildings. The Rowley Mile strip can also be used.

Major Races and Charges

Newmarket has made considerable and strenuous efforts to rejuvenate its facilities for the enjoyment of all. Sponsorship will continue to be a strong feature at this course and the list of corporate supporters reads like a Who's Who of business. Major races include the two Classics, the 1,000 Guineas, and 2,000 Guineas and the Autumn Double with the Cesarewitch and the Cambridgeshire. Other highlights include the Craven Stakes, The July Cup, The Cheveley Park Stakes, The Middle Park, and the Dewhurst. Prize money for the 1993 season totalled over £4 million. The ambience of the two Newmarket courses—the Rowley Mile and the July Racecourse—is totally different with the former featuring racing in spring and autumn in a highly professional manner and the latter creating an excellent atmosphere in beautiful surroundings for the more relaxed summer meetings. Attending one of the popular evening meetings on the July Course is a tremendous way to relax and forget your troubles, with the racing enlivened by some spectacular entertainment which takes place after racing this is provided free. If you haven't been you've missed some great nights!

In 1993, membership rates were as follows: £160 for an annual member's badge which includes free admission, car parking on all 31 days and one reciprocal day's racing at Cheltenham. An alternative subscription of £85 entitled members to a £6 entry at any meeting attended but includes all the other extras. For Juniors (17-25), a badge was well priced at £65. Inaugural membership requires an additional entrance fee of £35 for senior members and £10 for juniors. Daily prices vary; on the classic days and other principal meetings, prices for the Member's Enclosure range between £17 and £20. All other days are likely to cost £13. The Grandstand and the Paddock badge was priced at £11 for the major days and £9 on other occasions. The Silver Ring enclosure had a similar system—£5 and £3 being the respective asking prices. Parties of 10 or more are offered a 20 per cent discount if arranged in advance with the Racecourse. If parents wish to take children under 16 years, then they will be happy to learn they are admitted free. They may also be happy to know that fully trained Red Cross personnel are on hand to look after young racegoers while parents get down to the task of finding the day's winner—a fully equipped playground is available throughout the season. One of many recent developments at Newmarket is the introduction of a Triple Crown ticket that includes admission to the racecourse, the National Stud and the National Horseracing Museum which can be purchased from any of the three venues. In 1994, the introduction of a 16-25 club will allow discounted addmissions to the younger generation—the discounts can be up to 50% and represents excellent value. You only need to present proof of I.D. such as a driving licence. At the other end of the age scale, pensioners are admitted at half price to the Grandstand and Paddock for the Craven, July and October Meetings.

Racecourse Facilities

The Rowley Mile racecourse now incorporates new stands, 10 private boxes, 15 luncheon rooms and a new restaurant, The Guineas. Seven new boxes were also opened last year on the July course. All manner of conference rooms, marquees and chalets can be arranged through the course, and it continues to attract a tremendous selection of companies who wish to entertain. On the July course the oak panelled Queens Room and the Jockey Club Dining Room are also available for hire. As the entertainment facilities are so comprehensive it is advisable to contact the Racecourse for full details and advise on the most appropriate way of fulfilling your requirements. The racecourse caterers Letheby & Christopher, tel: (0638) 662750 are also happy to assist with any catering problems. The old thatched bar on the July Course has been replaced by the splendid Dante Bar and will soon be complemented by a refurbished and adjoining New Member's Bar.

Telephones are available as are banks as well as extra betting facilities. Disabled people have lavatories, escalators help the elderly and overall, everyone from junior to senior is well catered for. Newmarket is a well run racecourse—and a delight to visit. Long may the improvements continue at the headquarters of British racing.

Local Favourites

I cannot recommend a visit to Newmarket more highly. The town revolves around the sport of horse racing. From morning gallops to evening stables the hoof beat is never far away. Naturally, the crescendo is greatest in the spring through summer into autumn. If you want to stay in style and don't mind a short drive, **Swynford Paddocks** (0638) 70234 is ideally situated. The hotel is actually located in Six Mile Bottom and is an outstanding establishment. The bedrooms are elegant and the restaurant well recommended. Closer to home, the High Street of Newmarket offers a number of places to stay. **The Rutland Arms** (0638) 664251 and the **White Hart** (0638) 663051 are both comfortable and convenient, while on the Bury Road, **The Bedford Lodge** (0638) 663175 is a really popular racing location. Bar snacks in all the above hotels are good and dining is also available. A less extravagant, although still highly recommended establishment is **Hill Farmhouse** (0638) 730253 which can be found to the south of the racecourse in Kirtling. A modern, but well located hotel is **The Moat House** (0638) 667171—ideal for early morning gallops. There are many really outstanding hotels in East Anglia, one thinks of **Le Maison Talbooth** (0206) 322367 in Dedham near Colchester (note the outstanding Talbooth restaurant—really first class). In Woodbridge, **Seckford Hall** (0394) 385678 is a supremely comfortable country house hotel, while closer to Newmarket in Bury St. Edmunds, **The Angel Hotel** (0284) 753926 is a fine house with a first class restaurant—note its Dickensian past. Further south in Broxted, **The Whitehall Hotel** (0279) 850603 is another appealing manor with a splendid restaurant. **The Great House** (0787) 247431 at Lavenham should not be forgotten either with delicious French and English cooking. Meanwhile at Hintlesham, one finds **Hintlesham Hall** (047387)334—a classic stayer which boasts a golfcourse and some excellent cuisine.

People who are inclined to enjoy a drink or pub food will also be spoilt. Moreover, they will be pleased to hear they do not have to travel miles in order to find it. In Dullingham, **The Kings Head** (0634) 842709 is a friendly, busy racing pub which also has an excellent restaurant. In nearby Woodditton, another popular good pub is **The Three Blackbirds** (0638) 730811, a mere five minute's drive from the Rowley Mile racecourse—can't be bad. Other excellent establishments include **The Plough** at **Ashley, The Afflec Arms** at Dalham and the **Star** at Lidgate.

Two Cambridge hotels that are often used for busy Newmarket meetings are **The University Arms** (0223) 351241 and **The Garden House Hotel** (0223) 63421. The one overlooks Parkers Piece and the other the River Cam—both are excellent and make ideal bases for racing at Newmarket. Cambridge is also the perfect town in which to leave the person who may find a day or a week at the races a trifle tedious. An excellent restaurant to note in the City is **Midsummer House** (0223) 69299 on Midsummer Common—ideal for pre-sales, or post-racing discussions.

For people who really enjoy the modern facilities to be found in an hotel you should try **The Post House** (0223) 237000 at Impington—it should suit you extremely well. Other restaurants to consider include **Bradfield House** (0284) 86301 at Bradfield Combust—excellent English cooking, but do note the restaurant closes for lunch on

Saturday. **The Hole in The Wall** (0223) 812282 in Wilbraham is a fine restaurant, but please remember to book in advance. Also in Bury St. Edmunds is the **Butterfly Hotel** (0284) 760884, with a modern, continental feel, and in nearby Ixworth **Theobalds Restaurant** (0359) 31707 is there for discovering, open fire and all. North of Newmarket one finds the superb cathedral at Ely. In the same town **The Lamb Hotel** (0353) 663574 is comfortable while **The Old Fire Engine** (0353) 662582 produces some outstanding food—well worth the trip. If Chinese cooking is your style then try **The Peking Duck** (0353) 662063. Another good hotel near Ely is the aptly named **Fenlands Lodge** (0353) 667047, which is comfortable and the restaurant is also good. In Glemsford, a restaurant to short list is **Barretts** (0787) 281573—excellent sauces and a fine wine list. Stocks Restaurant in Bolisham also comes warmly recommended by a man in the know.

In case you have time between racing and opening time, or whatever you happen to be awaiting in Newmarket, we would strongly recommend you visit the National Horseracing Museum, a well thought-out establishment which owes much to the support of Britain's best known owners. It goes without saying, therefore, that the relics exhibited within are well worth seeing. The High Street reveals all manner of interesting shops: saddlers, tailors, bookshops, galleries are all to be found. Any remaining time before racing can profitably and entertainingly be whiled away at the splendid Equus Art Gallery (0638) 560445 also in Newmarket.

With the fabulous array of weekend meetings as well as mid-week occasions we will endeavour to recommend some pleasant inns, or pubs with rooms nearby. In Kennett, north of Newmarket, **The Bell** (0638) 750286 is an idea, while to the south, in Kirtling, **The Queens Head** (0638) 731177 will not disappoint. Further afield in Lavenham, **The Swan** (0787) 247477 is a delightful 14th century inn which also boasts a first class restaurant. While in Long Melford, three establishments are worth considering:- firstly, the excellent **Black Lion Hotel** (0787) 312356 is highly recommended and secondly, **The Bull Hotel** (0787) 78494. Finally, Chimneys is a restaurant with an excellent reputation. Returning towards Newmarket, **The Bell** (0638) 717272 at Mildenhall is a fine all-rounder and is pretty good value. The visitor to Newmarket is spoiled by a whole selection of excellent establishments—not least the racecourse itself. A visit is therefore essential.

One final thought for the racing enthusiast who also enjoys golf and has a taste for style and elegance; try **Hanbury Manor** (0920) 487722. It is a fair distance from Newmarket but is outstanding in every way. A place to spoil your non-racing partner!

Racing at Newmarket is to be recommended from the bustling betting shop to the early morning gallops from a smoke filled boozer to wide open heath, Newmarket is quintessentially a racing town and if you are looking for a day or two away in 1994, Newmarket is a worthy favourite.

The course is managed by **Pat Masterson** and he will be able to provide details of all the goings on at Newton Abbot. The **Clerk Of The Course** is L Lang and all enquiries should be directed to **The Racecourse, Kingsteinton Road, Newton Abbot. Tel: (0626) 53235, fax: (0626) 336972.**

Travelling to the Course

If you are heading to Devon for a long weekend, or even a short one, then you will be happy to hear that the racecourse is easily accessible by road. The M5 is the answer and this can be joined by the M4 and M6. The course is located just off the A380 which joins the M5. If you are journeying from Cornwall then a number of A roads are convenient. The A38 from Plymouth and the A30 via Okehampton are two obvious selections. It is as well to try and time your journey well because the M5 can get ridiculously one paced on occasions. Despite the rural setting, the public transport services are good. Trains depart from Paddington and a bus can then be taken from the local station to the racecourse. Helicopters are welcomed at the course and car parking is free unless you wish to park beside the course rails.

Major Races and Charges

The feature races in a busy fixture list of National Hunt racing include The Claude Whitley Memorial Cup Steeplechase, Langstone Cliff Hotel Steeplechase and the William Hill Hurdle. The course holds an abundance of meetings in August. This caters particularly well for those holidaying in this beautiful part of the world.

Newton Abbot is one of the few racecourses for which there is no Members Enclosure. The two enclosures are Tattersalls for which a charge of £5 is expected to be levied for 1994 and £4.50 for the Silver Ring. Despite the absence of a Members Enclosure, a season ticket can be obtained for £90 which includes seventeen reciprocal meetings. A new annual badge holders and shareholders lounge was completed in 1990 but there are only 350 such badges available, so book early. People who are holidaying in groups and local people should note the following discount rates. Essentially, if you get 10 or more people together you will save £2 per head on admission into the Tattersalls Enclosure if you book in advance.

Racecourse Facilities

The course has a good selection of sponsors and they generally make use of the two private function rooms. Eight private boxes are also available for hire. However, if you do wish to organise a substantial party—do telephone the course to check on availability. An alternative if these rooms are unavailable is to have a marquee in Tattersalls. It is clear however that the course really relies on the passing racegoer and they will be pleased to hear that picnics can be enjoyed at the racecourse—a charge of £1.50 is made for cars parked alongside the rails. If self-catering sounds too much like hard work, then there is the Terrace Restaurant in Tattersalls along with a self-service carvery and more modest snacks in the bars located in

Tattersalls and the Silver Ring. Any prior enquiries with regard to catering should be made to the racecourse or alternatively, addressed to the racecourse's caterers Partyfare Ltd. (0404) 42502. Although children are admitted free, there are no special play areas for them. There are three public telephones and disabled people have the benefit of a viewing ramp and a lift in the grandstand.

For those racing fans looking for a long weekend in the country, this is a fabulous answer. The racecourse is extremely welcoming and the standard of racing is not bad. There are also many splendid hostelries nearby in which to spend your ill-gotten gains. What more encouragement do you need? Make a date for 1994.

Local Favourites
In Newton Abbot, the proprietors at **The Queens Hotel** (0626) 63133 are eager to welcome visitors before and after racing, as they are at the excellent **Langtone Cliff Hotel**. A reasonably priced alternative is **The Lamora Guesthouse** (0626) 65627. Also in Newton Abbot one finds **The Two Mile Oak** (0803) 812411—really filling bar snacks can be found here. Indeed, one of the hallmarks of Devonian hospitality is the staggering portions that one is expected to consume. One such pub in Kingsteignton is the **Old Rydon Inn** (0626) 54626.

If you do have the chance, visit Dartmouth, where **The Carved Angel** (0803) 832465 is the finest restaurant in the area. Another excellent port of call in this delightful naval town is the **Mansion House** (0803) 835474—outstanding. All along the coast one finds nooks and crannies to explore and eventually one arrives at the larger resorts of Paignton, Torbay and Torquay. If you are looking for a good holiday hotel then the **Imperial Hotel** (0803) 294301 here is definitely the one.

There are all manner of activities to be found in Torquay and having played golf, fished or even after a trip to the races one place to visit is **Remys** (0803) 292359, ideal for dinner. Further round the coast one comes to Teignmouth where you find a super Victorian house which has been converted into an extremely welcoming hotel, **The Lyme Bay Hotel** (0626) 772953. No less excellent is **Thomas Luny House** (0626) 772976, an award winning, yet relatively inexpensive guesthouse. For people not wishing to visit the coast there are a number of excellent and secluded places to sample. A quiet country inn in which to spend a night is **The Rock Inn** (0364) 661305 in Haytor Vale. In nearby Haytor, **The Bel Alp** (03646) 217 is an extremely welcoming country house hotel to consider, as is the excellent **Moorland Hotel** (0364) 661407. In Ashburton, **The Holne Chase Hotel** (03643) 471 is a superb place to stay and it also has a fine restaurant.

There are seven public houses by the name of **Church House** (0364) 42220 within a very small radius. One you should certainly visit is located in Rattery—a welcoming place for a drink and substantial bar snacks, typically cosy. Nearer to Newton Abbot is Woodland and the superb **Rising Sun**, together with the nearby **Old Rydon Inn** at Drewsteignton another distinguished favourite.

Nottingham is run by the **Clerk of the Course, Major Charles Moore** and the **Administration Manager, Jan Entwhistle.** Ann Whelbourne is the **Secretary** and the team can be contacted at Nottingham Racecourse, Colwick Park, Nottingham, NG2 4BE. Tel: (0602) 580620. Fax: (0602) 584515.

Travelling to the Course

So how do you trace this track? Well, the course lies east of the city off the B686 Colwick road. The M1, that infernally unpredictable road, offers good going but does suffer from the odd tailback; southbound travellers should exit at junction 26 head for the city centre and then follow the signs for Colwick or Colwick Park. Northbound racegoers exit at junction24 and from there use the A453 and follow the signs to the racecourse. The A46 from Leicester is an alternative although this road is renowned for one-paced lorries. From the A46, follow the A606 and the A612. The nearest railway station is in the city, two miles from the course (trains leave London from St Pancras). Buses (no's 20 and 21) leave the city centre every 15 minutes. A short taxi ride will be necessary to complete your journey. If you do take the wheels, you will be pleased to hear that all parking is free. Helicopters may land in the centre of the course by prior arrangement with the management.

Major Races and Charges

In the past, the course has offered a very full calendar of Flat and National Hunt racing with meetings in every month of the year, including evening meetings during the summer months. These events are particularly popular, and on a fine day take some beating. The fixture list for 1994 has not yet been finalised but in 1993, the major races over the course included the Nottinghamshire Champion Novices Steeplechase, the City Trial Hurdle, and on the flat and The Nottingham Stewards Cup. In 1993, entrance to the Members' Enclosure in the new Centenary Stand was £12, the Grandstand was priced at £8 while the Silver Ring was £3. Annual membership was priced at £120 (or £200 double) which included parking and use of the Centenary Stand and enclosure. Children under 16 are admitted free of charge if accompanied by an adult. For people who wish to organise a party it is worth noting that cheaper rates can be negotiated with the course management for Tattersalls.

Racecourse Facilities

The course has an excellent location in Central England and it will surely use this to capitalise on the growth in corporate entertainment at the races. The Centenary Stand has boxes and a new Members lounge. The Grandstand has also been refurbished. The private boxes at the course have capacities of between ten and fifty people. Packages are available to include badges, bar, bucks fizz and a meal and for further information you should contact the racecourse. There is space for a marquee which will take up to 600 guests. There is a restaurant here and you are advised to book. The caterers, Haydock Park Leisure can be contacted via the racecourse office, tel: (0602) 580620. Nottingham also provides more than adequate extra facilities; the children have a playground in the Silver Ring; disabled people have a viewing stand and a lift in the Centenary Stand; pay telephones abound although no extra credit is available through the high street banks. This may prove a problem if you get carried away in the off-track betting shops located in Tattersalls and the Silver Ring. Nottingham's management have a great enthusiasm for the sport—we wish them all good fortune in developing the potential of this East Midlands track. If originality of ideas, hard work and enthusiasm are anything to go by then even in these competitve times Nottingham should prosper.

Local Favourites

The better hotels in the city are essentially extremely modern affairs. **The Forte Crest** (0602) 470131 is a 13-storey hotel which boasts panoramic views of the city. Alternatively, The **Stakis Victoria** (0602) 419561 should not be ignored. The **Royal Moat House International** (0602) 414444 is another up-to-date hotel. The interior is well designed, appealingly for this day and age, and there are good leisure facilities here. It is also very conveniently placed for the Royal Concert Hall. Another cultural place to visit is The Playhouse (0602) 419419, a most successful repertory theatre. Outside the city, one hotel geared to the businessman's requirements is the **Forte Post House** (0602) 397800 which has good facilities and is extremely convenient for the M1 (junction 25). In Beeston, **Les Artistes Gourmands** (0602) 228288 is a particularly well regarded French restaurant. **Le Tetard** (0602) 598253 is also French and is convenient for the racecourse (a three-mile drive).

Outside the town, one place to definitely try to visit is the outstanding public house in Old Dalby, **The Crown** (0664) 823134. If you're a real ale man then this is the pub for you. And those on lager or spirits will be equally delighted to hear that the pub food in this gorgeous converted farmhouse is excellent. There is also a restaurant in which you can dine in the evenings. Although it is a bit of a trek, **Stapleford Park** (0572) 84522 just outside Melton Mowbray is unparalleled in excellence. Although expensive, this 16th century marvel is worth every penny for a luxurious stay and good food. The town of Langar is also a little way from the course but the comfortable **Langar Hall** (0949) 60559 is well worth a visit. In Plumtree, **Perkins Bar** (0607) 73695 offers a tempting menu off the blackboard and this makes for an ideal spot post-racing. Not far away, in Cotes, you should note The **Cotes Mill**, a pleasantly converted water mill which is well worth a visit. Another quiet pub in which to reflect on the day to come, or just gone by, is **The Star** at West Leake. Many people may be heading back to that highway of modern life, the M1. If so, **The Cap and Stocking** in Kegworth is relaxing, and **The White House** has a fine setting, overlooking the waters of the River Soar and the **White Lady** in Newstead Abbey is a restaurant worth paying a visit. In Castle Donington, **The Cross Keys** has good food and a cosy atmosphere....can't be bad. Finally, the **Royal Horseshoes** (0664) 78289 in Waltham-on-the-Wolds is a pleasant village pub with above average accommodation—ideal for lovers of England's countryside.

Perth

This friendly course is run by **Sam Morshead** who has the role of **Clerk Of The Course** while Jill Grant is the **Racecourse Secretary**. They can be found at **Perth Racecourse, Scone Palace Park, Perth PH2 6BB**. Tel: (0738) 51597 on racedays, and on non racedays the Secretary can be reached at **Penrose Hill, Moffat, Dumfriesshire DG10 96X**. Tel: (0683) 20131. Mr Morshead can be contacted through the racecourse office at Ayr (0292) 264179.

Travelling to the Course

Although Perth is Britain's most northerly racecourse, some 450 miles from London, it is fairly accessible from all quarters of the country. Edinburgh is 44 miles away and the M90 can be taken from Edinburgh via the Forth Bridge, making your way through the Ochill Hills and past Loch Leven—a wonderful drive. The A9 struggles through the beautiful Perthshire countryside via Aviemore, Blair Atholl, Pitlochry and Blairgowrie. Even the train picks out numerous beauty spots as it shunts north from Edinburgh and the distant King's Cross in London, and there is a bus service to the course from the station. Helicopters may be landed by prior arrangement while aircraft should be landed at Scone aerodrome some two miles away. Car parking at the racecourse is plentiful and free.

Major Races and Charges

The wooded parkland of Scone Palace is the setting for this superbly picturesque course. The fixture list is well designed and all the meetings are run over two days. Clearly, the administrators of the Jockey Club enjoy their racing in Perth! The sponsorship at the course is reasonably good and is improving and this, coupled with the general popularity of the course, ensures some good fields. Meetings take place in mid-April, late May (the evening meeting is particularly popular), late August, September, and early October. The main race of the year is the Highland Spring Handicap Chase.

The rates for the various enclosures in 1993 were as follows: Member's £11, £6 for the Paddock Enclosure and a mere £2.00 for the Course Enclosure—good value by racecourse standards today. The Annual Membership subscription in 1993 was set at £55 for a single badge with a £30 charge for an additional badge. There are discounts of £1 per person for parties of 20 strong or more. This, not surprisingly, only applies to the Club Enclosure and Tattersalls. All enclosures have excellent views of the course and its sweeping wooded turns. However, if you're one of those people who hate to be parted from your car then centre course parking is an option at a price of £5.00—good value for picnic lovers.

Racecourse Facilities

The Grandstand is delightfully compact and allows for a superb atmosphere as the well-backed favourite strides confidently to the last. There are areas which can be adapted to accommodate parties and the course makes an excellent place to indulge. Private boxes which will cater for 20-30 people can be arranged with the Secretary with full catering facilities to fit the required budget. There are restaurants in all the enclosures and the course caterers are Wheatsheaf Catering Ltd. There are telephones at the course and viewing ramps for the disabled but no special facilities for children.

There are various plans for development at the racecourse, but I feel sure they will not detract from the charm of racing at Perth. It may be Britain's most northerly track but it is also one of the country's most attractive—a visit in 1994 is strongly recommended for those of you who really enjoy getting away from it all.

Local Favourites

In Perth, **The Royal George Hotel** (0738) 24455 is a comfortable place in which to stay and has views over the River Tay and the Perth Bridge. **Timothy's** (0738) 26641 is a good choice for a snack or more substantial offering. The restaurant is handily placed for the Perth Repertory Theatre (0738) 38123 whose season runs from August to May each year. Excellent value accommodation is plentiful in Perth with **Clark Kimberley** (0738) 37406 and **The Clunie Guesthouse** (0738) 23625 providing comfort and style. A final thought for Perth is Number 33 (0738) 33771 in George Street. An hotel exceptionally close to the racecourse is **Murrayshall House** (0738) 51171 in New Scone. The hotel offers a fine restaurant and a championship standard golf course and comes thoroughly recommended. Close to Perth is Dundee and should you venture here then **The Angus Thistle Hotel** (0382) 26874 is a most comfortable city centre hotel. An alternative idea is to visit Auchterhouse where **The Old Mansion House** (0826) 26366 provides an outstanding hotel-restaurant double. People making use of the A94 should note Alyth and here, the **Lands of Loyal Hotel** (082) 833151 is a pleasant and reasonably priced country house hotel in which to stay. Eastwards, one finds Blairgowrie, home of a wonderful golf course, Rosemount. South of the town in Kinclaven by Stanley, **The Ballathie House** (0250) 83268 has another gorgeous Tayside setting. Another outstanding hotel to consider is **Dalmunzie House** (0250) 85224, family run and welcoming—cottages are also available in the grounds for those who prefer the more independent life. **Dunkeld House** (0350) 727711 also enjoys a fine setting and is well thought of.

Another majestic place is, of course, **Gleneagles Hotel** (0764) 62231. Not only are there superb golf courses but the hotel exudes class—a first rate establishment in every way. More modest but still friendly accommodation can be found in Glenfarg's **Bein Inn** (0577) 3216. You may care to sample it en route to the next delightful port of call, St. Andrews. Some distance from Perth but if you are in the area, why not let your hair down? North of Glenrothes, in Freuchie, lies the highly recommended **Lomond Hills Hotel** (0337) 57329. En route to England, try Cleish near Kinross, where **Nivingston House** (0577) 5216 offers an inviting restaurant and some comfortable accommodation. Finally, we should alert you to three outstanding establishments, one at Dunblane, the other at Dunkeld. **Cromlix House** (0786) 822125 is superb and the restaurant is one of Scotland's finest. **Kinnaird House** (0796) 82440 is another hotel and restaurant that oozes class and is a great place to celebrate if the right horse wins. **Culcreuch Castle** (036086) 228 is well situated for all Scottish racecourses. It is family run, extremely welcoming and thoroughly relaxing. Ideal after a tight finish in the last.

Plumpton

Plumpton is a well run friendly racecourse in easy striking distance of London. Cliff Griggs acts as Clerk of the Course here whilst the racecourse is under the Management of Pratt & Co, 11 Boltro Road, Haywards Heath, Sussex. Tel: (0444) 441111. The number of the racecourse itself is (0273) 890383.

Travelling to the Course

Plumpton lies approximately 50 miles from London, midway between Haywards Heath and Lewes. The M23 is the best route south but after this, the motorist is left with various A and B roads. The A23, the A273 and the B2112 seem the likely routes to punt on. From Brighton and the South Coast, the A27 Lewes road coupled with the A273 should oblige. The course lies in the village of Plumpton Green. The quaint name of this village reflects its unspoilt character but the quiet is occasionally broken by the train. This is good news for racegoers as the station lies beside the course. The best idea is to catch the Victoria-Brighton train to Plumpton Station. If you can't spare the time to train it, helicopters are able to land at the racecourse. For parking, there is a charge of £1 per car unless you venture to the centre of the course with a picnic in mind, in which case, your motor will cost you £3.50, and alas a further £3.50 per occupant.

Major Races and Charges

1994 should follow the same pattern as last year with 17 days racing and, as with many of the smaller National Hunt courses, the Easter and August Bank Holiday meetings prove to be the most popular.

The prices for entry through the gates into Plumpton's Members' Enclosure were £11 in 1993 and for children (12-16) £2. The under 12's are allowed in free. In Tattersalls, children under 16 are not charged but adults are required to pay £8. A similar arrangement exists in the Course Enclosure where adults pay £3.50. If you wish to join the Members of Plumpton on an annual basis, then expect to fork out £90 plus a further £10 if you wish to have the privilege of joining your fellow Members in their private car park. You will also be entitled to reciprocal days racing at Warwick, Fontwell, Huntingdon and Chepstow. Further news to report is that parties of 20 or more will receive a 20 per cent discount in any of the three enclosures.

Racecourse Facilities

For people wishing to do some entertaining, Plumpton racecourse may have the answer. Groups of up to 20 can be accommodated in a selection of private rooms—bookings for these areas should be made through Pratt & Co and the cost of a box is about £150 per meeting. If you wish to organise a larger party then there are luncheon rooms for up to 60 guests and areas where marquees can be erected if this is more your style.

Snacks are available throughout the enclosures, the racecourse caterers being Letheby and Christopher (0273) 602987. The Members restaurant, The Regency, has recently been enlarged as has their bar. The racecourse informs us that they will provide packages in the restaurant for parties of six or more who do not wish to hire private boxes. There are bars in all the enclosures and a speciality seafood bar in Tatts. Although the course allows for children in its charging structure, special facilities are only available in summer to keep the kids occupied when they get tired of watching the gee-gees. Similarly, facilities for the disabled are somewhat limited. Perhaps this is one area that might be looked at in 1994.

This delightful course, whilst devoid of any grand pretensions, does provide good entertainment and we are delighted to hear report its continued developments which include a much improved oncourse betting shop in Tatts. If you have not visited Plumpton before, we would warmly recommend a mid-week winter afternoon where good racing in a pleasant atmosphere is assured.

Local Favourites
We start at a pinnacle of excellence, some way north of Plumpton— **Gravetye Manor** (0342) 810567 in Gravetye, south of East Grinstead. Another top hotel can be found at Cuckfield, **Ockendon Manor** (0444) 416111—the building is 16th Century and the traditional open fires and panelling add immense charm to the excellent facilities. The restaurant is also particularly well thought of. Ashdown Forest has some delightful scenery and an excellent base from which to explore is the **Chequers Inn** (0342) 824394 at Forest Row. In Lower Beeding, **South Lodge** (0403) 891711 is an attractive restaurant and boasts some excellent accommodation within. For lovers of luxury, a final recommendation here is for **Horsted Place** (0825) 750581 near Uckfield, where both the rooms and the restaurant are of a standard seldom equalled.

Much further south, one arrives in the extremely pleasant Sussex town of Lewes. Here one finds an hotel engulfed by a roaming creeper—**Shelleys** (0273) 472361. There are a number of restaurants in Lewes:- **Kenwards** (0273) 472343 is a fine one where imaginative cooking ensures delightful eating. Staying in this part of the world need not cost a fortune and for the avid bargain hunters, **The Bull Hotel** (0791) 83147 should fit the bill. While restaurants come and go, pubs generally stand their ground. In Fulking, **The Shepherd and Dog** is a pleasant small country pub and the bar snacks here are excellent. Closer to the racecourse at Clayton, **The Jack and Jill** is also a friendly place while the **Rainbow Arms** in Cooksbridge is welcoming and provides good bar snacks too. Another pub with a good restaurant is aptly named **The Stewards Enquiry** on the Lewes Road near Ringmer. **The Highlands** in Uckfield is another establishment patronised by those in search of good fayre. Not too far away we find Chiddingleys **The Six Bells**—most appealing with old beams and excellent snacks as well as some good beers. In Horsted Keynes, try **The Green Man** or **The Oak** at Ardingly, more excellent snacks in an ancient and traditional free house. Another fairly convenient stop could be made at the **Hare and Hounds**, a pleasant village pub east of Uckfield. Finally, racegoers who like country pubs with charm, should try **Juggs** in Kingston. Rustic to the core, it is a country pub for a country course. One to consider when planning your racing in 1994.

A lot of hard work goes into making Pontefract one of the most popular racecourses in the north of England. The man in charge of this most progressive of courses is **Norman Gundill,** who acts as **Clerk, Manager** and **Secretary** . He can be contacted at **The Racecourse, Pontefract Park, Pontefract. Tel: (0977) 702210** (racedays only) or at **33 Ropergate, Pontefract. Tel: (0977) 703224.**

Travelling to the Course

The course itself is marvellously situated for motorway access, the entrance being only half a mile from junction 32 of the M62 making it an excellent location for racegoers from almost all areas of the country. Leeds lies nine miles west of Pontefract and the A1 and M1 and M18 are all within ten miles of the course. Although there are plenty of busy rail stations nearby; Doncaster, York and Leeds, Pontefract is not on a main line station so this is probably a course where one should take the car. There are vast car parking areas and all parking is free, other than the Special Reserve Park, where a charge of £10 is levied. Buses are an option too, with those from Pontefract and Leeds passing the gates. If you are in a particular hurry, there are ample open playing fields in the park in which to place one's helicopter. You must check with the Secretary first though, just in case some other activity is taking place!

Major Races and Charges

The course itself is compact and, despite its length, the whole circuit is visible from each enclosure. Charges for 1994 will be in the region of £12 for a daily membership, £7 for entrance to Tattersalls, £3 for the Silver Ring and £1.50 for the Third Ring. The best value, however, may be the Third Ring car park which costs £5 per car and this includes up to four people. If you wish to become an Annual Member the adult single badge is priced at £95, whilst a husband and wife team can be members for the more reasonable sum of £130. In 1993, a Junior Annual Membership for those aged between 16 and 21 was introduced priced at £45. Annual Members are also entitled to reciprocal meetings at Thirsk, Doncaster, Haydock Park, Beverley, Newcastle, Market Rasen, Nottingham and Catterick. The racecourse Executive is to be applauded for reciprocal meetings at a variety of Yorkshire County Cricket Club venues including Headingley and Sheffield. The course also offers special discounts for parties in all racecourse enclosures. Contact the Secretary for further details.

Racecourse Facilities

For those wishing to entertain guests at Pontefract there is a Club chalet with its own private lawn and terrace which can accommodate up to 30 people for a sit down lunch or supper. The Private Room in the Main Stand looks directly out over the course whilst larger parties can be accommodated in the Entertainment Suite. Charges vary so it is best to contact the racecourse for details. The racecourse would certainly be a tremendous place to have a company summer party with a difference. Catering arrangements should be made directly with the racecourse caterers, Craven Gilpin & Sons, tel: (0532) 311221. Snack bars can be found throughout the course and more substantial food can be found in the Club and Tattersalls restaurants. Finally, should you wish to have a picnic, the place to go is the Third Ring car park on the stands side. Other points of interest are that there is a special playground for the youngsters in the Third Ring and if under 16 they will be admitted free when accompanied by an adult.

Another successful innovation in 1993 was the introduction of a fully supervised creche in the Third Ring at holiday meetings during Easter and at the two evening meetings in July and August. This venture will be repeated in 1994.

Local Favourites
Pontefract is ideally placed for venturing farther north, and one place that should be visited is Ilkley—a little distant but well worth the trek. Here, **Rombalds** (0943) 603201 is a really excellent place to stay—home comforts and a warm Yorkshire welcome are the order of the day. What's more, if you happen to wake up a little hungry on Sunday morning after an evening at Pontefract, fear not, their Edwardian breakfast is an absolute monster and should keep the largest of wolves from the door. Ilkley is cluttered with some delightful antique shops and if you are fortunate enough to dine at **The Box Tree** (0943) 608484 then expect something out of the ordinary, although the restaurant has experienced several management changes of late.

Returning to more local spots, one should consider some places in which to have an ale or two. In Ledsham, **The Chequers** is an enormously popular free house, resplendent with oak beams and open fires. In Ledston's Main Street, one finds an equine establishment, **The White Horse** and another warm welcome and fire, so I understand. In Wentbridge, the **Wentbridge House Hotel** (0977) 620444 is a glorious, early 18th century hotel, very cosy and well-appointed, standing in 15 acres of grounds. The restaurant here is absolutely outstanding, a fine place to visit prior to the racecourse and perfect for a post race celebration.

Parkside Innes sponsor meetings here and we are happy to list three of their establishments convenient to the racecourse, recommended by Pontefract's Manager. They include **The Parkside Inne** (0977) 709911 which lies opposite the one and a half mile starting post and provides good pub food as well as a retsaurant and motel accommodation. **Rogerthorpe Manor** (0977) 643839, Badsworth comes from the same stable and lies three six miles south of Pontefract, just off the A639. This is a country house hotel of some quality. The **Swiss Cottage Restaurant** (0977) 620300, in Wentbridge is our final suggestion for those who enjoy a post race gathering. We wish this group and the racecourse well in 1994.

The team in charge at Redcar is headed by the **Chairman and Managing Director, Lord Zetland, Clerk of the Course,** John Cleverly, and the **Secretary, Mrs M. Rose.** They can be contacted at **Redcar Racecourse, Redcar, Cleveland, TS10 2BY. Tel: (0642) 484068.** They form as able a team as you will find in racecourse management and continuing improvements at the racecourse are evidence of this.

Travelling to the Course

Redcar Racecourse is located in the south of this coastal town to the north east of the Yorkshire Moors. Redcar is accessible by road from the A19 dual carriageway, which passes within 15 minutes of the racecourse (via the Parkway). The A19 links to the south with the A1 at Dishforth and to the north at Newcastle. Travellers from the east will find the A67 and the A66 routes the most direct into Redcar and the racecourse. The nearest railway station is in the town itself, a distance of approximately half a mile from the track—a five minute walk at the most! A fast train service runs from Kings Cross to Darlington where you can catch the local train to Redcar or a 268 or 269 bus. The bus station is a mere 150 yard hike from the Grandstand—perfect. There are ample free parking facilities with three major areas for cars and coaches. People using Light aircraft should ring Mr Towers on (0642) 484340. There is a landing strip 660 metres long. Full details are available from the aforementioned Mr Towers, but beware the 250 volt powerlines to the east! Helicopters may land on the course with prior warning.

Major Races and Charges

Racing here is likely to follow the same pattern as 1993, Levy Board changes allowing. The principal days include the Spring Bank Holiday Monday with other days in June, August and September. Two of the feature races are the Zetland Gold Cup, which will be worth some £25,000 in prize money, and also the Tote Two-Year-Old Trophy which is a fine part of Redcar's racing calendar.

Annual Membership in 1993 was priced at £92 and £46 for Juniors (under 21). A married couple are charged £135 for Joint Membership. Annual Membership includes a free racecard and car pass for each meeting plus the use of a private room, bar, catering and Tote kiosk. The use of a private bar is an excellent concept and one which all the racecourses should adopt for their annual patrons. The daily admissions for the Members', Tattersalls and the Course were priced at £12, £7 and £2.50 respectively. At the time of writing, we are unable to inform you as to whether these charges will be increased for 1994, but changes are likely. The stand facilities are good and the colourful flower beds form a cheerful feature—all further indications of the management's eagerness to please. The racecourse offers a £1.00 discount for parties of 20 or more, plus a free pass for the organiser and £1.50 for parties of over 40 with two free passes and a bottle of whisky. Discounts only apply to Tattersalls.

Racecourse Facilities

The course will be happy to provide information with regard to boxes, conference suites and rooms for smaller gatherings. The popular Saddle Room, with private bar and viewing facilities, is only strides away from the welcoming Members Dining Room. The Paddock Rooms have added a new dimension to Redcar's facilities as a fully self-contained entertainment centre with magnificent spectating facilities and boxes to cater for between 35 to 140. The Members' Dining Room, Tattersalls Restaurant and Course Cafeteria all offer good food for the punter and there are comprehensive snack bars. Practically all the facilities at the racecourse have been improved dramatically in recent years, ensuring that individual racegoers, as well as companies entertaining guests, can relax in the knowledge that they will be ably looked after. Catering is in the capable hands of Ring and Brymer who can be contacted through the racecourse office.

The racecourse has a children's playground and they are admitted free if under the age of 16 and accompanied. Other facilities include a viewing ramp for the disabled opposite the winning post and lavatories for the disabled in all enclosures. Although there are no special banking facilities, public telephones are available for any necessary credit punts and there is a Tote betting shop. We are constantly told of the recession in racing and it is of course worrying, but innovative management will help and there are few more competent than those at Redcar. If in 1994 the clouds of economic misery lift, surely this course will benefit more than most—it certainly deserves to.

Local Favourites

The North East of England may not enjoy the most illustrious of reputations elsewhere, but in this case ignorance is not bliss. Few who venture this far north are in any hurry to leave. In Crathorne, near Yarm, there is an extremely fine hotel **The Crathorne Hall Hotel** (0642) 700398. The hotel enjoys a splendid setting and it is thoroughly welcoming—a good choice. In Yarm itself, **Santoro** (0642) 781305 is a good Italian restaurant to note. At Staddle Bridge, **McCoys at the Tontine** (060 982) 671 is a great name for a truly delightful hotel run by the McCoy brothers with a genuine 30's feel and an outstanding restaurant. In Stockton-on-Tees, the **Swallow Hotel** (0642) 679721 boasts extremely comfortable accommodation and is high on the list of visiting business people.

If the bustle of the city centre hotels are not to your liking then you may care to try **The Grinkle Park Hotel** in Loftus (0287) 40515—the parkland setting of this Victorian hotel is especially attractive. Alternatively, why not sample what is probably the best hotel in the area, the superbly luxurious **Ayton Hall** (0642)723595 in Great Ayton. One of the most commendable points about this particular hotel is the thoughtful attention to detail. Farther afield in Goathland, **The Mallyan Spout Hotel** (0947) 86206 is recommended.

There are several pubs to note in the area and one such establishment is the **Ship** at Saltburn-by-the-Sea, splendid sea food, snacks and good views—well worth a trip out. Farther west in Egglescliffe, **The Blue Bell** (0642) 780358 has good food as well as fine views of the River Tees. A joyous atmosphere in which to peruse your

Ripon

The authorities are headed by **Mr M.C.H. Hutchinson** who acts as Managing Director and is assisted by **Clerk of the Course, Mr J** Hutchinson. They can be contacted at **77 North Street, Ripon, North** Yorkshire, HG4 1DS. Tel: (0765) 602156. Fax: (0765) 690018.

Travelling to the Course

The most obvious way to get to Ripon is by car for there is no train station at Ripon and while trains do stop at Harrogate, the nearest major station is at York which is some 22 miles away. If you do wish to travel by train then the King's Cross line is the one to board. London itself lies 200 miles away and the best way of reaching the racecourse from the south is to use the A1/A1(M). The course itself is two miles east of Ripon, off the B6265 which in turn is just four miles from the Great North Road (A1). The A61 from Leeds and Harrogate is a useful road from the south and this, together with the A19, will assist racegoers from the North East. Similar assistance is provided by the A61 from Thirsk for those travelling from the East. There are ample parking areas at the racecourse and this is provided free. If people are hurrying to the course then helicopters are a welcome option provided you've given prior warning. This may be singularly appropriate as the A1 is being elevated to motorway status but for the near, and not so near future, chaos will reign supreme.

Major Races and Charges

The spring and summer months play host to Ripon's race meetings and August is particularly crowded with excellent fixtures although fixtures for 1994 have not yet been finalised. The Tote Great St. Wilfrid Handicap (£20,000) is the feature race whilst many a good two year old is attracted by the Champion 2 Year Old Trophy (£12,000). Lovers of the summer sports who enrol as Members of Ripon will also be offered a taste of another splendid summer game—cricket. Annual Members are given eleven days' complimentary cricket at nearby Headingly. As well as this, four reciprocal meetings are thrown in at Newcastle, Haydock, Doncaster and Market Rasen. Membership runs as follows: a husband and wife team is charged £100, a single badge £65 and a Junior (under 21) is required to pay a £45 subscription. If you are only able to justify the occasional visit to Ripon then daily badges cost £12 in the Club, £7 in Tattersalls, and £3 and £2.00 in the Silver Ring and Course Enclosures. These are the prevailing rates at the time of pblication, but may be increased for the 1994 season.

There are various group discounts available for Tattersalls and the Silver Ring. The discounts start for parties of 20 or more and become more generous as the numbers increase. A 50 per cent discount is given to parties which can scramble together 250 people ... quite an effort I would have thought.

Racecourse Facilities

If you are looking for an afternoon with slightly more than the average entry badge allows, then a range of boxes are available for hire. They have a capacity for between 25 and 100 people. If you require precise details, contact the course as they have an excellent printed handout. It is clearly good value but don't forget to sort out the catering at the same time. For bigger parties a marquee area is available in the Paddock but there is not too much room and if you are organising a bigger event, there is also a location available in the car park adjacent to the Paddock. There are restaurants and snack bars in all enclosures—parts of the Members' and Tattersall stands have been rebuilt, increasing and improving the facilities available. Apparently, Ripon was the first course to have a children's playground and there are now two—one on either side of the course—marvellous. Other details to note are that there are telephones in the Paddock, Silver Ring and Course enclosures. Disabled racegoers have ramp assisted viewing and there are two betting shops in the Paddock. Those of you who have not visited Ripon should give it a try, it is fondly called the 'Garden Racecourse'.It is one of the most pleasing in the country.

Local Favourites

Ripon's leading hotel **The Ripon Spa** (0765) 602172 is a particularly racing orientated abode. Less glamorous, but quite agreeable accommodation can also be had at **The Crescent Lodge Guesthouse** (0765) 602331. When we talk of style and Yorkshire we must surely consider Harrogate. A number of hotels in Harrogate will make a good base while you visit Yorkshire. Style is the order of the day in Harrogate's most striking hotel, **The Hotel Majestic** (0423) 568972. An eighteenth century building with an extremely attractive setting is a fair description of the splendid **Old Swan** (0423) 500055 where a really excellent restaurant is complemented by comfortable accommodation. The value of staying in Harrogate as opposed to the nearby countryside is that firstly one can leave one's non-racing partner in a delightful town in which to browse and secondly, in the evening one has a number of restaurants to visit. **The Drum and Monkey** (0423) 502650 is good, downstairs—a bustling bar and superb food, upstairs a more formal and extremely popular dining room. The **Bay Horse** (0423) 770230 is also well recommended - excellent value.

Further north, one arrives at an hotel of distinction—**Jervaulx Hall** (0677) 60235. Closer to Ripon in Markington **The Hob Green Hotel** (0423) 770031 is another good extremely restful place to stay. Great character and some good value accommodation can be found in the **Sportsman's Arms** (0423) 711306 in Wath-in Nidderdale—if you love the country, stay here—it's a charming setting and the food is also first class. **The Crown** (0423) 322328 in Boroughbridge, an ancient coaching inn with twentieth century additions, is also worth a pre-race inspection. For people who have to rush home the same day then a few options before you set sail. In Staveley, **The Royal Oak** (0423) 340267 is a welcoming country pub with good food while in Roecliffe, **The Crown** (0423) 322578 is another great little pub. Other public houses handy for the A1 include the **Olde Punch Bowl** in Marton cum Grafton and **The Ship at Aldborough** (09012) 322749—note the Roman connection here. Another tip before we leave this area—**Cragg Lodge** at Wormald Green (0765) 677214, with the most incredible collection of malt whiskies! Careful with your pre race binge, racing at Ripon can be competitive and will need a clear head. A trip in 1994 is to be recommended.

Salisbury is an enchanting racecourse and keen racegoers should definitely make the effort to attend a meeting here in 1994. Ian Renton runs Salisbury as the Clerk of the Course. He can be contacted at Salisbury Racecourse, Netherhampton, Salisbury SP2 8PN or on (0722) 326461/327327.

Travelling to the Course

The Racecourse is located three and a half miles south west of Salisbury on the A3094. The best plan is to aim for the town and from there you should follow the signs to the Racecourse. The A360 is the best route from the north. For people heading from the east or the west of the country the A30 is ideal. Other modes of transport to be considered are the train/bus double. The first leg is the Waterloo-Salisbury line which should be coupled with a bus from Salisbury Station to the racecourse. If you wish to use the helicopter then there is no problem—as long as you telephone the management in advance. There are excellent car parking facilities at the course which are provided free of charge.

Major Races and Charges

In 1994, racing will follow the same format as in 1993 with the major meeting again being the Bibury Meeting which takes place in late June. The feature race on the card is the Veuve Clicquot Champagne Stakes worth £17,500. Other seasonal highlights include two extremely popular evening meetings in July and August where 'Kids Kingdom' provides entertainment for the children and jazz bands and barbecues add a certain spice to some competitive racing.

Admission prices should remain the same as 1993 when they asked £12 for the Members', £8.00 for Tattersalls and £3.50 for the Course Enclosure. Children are admitted free, if accompanied. If you wish to become an Annual Member the rate is in the order of £80. However, in addition you receive a car pass and 19 reciprocal meetings plus, of course, the prestige of belonging to the oldest known racing club still in existence—The Bibury—which can't be bad!

Racecourse Facilities

If you wish to organise a party at Salisbury, and it's a special place to have one, discounts are available subject to numbers. Private hospitality boxes located above the Members' Bar are available for hire daily or on an annual basis. Daily sublets can be arranged, depending on the day and the box required. In addition, there are three small Private Rooms to accommodate between 20 and 40 guests which are very popular too. These range from £150-£300 per day. Whatever you decide, book through the racecourse office. The best idea however, may be to organise a marquee or chalet—located adjacent to the parade ring and the winning post. Other racegoers may wish to take advantage of the Members' Restaurant in the Bibury Suite. Despite the fact that this has been doubled in size, one is still advised to book. Please contact the racecourse caterers G.F. & K.M.Woodland Ltd (0225) 702905. There is also a snack bar located in the Bibury Suite if you fancy something less substantial and other

snack bars can be found throughout the enclosures. On the drinking front, Members can enjoy the 'Wessex Bar', while in Tattersalls, a temporary Pavilion Bar is erected to cater for the larger crowds in July and August. Disabled people are given the opportunity to enjoy racing by virtue of a raised viewing area—situated in the Members' Enclosure. A Tote betting shop is located in Tattersalls and telephones are available. An evening or afternoon at Salisbury is thoroughly recommended.

Local Favourites

Hampshire, Dorset and Wiltshire are home to an inticing array of country pubs. Here is a quick listing of some of the possible contenders: **The Compasses** (0722) 70318 in Lower Chicksgrove has bar snacks and a traditional atmosphere as well as a separate restaurant and cosy rooms if required. Another pub-restaurant ideal for informal post-race nosh is **The Black Dog** (0722) 76344 in Chilmark. **The Black Horse** (0722) 76251 in Teffont Magna has super food and pleasing accommodation. The same can be said of a critter—**The Fox Inn** (0258) 880328, a lovely village pub. In Broad Chalke, **The Queen's Head** (0722) 780344 is a good stayer and in another gorgeous village, Fonthill Bishop, **The King's Arms** is a picturesque alternative, while the **Victoria and Albert** in Netherhampton is very convenient. The list goes on and on. If you love the country and it's traditionally copious cuisine, then this is an area for you. Three local tips worth following are the **Rose and Crown** at Harnham, the **Pembroke Arms** at Wilton and **Cricket Field Cottage** (0722) 22595. All three also offer good accommodation. We then come across a couple of tools. Before you take offence, relax..merely a reference to two other excellent pubs in the vicinity; **The Malet Arms** in Newton Toney, and **The Silver Plough** in Pitton, a tremendous hostelry with a restaurant.

Then there's Salisbury. A charming city and the county town of Wiltshire. The rivers Avon, Bourne, Wylye and Nadder converge here. Many people visit the area to see the cathedral or shop in the market and the town is a busy and thriving focal point. **The Rose and Crown** (0722) 327908 has a lovely setting on the banks of the River Avon, overlooking the cathedral. The accommodation here is comfortable and the English cooking is good. The **Old Bell Inn** (0722) 327958 also has pleasing bedrooms and two lovely fourposters and the bar is a civilised meeting place. Finally, the **White Hart** (0722) 327476 has great character and is a first class place to stay before racing at The Bibury Club. If you are in search of a pub then **The Haunch of Venison** (0722) 322024 exudes character and provides good food while the Tudor **King's Arms** (0722) 327629 offers good-value accommodation. The **Coach and Horses** (0722) 336254 also offers good food. Outside the town, a really super pub to note is the **Fox and Goose** at Coombe Bissett—well worth a post race pint.

Some distance from Salisbury, but a definite must if you have time, is **The Sign of the Angel** (0249) 73230 at Lacock—also a possibility for Newbury. Marlborough offers the splendid **Ivy House Hotel** (0672) 515333 which is thoroughly recommended, as is **The Sun** (0672) 52081, a charming pub with good bar food and uncomplicated accommodation—an ideal port of call for those of you wishing to break the journey before racing at Salisbury.

Sandown Park is ably **managed** by **Nick Cheyne** who acts as **Clerk** as well. **Karen Winterborne** is **Club Secretary** here and if you wish to contact them, write to **Sandown Park Racecourse, Esher, Surrey KT10 9AJ.** Tel: **(0372) 463072.** Fax: **(0372) 465205.**

Travelling to the Course

The racecourse is a mere 15 miles from the centre of London in true suburbia, Esher. The best route from the capital is to take the A3 out of central London itself. The A308 and the A309 are trunk roads that run nearby, and the racecourse itself lies off the A307, the Portsmouth Road. Racegoers from London are strongly recommended to use the Esher—Waterloo / Clapham Junction line as it passes the course. If you live closer to the course, buses from Kingston, Guildford and Staines all go to Esher and stop in the High Street. Assuming that you are in a car, you will find free parking off the Portsmouth Road. Parking in the members car park carries a charge of £2. If time is of the essence and you can take the company 'copter, land on the golf course in the centre of the track—but please check with Mr Cheyne beforehand.

Major Races and Charges

Fixtures for 1994 are expected to remain the same as last season. There are 16 flat, 10 National Hunt and the celebrated mixed race meeting. The Coral Eclipse always produces a thrilling clash, whilst the Whitbread Meeting with the Classic Trial and the Whitbread Gold Cup is one of the best racing days of the year. The feature race inevitably attracts a top class field which nearly always produces a tight finish. However, there are now course restrictions on numbers at this meeting so you are advised to book tickets in advance wherever possible. Other highlights for Sandown include the Gardner Merchant Mile and the Agfa Diamond Chase.

Feature days in 1993 demanded charges of £22, £13 and £4 for the Members, Tattersalls and Silver Ring whilst most other days were priced at £13, £9 and £31 respectively. Annual Membership was priced at £180 and this includes free car parking and reciprocal days at eight other venues including Lingfield Park, Warwick, Newton Abbot, Wincanton and even Hickstead. Juniors (16—25) are charged the reduced sum of £75. Finally, if it is your intention to organise a party to Sandown then contact the course for the full range of discounts available to you.

Racecourse Facilities

The 36 Boxes at Sandown are let on an annual basis. However, you may be lucky enough to sub-let one of these and should phone the Club Secretary to see what is available. Numerous private rooms are also available to rent and marquee sites can be organised. Caterers here are Ring & Brymer who can be contacted on (0372) 465292. The Members Restaurant, located at the top of the Members Grandstand, will set you back approximately £25 and you are advised to book. As well as the Tack and Saddle restaurant in the Grandstand, costing approximately £6.50 per head, there are all manner of snack bars at the course but these can be rather pricey. You may prefer to take your own picnic to enjoy in the car parks. Given the high standard Sandown has set in past years, it can be strongly recommended as a place to entertain. It is often said nowadays that sponsorship and entertaining go hand in hand, if you want the best of both worlds you would have to look carefully at Sandown Park.

Plans to redevelop the Park area are still being considered but we are happy to report the completion of a new stable lads hostel and weighing room complex. No doubt the stable lads and jockeys are delighted too. All too often it seems the behind the scenes facilities are ignored and in certain cases, these are downright archaic. The courses who forget the stable staff are more often than not the courses who provide the poorest service all round.

Children under 16 are admitted free to the course and are well catered for at Sandown with a large playground. A creche has now been opened providing first class facilities free for young children. Similarly, facilities for the disabled here are excellent with specially equipped toilets, viewing areas, reserved parking and access ramps to all areas.

Sandown is a tremendously well run racecourse in a delightful setting and if you haven't sampled racing here then do make the effort. Evening racing is a particular delight, and what a different way to spend a long summer's evening.

The whole concept of evening racing is fascinating—it has to be one of the most successful additions to the racing calendar the sport has made. Unlike so many afternoon meetings when potential punters are busy working, the evening provides a time to relax, meet friends and generally have a good time. British racing must realise how popular these meetings are and how they could be developed further. Let us hope that, with the opening of betting shops in the evenings, that the increase in turnover will benefit the sport at every level. Sandown Park is an excellently rounded racetrack; whether you are the chairman of a P.L.C. or Joe Bloggs in the jolly old Silver Ring, you're almost certain to have a good day especially if you can find a winner or two. We wish you well while travelling the turf here in 1994.

Local Favourites

Because of Sandown's proximity to London, many race-goers will inevitably be heading back to the capital after a day at the track so it is difficult to know where to start a selection of hotels and restaurants. For those who want luxury and have the money to spend, **Blakes Hotel** 071-370 6701 in South Kensington is quite superb as is

the renowned **Browns Hotel** 071-493 6020, that bastion of old-fashioned English values. **Claridges** 071-629 8860 on Brook Street needs no introduction; its discreet luxury and elegance are quite unsurpassed. Park Lane delivers a number of excellent hotels. **The Dorchester** 071-629 8888 has recently been totally refurbished and is crying out for a pre-race inspection. The **Grosvenor House** 071-499 6363 is another impressive hotel and a star performer for the Forte stable. The **Inn on The Park** 071-499 0888 and **The Hyatt Carlton Tower** 071-235 5411 are two other thoroughbreds with outstanding restaurants as well. If the above are slightly out of the range of the impoverished race-goer, then it goes without saying that London provides a veritable multitude of accommodation at vastly varying rates. One highly recommended establishment that combines comfort and value is **The Aston Court Hotel** 071-602 9954.

A tasty meal may well be the order of the day, in which case one could do a great deal worse than head for Rue St Jacques 071-637 0222 on Charlotte Street, or L'Escargot 071-437 2679 on Greek Street.

So far, the emphasis has been on central London, and what with the traffic and parking problems that beset the capital, perhaps the outer regions are more than worthy of consideration. On Wimbledon Common, **Cannizaro House** 081-879 1464 is an unexpected delight, a true country house overlooking the Common and superbly appointed throughout. Wandsworth may sound like an unlikely venue after a day at Sandown but there really are some excellent restaurants here, most notably, **Harveys** 081-672 0114 and **L'Arlequin**. Both restaurants are expensive but if you are planning a celebration you will not be let down. Staying south of the river, **Prima Donna** 071-223 9737 in Battersea is a hot favourite—delicious Italian food and very good value.

Quite a few ideas, therefore, for the London-based visitor to Sandown, but what of those who prefer to stay in the Esher area to sample the local delights? The **Dining Room** (0932) 231686 at Hersham serves good English food, whilst the **Hilton National** (0932) 64471 in nearby Cobham has excellent facilities such as saunas and whirlpool baths. If you are lucky enough to fly to Sandown by helicopter, then you will be pleased to know that your chopper is also welcome here. Elsewhere, in Coatham **The Woodlands Park Hotel** (0372) 843933 is an improving type and an excellent choice for visitors to Sandown who are not keen on the big smoke. Slightly farther afield,in Weybridge, The **Warbeck House Hotel** (0931) 848764 is unpretentious but highly recommended. The **Oatlands Park Hotel** (0932) 847242 is a strong local fancy and a recent upgrading makes it a handy favourite.

Finally, Sandown and Kempton are twinned not only by their association with United Racecourses, but also by very close proximity to one another. So, if you are still fishing for more ideas and suggestions of where to eat or stay, then the Kempton section should provide all you require.

The team in charge here are **Clerk of the Course, J.G. Cleverly** and **Manager** and **Secretary, D. Riley**, who can be contacted via the **Sedgefield Steeplechase Company, 23a The Green, Billingham, Cleveland.** Tel: (0642) 557081.

Travelling to the Course

The racecourse is approachable from Middlesbrough and the east via the A177, while the A1(M) makes the racecourse easily accessible for both northbound and southbound travellers. For racegoers from the larger conurbations to the south-west the M62 and the A1(M) provide good routes to the racecourse. Despite its proximity to the Great North Road, the track has a remote and quiet setting. Major train routes run to the centre of Darlington some 250 miles from London. The closest rail stations are at Stockton-on-Tees (9 miles away), Durham (12 miles) and Darlington itself. There is ample free parking for a variety of vehicles, although there is a charge of £2 in the Paddock car park. Helicopters are also able to land at Sedgefield, but do please call in advance.

Major Races and Charges

There are approximately 21 fixtures on offer in 1994, a great many of which take place on Tuesdays. The course's major race in 1993 was the Durham National Handicap Steeple Chase and it should be noted that the management here have managed to attract excellent sponsorship support to boost the prizes which could otherwise be fairly minimal.

The course has only two enclosures: a combined Paddock and Tattersalls area which is very reasonably priced at £7, (OAP's £3.50) and the Course Enclosure which is equally good value at £2.00. Prices rise for the Boxing Day fixture to £8.00 (OAP's £4.00) and £2.50 respectively. The course also offers special party rates with a 50 per cent discount for groups of 40 or more in the Paddock. Children under 16 are admitted free.

Racecourse Facilities

During recent years the racecourse management have spent over £1,000,000 on improvements to the track, stabling and public amenities. A brand new Pavilion has been built to house a new bar, snack bar, a restaurant and private boxes with new Tote facilities. There are now a total of ten private boxes, the six new ones situated within the new pavilion. All have excellent views of the winning post. Two sponsors' suites are available for hire, the first seats up to 100 while the smaller one seats up to 40. The caterers are Ramside Estates Group and they can be contacted on (0740) 20253. Good value lunches are available at Sedgefield in the Pavilion Restaurant which seats between 75-100. A new fish and chip restaurant has also opened here and there are various other snack bars to keep the hunger pangs at bay.

There are no special facilities for children, except on the Family Evening. However, the disabled racegoer has special ramps to ensure a pleasant day. An on-course betting office is in existence as well as telephones, although no banking facilities are available. Sedgefield is well supported by the local community and visitors from further afield are encouraged to visit this unspoilt, well run racecourse which has been significantly re-furbished in recent years.

Local Favourites

Nearby, Darlington grew up around the railway expansion of Victorian times. **The King's Head Swallow Hotel** (0325) 380222 dates from this era and today its a particularly welcoming hotel that makes an ideal meeting place. A restaurant nearby of note is **Bishop's House** (0325) 286666, excellent cooking which given the quality, is well priced. In order to reach Sedgefield we should be heading north. However, a quick diversion south to Neasham is in order. Here the **Newbus Arms Hotel** (0325) 721071 is particularly charming and friendly and therefore thoroughly recommended.

Returning north in the right direction for Sedgefield racecourse one may come across Stapleton; here the **Stakis White Horse Hotel** (0325) 382121 is not grand but comfortable and convenient. If you feel like spoiling yourself with an excellent post-race nose bag try the **Black Bull** (032577) 289 in Moulton; it's a mile and a half off the A1 at Scotch Corner and is one of the most celebrated fish restaurants in the country. In Rushyford, three miles from the course, one finds the **Eden Arms Swallow Hotel** (0388 720541) which receives promising reports from locals in the know. On the doorstep of the racecourse itself, **The Dun Cow** (0740) 20894 will provide for your every reasonable need!

Leaping somewhat randomly to Durham we find ourselves in the county town. Here the cathedral is outstanding and the castle's also worth a look—if you're going to stay here then the better hotels include **The Royal County** (091) 3866821 which overlooks the River Wear and the **Three Tuns** (091) 386 4326, a large hotel where your every comfort is assured. Further south in the less busy Croxdale lies **The Bridge Hotel** (0385) 3780524. This is one for the busy businessman who may wish to escape from his journey up the A1. In Coatham Mundeville, a 15-minute drive from Sedgefield between Darlington and Newton Aycliffe, one finds a hot favourite—**Hall Garth** (0325) 300400, a well-appointed 16th century mansion—thoroughly recommended.

There are two places nearer the course that should also be considered in your each-way plans. Firstly, **Hardwick Hall** (0740)20253, which lies one mile west of the town making it most convenient for early morning race enthusiasts. Secondly, **The Nags Head** (0740)20234, an extremely friendly pub which offers good bar snacks as well as having a separate restaurant. A good idea for a pre race rendezvous when travelling the turf in 1994.

The **Clerk of the Course** at Southwell is **Ashley Bealby**, the **Secretary** is **Mandy Boby** and the **Raceday Manageress** is **Linda Moulds**. They can be contacted at the **Southwell Racecourse, Rolleston, Newark, N525 OT5. Tel: (0636) 814481. Fax: (0636) 812271.**

Travelling to the Course

The racecourse itself has a splendidly scenic setting. A Midlands track, it is situated just outside the Nottinghamshire village of Rolleston some five miles from Newark and within access of various motorway routes. Westminster Abbey is some 138 miles away and the A1 is the most direct route to follow. Northbound travellers should exit for the racecourse on the A6065 and then pursue the A617. The A46, which runs from east to west, serves racegoers from those points of the compass. The A617 should be used by travellers from the north-west and is convenient owing largely to its connection with the M1, junction 29. Drivers should also note the new Newark By-Pass. If you do not wish to travel by car, then the train is a cert. In fact, Rolleston's station is one of the most convenient racecourse stations in the land. Nottingham is on London's St Pancras line and from here one can catch a train to nearby Rolleston. Some of the Mansfield/ Newark buses also stop in Rolleston a quarter of a mile from the course. As one would expect with such a rural track, there are plenty of parking areas in the fields around which are free. Helicopters may land in the centre of the course, subject to prior organisation with the management. There is a landing space for light aircraft four miles away with a shuttle service to the racecourse available.

Major Races and Charges

As a result of its new all weather racetrack, Southwell has experienced a whole new lease of life. The fixture list will follow a broadly similar pattern but Monday fixtures will be transferred to Southwell's sister racecourse Wolverhampton. Admission to the course in 1994 will be £10 for Daily Membership and £5 for Tattersalls. The cost of Annual Membership at Southwell in 1994 will be £120.00 for a single and £200 for a married couple. Membership includes parking, a racecard, reciprocal meetings and the use of the Queen Mothers Restaurant, paddock viewing balcony and Members' Bar and Restaurant. If you wish to take

a group of friends the racecourse offers some very attractive discounts to Tattersalls according to the size of your party—contact the racecourse management for details. For groups of 30–50 there is a £1 discount rising to £1.50 for groups of 50 or more. These discounts are restricted to Tattersalls only.

Racecourses Facilities

The new Club Stand comes complete with all the corporate trappings; boxes, suites, dining rooms etc. There are at present seven boxes available for parties numbering up to 30 guests. The cost of a box is £200 plus £10 per Members badge. Catering can then be tailored to your particular requirements. A raceday 'box package' at £945 plus VAT includes sponsorship, a full meal for 20 and parking. If you should need larger facilities, then there are grass areas for marquees which should fit the bill. Also of note is the area for trade stands in the Southwell Arcade. Booking is required in the Queen Mother Restaurant but for the less extravagant but good snack bars are dotted throughout the course and a wide variety of food is available from fish and chips and a bar-b-que to a sweet stall and shell fish bar. There are several different caterers here too which is unusual but no doubt a good idea as 'variety is the spice of life,' or so they say.

Other details to be noted when considering a day's outing at Southwell; children under 16 are admitted free if they are accompanied by an adult. If the racing does not grip them then they will be delighted to hear that there is a children's adventure playground. There are two telephones in Tattersalls and two in the Members' Bar and Weighing Room. Facilities for the disabled are good, both floors are pirpose built with lavatories, a lift and viewing platform. there is a Tote betting shop in the Grandstand too.

This is a developing racecourse with a constant eye to the future. It boasts a small hotel with a nine hole golf course and all manner of other facilities from squash to archery. There are also American-style training barns. With a constant eye ahead, R.A.M. Racecourses Ltd. are reconditioning this essentially rural track—they are experts in the art and we wish them well.

Local Favourites

The Saracen's Head Hotel (0636) 812701 is the ideal starting point for visitors to Southwell racecourse. The inn dates from the 16th century and its Stuart heritage is displayed in many paintings_but mind your head, oak beams abound. Southwell also boasts **Upton Fields House** (0636) 812303 an excellent Bed & Breakfast establishment. **The George** (0780) 55171 at Stamford is a magnificent old coaching inn whilst **The Cavendish** (0246) 582311 occupies a superb setting in the grounds of Chatsworth and has a fine restaurant with venison a speciality. In Stamford, a super old market town, note **The Lord Burghley**—a lively pub renowned for its fine ales. Other places to stay include the **Bull and Swan Inn** (0780) 63558 and the **Crown Hotel** (0780) 63136—both are marvellous old inns and make for a pleasant place to stay. For those heading south, the Ram Jam Inn on the A1 is convenient and well recommended as a good stopping place.

The French Horn at Upton, is certainly worth visiting for its good-value, quality pub food and is especially convenient for Rolleston and the racecourse. In Maplebeck, a little further north, **The Beehive** village pub is worth a visit despite or perhaps because it is a little out of the way in the Nottinghamshire country-side. Travelling in the same direction, the medieval village of Laxton offers the hospitable **Moorgate Farmhouse** (0777) 870274. In Marston, **The Thorold Arms**, which is convenient for A1 travellers and for **Marston Hall**, offers a particularly good drop of ale and nice bar meals. In Bottesford, due north of Belvoir Castle, one finds an excellent and intimate restaurant—**The Thatch** (0949) 42330. Other than Belvoir Castle itself, Newstead Abbey is a sight worth seeing. The most famous part of this stately home of the poet, the sixth Lord Byron, is a fascinating gallery housing numerous personal articles; but the gardens too are ideal for a diversion for the less than enthusiastic racing partner. In Grantham, **The George** (0400) 72251 offers good bedrooms and breakfasts, and also note **The Angel and Royal** (0476) 65816. Four miles north you find **Barkston House** (0400) 50555 in Barkston, a charming restaurant with rooms. South of Southall at Lowdham, **The Springfield Inn** (0602) 663387 has some attractive bedrooms and is a comfortable place in which to stay, as is **Langar Hall** (0949) 60559 in Langar. At just £30 per night, Southwell's **Racecourse Hotel** (0636) 814481 is excellent value. The **Full Moon Inn**, just one mile from the racecourse is also a newcomer of note. Finally, we would recommend two local favourites; **Fiskerton Manor**, Fiskerton and **The Old Forge** (0636) 812809.

Clerk of the Course at Stratford is Lt.Commander J W Ford and Mrs Alison Gale is the Manager and Secretary. They can be contacted via The Racecourse. Luddington Road, Stratford-Upon-Avon. CV37 9SE. Tel: (0789) 267949.

Travelling to the Course

Stratford is fairly easy to reach from all directions. It is sandwiched between the M5 to the west and the M1 to the east. The new M40 is also useful for traffic coming into Stratford from the south and west. The A46 is the most direct route for north and southbound travellers whereas the A422 serves east and westbound travellers. The course itself is situated a mile south-west of the town and this makes trains and buses a little inconvenient. However, for those who do travel by car, the new Stratford by-pass is a great help and there are A.A. signs to the racecourse to further assist on racedays. If you do wish to travel by train from London then you should aim for Stratford-upon-Avon from Euston, changing at Coventry, or Paddington changing at Leamington-Spa. However, there is no bus directly from the station to the course although buses from the town heading to Evesham pass the entrance to Luddington Road. There is ample parking at Stratford with a large free car park in the centre of the course. A charge of £2 is made for cars parking next to the stands. Members park separately. There are also good facilities for coaches but limited scope for helicopters so please arrange with the racecourse in advance should you wish to buzz in.

Major Races and Charges

In 1994 racing should follow the same pattern as it did last year although there is still some uncertainty over the fixtures at the time of writing. The major race day is still likely to be the Horse and Hound Cup Final Championship Hunters Steeplechase a really first class day. In 1993, Annual Membership badges cost £75 with an extra £5 required for an annual car park badge. Prices will be reviewed for the 1994 season. Daily Membership is now £11. Entrance to Tattersalls is £8.50, whereas the Course Enclosure costs £3.50. If you are planning a party, then 12 is the minimum figure required for a 20 per cent reduction. For further details, contact the Manager. If you wish to take children under 16 racing, the racecourse welcomes them at no charge.

Racecourse Facilities

There is a new hospitality room at Stratford and the course does have plenty of facilities in the way of boxes, conference areas and function rooms. The Avon Suite is specifically designed for corporate hospitality, catering for up to 90 people. Specific requests for these facilities should be directed to the racecourse management. The outside caterers are Jenkinson Caterers Ltd and they can be contacted on (0785) 52247. The course has several bars which have recently been refurbished and provide snacks. The Paddock Suite Restaurant is also available and there is no need to book. There are some amenities for disabled racegoers at Stratford for whom a small stand is provided. Telephones are located in the members enclosure but there is no bank at the course so bring your readies with you.

Stratford Racecourse is a good track. The opening of the M40 extension makes the trip far speedier for many visitors and this will hopefully boost attendances. There are all manner of reasons for going racing; a day in the fresh air, a rendezvous with friends, a tilt at the ring or if you are lucky to watch your own horse run. Stratford does not profess to being Britain's foremost racecourse but it provides good racing in a convenient location and a visit should be considered in 1994.

Local Favourites

The first production of the charming Midsummer Night's Dream apparently took place in the grounds of **Alveston Manor** (0789) 204581. This charming hotel is particularly pleasant and golfers may wish to take advantage of the nine holes on offer here. A Georgian hotel which lies conveniently for the theatre is **Stratford House** (0789) 68288, a pleasing and somewhat less expensive place to stay with an excellent restaurant. On the Warwick road outside the town the **Welcombe Hotel** (0789) 295252 is another extremely well thought of hotel, more golf—18 holes on this occasion, some delightful rooms and a first class restaurant. Pride of place for the area goes to **Ettington Park** (0789) 740740 in nearby Alderminster. The hotel is magnificent, the bedrooms are charmingly furnished and the bars and library comfortable and relaxing. Among the wealth of guesthouses that form an equally important part of Stratford's accommodation industry, **Broad Marston Manor** (0789) 720252 will satisfy the most discerning international hotel hopper. Another hotel of acclaim outside Stratford-upon-Avon is located at Billesley—**The Billesley Manor** (0789) 400888; a fine gabled manor house.

People who prefer a day out without an overnight stay might wish to sample any one of a number of pubs. In Wellesbourne, **The King's Head** (0789) 840206 is a good place for lunch and **Charlecotte Park**, a superb Elizabethan mansion, lies close by and can be viewed between April and October. **The Butcher's** Arms at Priors Hardwick, more of a restaurant than a pub, is handy for the A41 while the A34 reveals the **White Bear** (0608) 61558 at Shipston-on-Stour, an excellent place to have a bar snack. In Oxhill, **The Peacock** is an extremely hospitable village pub as is the **Royal Oak** in Whatcote. Traditionalists will enjoy the **King's Head** at Aston Cantlow, another tremendously atmospheric pub. In Wilmcote, the **Masons Arms** is also splendid with an excellent and varied menu. If you are keen to enjoy the Cotswolds after the Stratford steeds then a reasonably priced and extremely relaxing hotel to visit is **The Three Ways** (0386) 438429 at Mickleton—the restaurant is also quietly civilised with a fine wine list. In Chipping Campden, two establishments most worthy of note are the **Cotswold House Hotel** (0386) 840330 and the delightful restaurant **Greenstocks**. Close by at Charingworth, **Charingworth Manor** (0386) 78555 provides accommodation and service of the highest standard. Final thoughts for this racecourse is the Chase Hotel (0789) 740000, Ettington, more good value and a fine restaurant to match while the **Houndshill** (0789) 740267 is a pleasant inn on the A422 and is an ideal place to stay.

The irrepressible **Tony Shewen** acts as **Clerk of the Course, Manager** and **Secretary** and can be contacted via the course at **Orchard Portman, Taunton. TA3 7BL. Tel: (0823) 337172.** There are few racecourse managers who are so genuinely enthusiastic and it is with regret that the racecourse has raised its prices. Despite this, we strongly recommend a visit if you are exploring the south west in 1994.

Travelling to the Course

'The Paddington route is not just fairly good, it's bloody marvellous,' so says the racecourse Secretary. It is 100 minutes from London on a fast train with a direct service from Plymouth and down from the North and Midlands. Furthermore, Taunton is situated close to the M5, 50 minutes south of the M4 intersection, while the A303 is fast achieving near motorway status as a major trunk route giving access from the South coast. Why not travel the day before racing and spend the night in a local hostelry? Buy your day badge and a plentiful supply of Tote vouchers in advance from the racecourse secretary and you won't need to worry about living it up overnight in the Cider County. So our punter will settle himself comfortably into his Pullman seat on the Paddington train secure in the knowledge that his day badge will be £10, Paddock £8.50 or Course £4.00. Cars race free—unless they go onto the centre of the course as the base for a family picnic or portable grandstand, in which case have £3 handy.

Major Races and Charges

You are bound to enjoy your day at Taunton so much that an annual badge will be a must. 1994 prices are likely (please note the proviso!) to be: £70 for 24 days racing , 12 at Taunton and 12 reciprocal meetings at Cheltenham, Kempton, Newbury and West Country neighbours. And if that isn't good value—even better is £115 for a double badge to include the wife (or hubby). That's 48 days racing at less than £2 a day.

Racecourse Facilities

No matter how the punter travels, a cup of coffee and a little something to keep the wolf from the door will necessitate an early visit to one of the many bars and snack counters. The local caterers have a coffee and tea room where you can put your feet up and study the form and in addition to a good line in snacks, there is a 'Racegoers Special' two course, quick service lunch in the Orchard Restaurant. Perhaps you want to indulge yourself by taking a Restaurant Window Table with a birds eye view of the course, in which case £30 provides an all-day table for your use with a three course lunch, afternoon tea, bar service and all the coffee you need—book in advance and for an extra £5 your admission will be free. These seats offer an unrivalled view of the course and make for a great day. Catering is in the hands of Aspen Catering (0823) 325035. It is also good to report the recent opening of the new Owners and Trainers Bar which is situated next to the Parade Ring with a fine view of the course.

The course betting shop is run by Peter Jolliffe and this and the Tote betting shops are in Tattersalls, together with two public telephones for credit punters. The course has reserved a prime viewing area next to the restaurant for the disabled person, and all the public parts of the course have this enthusiastic band of racegoers in mind. Tony Shewen is a wonderful enthusiast and a man who clearly loves his racing—if you love yours, take a trip to Taunton and you won't be disappointed. An example of this dedication is the racecourse Secretary's pledge to 'get on his bike' and review the catering at any course his visitors deem superior to that of Taunton. Dedication indeed, but knowing the gentleman in question, you can guarantee he will do it! A visit in 1994 is as highly recommended as ever.

Local Favourites

In the town itself, the **Castle Hotel** (0823) 272671 on Castle Green is excellent in every way. Elsewhere in town, **The County** (0823) 337651 is a pleasant old coaching inn with a good-value Taste of Somerset lunch worth sampling. One mile outside the town lies the outstanding (and outstandingly reasonable) **Meryan House Hotel** (0823) 337445. The city centre is changing nearly every day but restaurants are a little thin on the ground. Some of the many pubs in the area are obviously good places to meet for a post-race beverage. In Staple Fitzpaine, close to the racecourse, **The Greyhound** (0823) 480227 is a splendid little pub serving an excellent pint and good bar snacks. It also has an adjoining restaurant, a fine place for post-race dinner. **The Volunteer** at Seavington St. Michael is a good place both for its cooking and for that extraordinary stuff, Scrumpy. Another good-value food pub is the **Square and Compass** (0823) 480467 in Ashill. Breaking momentarily from the pub scene, it is well worth seeking out Hatch Beauchamps **Farthings Country House Hotel** (0823) 480664, an attractive Georgian house which is convenient for the racecourse.

Many people racing at Taunton are locals just out for a quick day's sport. If, however, you have made a bit of an effort to go to Taunton races, then one great place to reward yourself is **The Kingfishers Catch** (0823) 432394 at Bishops Lydeard on the A358 and en-route to the splendid Dunster Castle. An hotel which affords great comfort is **Langley House Hotel** (0984) 23318, near Wiveliscombe on the A361. With sofas, an array of fresh flowers and some splendid views, one really feels the closeness of the countryside. To the west of Taunton along the A361, **Huntsham Court** (0398) 6210 at Huntsham is both comfortable and somewhat eccentric—you can help yourself to your own drink at the bar or listen to a pre-war wireless in the bedroom. For an informal stay and personal attention, this cannot be beaten. Take a trip this year to the south west—it's a delightful part of the country.

John Smith, Clerk of the Course at York, now also performs the Clerk's role at York's neighbour—Thirsk. Mr. Smith and the Manager and Secretary, Mr. Christopher Tetley, can be contacted at Thirsk Racecourse, Station Road, Thirsk, North Yorkshire,YO7 1QL. Tel: (0845) 522276.

Travelling to the Course

The racecourse is situated just off the A61 west of Thirsk. The best route for travellers from the South is to use the A1 northbound and then follow the A61, or the A19 if journeying from York. Southbound drivers should also use the A1, the A61, or the A19. If travelling from the east, the A170 is convenient whilst eastbound journeyers should take in the M62 and the A1 north. There is ample car parking to be found on arriving. If you wish to travel by train, the King's Cross line is pretty nifty and Thirsk Station is a mere 6 furlongs away. Buses from Thirsk will take you to within a quick canter of the track but there are no special race buses. One other point that should be noted is that there are facilities for helicopters if you're lucky enough to have one. One constantly hears of jockeys missing races due to the delays on the A1 so make sure you set off in good time.

Major Races and Charges

With so many weekend fixtures, the Thirsk racegoer is thoroughly spoilt. The 2000 Guineas Trial, the oldest classic trial in the country. The Thirsk Hunt Cup is also good value. There are some 12 racing days provisionally scheduled for 1994 with the meetings in April, May and August likely to be the most popular.

There are four enclosures at Thirsk: the Members', Tattersalls, the Silver Ring and the Course Enclosure. In 1993, prices were £12, £7, £3 and £2 respectively. Party bookings are encouraged and various arrangements and discounts can be agreed with the course. This largely depends on your ability to gather troops to the fray. Basically, the more the merrier. However, these party terms do not apply to the Members' Enclosure. In 1993, Membership cost £65, whilst Associate Membership cost £110—this apparently means a man, plus another member of the family—family is not defined! Juniors are welcomed and the Annual Membership subscription is good value at £35. These prices may increase in 1994. Your membership also entitles you to five reciprocal meetings and a number of days courtesy of Yorkshire Cricket Club. Cars can be parked beside the course in the number three enclosure on all days except the most popular August meeting.

Racecourse Facilities

The racecourse rests at the foot of the Hambleton Hills and has an excellent setting, subject naturally to the weather. There are several snack bars around the course and a more substantial restaurant can be found in the Members' Stand. Bookings for lunch should be made through Craven Gilpin & Sons in Leeds (0532) 311221. Bars in both the Members' and Tattersalls have also been improved. If you wish to have a picnic then the racecourse welcomes this and if you want to order a box this can also be arranged—there are a choice of five and they can hold from ten to twenty people. For large functions there is an ideal place near the Paddock for a marquee as well as a private dining room for up to 50 people. Again, arrangements and bookings can be made through the racecourse. This is a friendly racecourse in a beautiful part of England—well worth a visit.

Local Favourites

In Thirsk itself, the **Golden Fleece** (0845) 523108 is a very satisfactory and convenient place to stay. The hotel is an old coaching inn and it faces onto a cobbled market square. Another idea is nearby Sowerby. Just outside the town is the small, but cosy, **Sheppard's** (0845) 523655. Climbing into the Hambleton Hills one arrives at Helmsley. Here, there are a number of excellent hotels, pubs and another scenic market place. This is an ideal base for exploring the nearby Dales and two sights that should definitely be seen are the ruins of Rievaulx and Byland Abbey. **The Black Swan** (0439) 70466 is extremely comfortable with a fine restaurant. Another good hotel is the **Feversham Arms** (0439) 70766—good value and a superb place for a bar snack. Alternatively, try the extremely welcoming market place hotel **The Crown** (0439) 70297—not so stylish, but extremely pleasant. A similar accolade befits **The Feathers** (0439) 70275.

Another good spot is the **Fauconberg Arms** (03476) 214 in Coxwold, a first class pub popular locally (always a good sign), with some good bedrooms. An excellent pub restaurant can be found in the **Star Inn** (0439) 70397, Harome. In Kirkbymoorside, **The George & Dragon** (0751) 31637 is an excellent establishment for a bar snack and some cosy bedrooms make it an ideal place to stay.

The Plough (0751) 31515 in Fadmoor is first class. Other good restaurants can be found near Northallerton. In the High Street itself, **Romanby Court** (0609) 8277491 is a splendid restaurant with an Italian bias to the cooking. In nearby Staddle Bridge, an outstanding restaurant is **McCoys** (0609) 82671. An evening here will be one to remember. In Pickhill, the appropriately named **Nags Head** is a great favourite. The **Bay Horse** in Rainton and the **Fox and Hounds** in Carthorpe are also very popular. Another interesting alternative is the excellent **Solberge Hall** (0609) 779191 in Newby Wiske, a really appealing place with delightful views of the moors. A little further afield, but extremely conveniently situated for the A1 is the **Crown Hotel** (0423) 322328 in Boroughbridge.

A number of new selections in this excellent field include; the **Crab and Lobster** (0845) 577286 at Asenby, the **Carpenters Arms** (0845) 537369 at Felixkirk and the **Whitestonecliffe Inn** (0845) 597271, Sutton under Whitestonecliffe. All are approximately five miles from the course. Slightly further afield, in Kilburn, is the **Forresters Arms** (0347) 868386. Kilburn is the home of the famouse 'Mouse Man' furniture maker. Finally, we come to **The George and Dragon** , Melmerby, (0765) 640303. This is a small inn located between Thirsk and Ripon—ideally placed for two of Yorkshire's quite excellent race tracks.

Hugo Bevan holds the dual position of Clerk of the Course and Racecourse Manager. The Racecourse Secretary is Philip Brangwyn. Contact can be made with the authorities by writing, care of The Racecourse, Easton Neston, Towcester, Northants, NN12 7HS. Tel: (0327) 53414.

Travelling to the Course
The racecourse itself is situated one mile south east of the town of Towcester which lies at the intersection of the A43 and the A5. Although the course itself has a tremendously tranquil setting, the busy M1 is only a few miles away. People travelling from both the north and south should get on to the M1 and exit at junction 15a. The A43 towards Oxford should be followed for some six miles until the junction with the A5. From the town centre, follow the signs for the racecourse. The major train routes leave Euston and racegoers are advised to go either to Milton Keynes or Northampton. The former is some 11 miles away and the latter nine. Bus services run from Northampton but only as far as Towcester, half a mile short of the racecourse. A better bet would be to take a helicopter, but make arrangements with the racecourse beforehand. There is ample free parking space ideal for picnics and there is a roped off area for Members parking.

Major Races and Charges
The fixture list for 1994 should follow much the same pattern as 1993 with some 14 fixtures. The bank holiday meetings at Easter and in early May are always popular—6,000 racegoers wisely decided to spend last Easter Monday at Towcester—and evening meetings also bring out the locals in droves.

Day badges in 1994 will be; £12 for the Members', £8 for Tattersalls and £4 for the Course Enclosure. There is one rider to this, namely the car. Take a car and pay £15 per load. What you interpret as a load is not defined, but one does not need to work for Price Waterhouse to realise that cramming the car would lead to significant savings. People lucky enough to justify an Annual Membership had to be prepared to spend £85 in 1994 (no junior rates). There are four reciprocal days thrown in; one each at Uttoxeter, Market Rasen, Newbury and Fontwell. If you are wishing to take a party racing then do contact the racecourse for discounts. Parties in excess of 30 will receive a discount of 30 per cent, whilst if you arrange a get together of 100 people they will all be allowed in at half price.

Racecourse Facilities
If you prefer more exclusive comfort then there are three chalets for daily hire. Each chalet can hold 12 people comfortably. In addition, there is a Pavilion which holds up to 50 people and a suite in Tattersalls which can comfortably house 300. Catering can be arranged should you desire this. The racecourse caterers are Drewetts of Rugby; tel: (0788) 544171.

The racecourse has the standard telephone and betting facilities in Tattersalls and a small stand for disabled viewing. There are no banking facilities available. Towcester has much to commend it, not least its marvellous setting. It is surely one of the most charming country courses in Britain. A visit for 1994 is an absolute priority.

Local Favourites

If you should wish to make a weekend trip to Towcester, and why not, then the following hotels are to be noted. In Northampton, a hotel that is extremely popular with many business people who use the M1 is the **Northampton Moat House** (0604) 22441. Another to remember is the **Swallow Hotel** (0604) 768700. The hotel is modern in design but luxurious and the leisure facilities most impressive. Cheaper alternatives worth a second glance include **The Poplars Hotel (0604) 643983 and The Fish Inn** (0604) 234040.

Another excellent newcomer to the Towcester stakes is the **Farthingstone Hotel, Golf & Leisure Centre** (0327) 36291 The hotel is extremely well placed for the racecourse. In Towcester itself, **The Saracen's Head** has re-opened after substantial improvements. **The Plough** (0327) 50738, on the road out of Towcester, is well worth a post-race quickie. In Stoke Bruerne a canal-side stop-off reveals **The Boat Inn** (0604) 862428. The pub itself has a fairly modern interior but the welcome is genuine as is the restaurant—a sound each way chance.

Only six miles from Towcester lies Roade, not the M1 or anything, but a village. The aptly named **Roadehouse Restaurant** (0604) 863372 has a pleasant situation in the village which is only 2 miles from junction 15 of the motorway. Venturing south of the blue line one may arrive in Horton, which is no bad thing for here the **French Partridge** (0604) 870033 is an outstanding restaurant. After a cold afternoon's racing, there could be nothing better than sitting down to some quite superb game—a really first class idea. The **Vine House Restaurant** (0327) 33267 also offers excellent cooking and some pleasing bedrooms. In Weedon, **The Crossroads** (0327) 40354 is convenient for the M1, junction 16, and is also extremely pleasant. (Breakfasts and coffees are served to non-residents). There are a number of pubs which have appeal: in Akeley, **The Bull and Butcher** (0280) 6257 is friendly and offers superb steaks, in Brackley Hatch **The Green Man** may be inspected, whilst Potterspury offers **The Old Talbot**. In Stony Stratford, **The Cock** is a popular local and if people are seeking a restaurant then **Stratfords** (0908) 566577 is set in an old chapel and offers some fine cuisine. Finally, for those really keen on having an outstanding weekend, two somewhat distant thoughts. **Hartwell House** (0296) 747444 is the first—seeing is believing—a classic country house hotel. Alternatively, lovers of quality food should try **Pebbles** (0296) 86622 in Pebble Lane—a first class restaurant in an ideal location in which to celebrate a visit to an unspoilt racecourse.

At Uttoxeter, **David McAllister** acts as **Clerk, Manager** and **Secretary**, ably assisted by **Jane Clarke**. **Gordon Brown** is the Commercial Manager with responsability for sponsorship, corporate and private hospitality, perimeter and racecard advertsising. Janyce Rhodes and Lynda Fletcher are the joint Club and Advance Booking Secretaries. All may be contacted at **The Racecourse, Wood Lane, Uttoxeter, Staffordshire, ST14 8BD. Tel: (0889) 562561.** Uttoxeter also has another extremely valuable asset in their 'hands on' Chairman, Stanley Clarke. He may also be reached via the racecourse.

Travelling to the Course
Uttoxeter is situated in the heart of the Midlands equidistant between Stoke-On-Trent and Derby. London is 135 miles away to the south east The course is situated three quarters of a mile south east of the town centre, just off the B5017. If you are travelling from either the north or the south of the country, the M6 is the motorway to aim for. One should exit at junction 14 and then use the Stafford ringroad. The new M40/ M42 link is also a possibility if you do not wish to tackle the M1/ M6 combination. Alternatively, catch a train. Uttoxeter station adjoins the racecourse and is on the Derby and Stoke line. By bus, Derby, Burton and Stoke all have routes taking in Uttoxeter. By air—helicopters may land in the centre of the course—please telephone first. Light aircraft may land at Tatenhill Aerodrome at nearby Needwood. Telephone the racecourse to arrange transport.

Major Races and Charges
Uttoxeter enjoys an average attendance of around 6,000 and recently broke Newmarket's hold on the regional racecourse of the year. The course has also been named the most popular small course between 1990 and 1992 and the most 'owner friendly' for the second year running. Prize money at the course has also risen quite dramatically and in 1993 added money topped £500,000 for the first time. Admission prices at Uttoxeter are being held for the third year in a row; £12.00 for the Member's Enclosure, £8.00 for Tattersalls, £5.00 for the Silver Ring and £3.00 if you are happy with the Course Enclosure—a great place to picnic with a point-to point atmosphere. Annual Membership rates may also be pegged at 1993 prices; £100 for a single badge or £150 for a double badge. Juniors pay £50. There are also eleven interesting reciprocal meetings included at; Ludlow, Wolverhampton, Doncaster, Southwell, Newton Abbot, Chester, Chepstow, Towcester, Nottingham, Exeter and Bangor-on-Dee—a tremendous selection. If you wish to take a party racing, then there are discounts on offer if booked in advance. Contact the racecourse for further details.

Racecourse Facilities
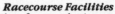
Uttoxeter is an ideal place for your business entertainment and it is worth considering taking a box here. The new £2 million stand is due to open in October 1994 and there will be 18 new boxes with spectacular views of the course.

The facilities at Uttoxeter are exceptionally well turned out and this progressive racecourse provides a setting in which companies can entertain in either a formal or informal manner. Rooms and boxes are available for parties of 12 to 60 guests and marquees for up to 600. Please ring the racecourse for details. From one extreme to the other—why not simply take a picnic? The racecourse welcomes this and the ideal place in which to enjoy your hamper is the centre of the course where cars can be parked alongside the rails. There is also the Members' Restaurant which now boasts a food court. However, tables may still be reserved in the Champagne and Sea food Bar adjacent to the Padock. Please ring the racecourse.

At the major meetings and on bank holidays youngsters have the benefit of a fun fair and a creche. This is an excellent way to distract the kids. There are three public telephone boxes and there is reserved parking on the rails for disabled racegoers as well as a viewing platform and loos. This is a thoroughly well run racecourse which offers fine racing.—well worth a visit in 1994.

Local Favourites
South of Stoke, in Stone, **The Crown** (0785) 813535 is an 18th century coaching inn which is set in lovely gardens and also offers a pleasant restaurant. **The Mill** is also a fine place to drink if this is more to your way of thinking.

If you wish to stay in nearby Dovedale, **Peveril of the Peak** (0335) 29333 is a charming hotel. **The Izaak Walton** (0335) 29555 is also a good place for a drink and/or a kip. There are many pubs hidden away in these parts and invariably they have superb views. **The Yew Tree** in Cauldon boasts a splendid array of antiques as well as some good food and beers and worth a detour. Another place that is well worth taking some trouble to find is **The Old Beams** (0538) 308254, Waterhouses. This is a really tremendous restaurant which has character and charm as well as some excellent food-thoroughly recommended.

In Uttoxeter itself, **The White Hart** (0889) 562437 is an historic coaching inn and the bar here makes a good place to meet if you are planning to see friends before the races. Anothergood inn is **Ye Olde Dog and Partridge** in Tutbury. The building dates from the 15th century and the bars here are typical of this kind of inn, welcoming and refreshing. Perhaps an even more enchanting place to stay can be found in Rolleston-on-Dove. Here, the **Brookhouse Inn** (0283) 814188 has charming bars, a good restaurant and extremely pleasing bedrooms. Another superb hotel and restaurant double can be found close to here; **The Dovecliffe Hall** (0283) 31818. Back in Uttoxeter, the truly excellent **Hillcrest Guesthouse** (0889) 564627 will undoubtedly gratify all intrepid bargain hunters. If you are seeking somewhere relatively inexpensive try **The Crown** (0283) 840227. The neighbouring town of Abbots Bromley contains farmhouse accommodation of character and comfort at **The Marsh** (0283) 840323. One final thought is the **Royal Oak** also in Abbots Bromley- this excellent establishment offers outstanding bar food and a fine restaurant—well worth a visit. Finally, the **Meynell Ingram Arms** (0283) 75202—the local 'in place' and a favourite of the management.

Both Edward Gillespie, **Clerk of the Course** for flat meetings and Peter McNeile, who combines the role of **Manager** with **Clerk of the Course** for National Hunt meetings, can be contacted at Warwick Racecourse, Hampton Street, Warwick, CV34 6HN. Tel: (0926) 491553. Fax: (0926) 403223.

Travelling to the Course
Warwick racecourse lies close to the junction of the A46 and the A41 and is convenient for the M1, M5 and M6, a mere eight miles from Stratford (which should be avoided in the summer) and 20 miles from Birmingham—following the M6—M42 (junction 2), thence on the A41. The A46 via Leamington Spa from the north and via Stratford from the south is most convenient. Travellers from the south and west might join the A46 from the A422, (Anne Hathaway's cottage marks the appropriate junction). Road travellers should also note the new M40 link as junction 15 is only two miles from the racecourse making it extremely handy for Londoners and those from the south east.

The somewhat difficult train journey from London has been improved and there is now an hourly service direct from London to Warwick and Leamington. The station is a 20 minute walk from the racecourse. There are special Raceday Buses running from Coventry Pool Meadow Station one hour before racing starts. The return trip in 1993 cost £2.30 (children under 16 travel free). The buses return to the same place one hour after racing ends. There is free parking for 3,000 cars. There is also parking in the Members' car park, but you will be charged £5 as a non-member for the privilege. Coaches are also welcome here with space for 100 altogether. Helicopters may land in the centre of the track at Warwick by arrangement but please avoid the cars! As for light aircraft, they are somewhat unwelcomingly sent to Coventry.

Major Racecourses and Charges
Racing in 1994 is likely to follow the same pattern as 1993 with 13 days of flat racing followed by 12 National Hunt meetings. Annual Membership rates for 1993 were £110 for a full badge and £65 for a National Hunt badge. Juniors (16 to 24) are charged £50 but please also note an extra £7.50 is asked for a car park badge for all members. A Half Yearly Membership may be purchased from June 1st at a cost of £55. However, in addition to racing at Warwick, full members are entitled to reciprocal arrangements at nine other courses. Each member is also given two vouchers which admit guests to the Club during the year—this seems an admirable gesture by the executive. The Daily Club badge in 1993 was priced at £12 (juniors £6), Tattersalls (Grandstand and Paddock) £8 and £5.50 for the Course Enclosure. Accompanied children under 16 are admitted free and there are discounts on a sliding scale for parties of 20 or more.

Racecourse Facilities

Warwick is extremely good for company entertaining and the addition of the new Paddock Suite facilities has given a further boost to the private facilities at the racecourse. Boxes in the Paddock Suite are available on a daily basis and enjoy spectacular views from within as well as from the balcony over the Paddock and racecourse. The elegant Castle Suite accommodates 60 for lunch or dinner and 80 for a buffet meal whilst the Chandler Suite, situated on the ground floor of the Members Enclosure, has a private viewing stand. The Suite may be divided into three rooms if required. The Spartan Missile Room is opposite the winning post offering entertaining views of the betting ring too. There are snack bars in all enclosures and two restaurants; the Paddock Bar andrecently refurbished Members' Bar. Booking is advisable on major race days and can be done by telephoning the course caterers, Drewetts. Tel: (0788) 544171 who will also be pleased to supply sample menus for parties in the above rooms. The Council Room in Tatts has also been refurbished and more upgrading is planned over the next few years. From the 1993/94 National Hunt Season an exclusive Owners and Trainers room will be available—an excellent idea.

There is a playground in the Course Enclosure for children to occupy themselves while father loses his shirt. Disabled people are provided for by means of a raised stand, ramps and lavatories in the Members Enclosure. There are no banks on site at Warwick so come prepared as there is a betting shop in Tattersalls and the Course Enclosue (open Saturdays and Bank Holidays only).

Local Favourites
If you are staying nearby, a number of hotels stand out. In Warwick itself **The Lord Leycester** (0926) 491481 in Jury Street is within walking distance of the racecourse—the restaurant is good here as are the bars. A modern but well thought of hotel is **The Hilton National** (0926) 499555, most convenient for the **A46** and the new motorway. We have also had a tip from one of Britain's former jockeys: **The Woodhouse Hotel** in Princethorpe (0926) 632131. If his expertise in the culinary stakes is as masterful as his work in the saddle this is definitely one for the notebook. A popular local watering hole is **The Racehorse** in Stratford Road.

Further north in Henley-in-Arden **Le Filbert Cottage** (0564) 7922700 is a French restaurant to note. An extremely friendly place to stay is the **Ashleigh House** (0564) 22315, an Edwardian country house with extensive views over the Warwickshire countryside towards the Cotswolds, small but good value. Alternatively try the splendid Tudor **Yew Trees** (0564) 24636—superb character and a very high standard. In Dunchurch, one finds a village inn of some repute, **The Dun Cow** (0788) 810233. The bedrooms are cheerful and the bars are an extremely good place to meet before dining in the Oakwood Restaurant. Perhaps the most outstanding place to visit in the area is **Mallory Court** (0926) 330214. Situated in Bishops Tachbrook, south of Leamington Spa, this is a picture of elegance. Bedrooms are sumptuous, while the restaurant provides exquisite French cooking. In the Parade of Leamington Spa itself, one finds a more modest, but no less welcoming hotel, **The Regent** (0926) 427231. For outstanding food, the **Old Mill** (0608) 61880 at Shipston-on-Stour simply has to be visited. One final tip for the Warwick visitor is **The Pheasant** at Charlecote—more good value.

Wetherby is an extremely popular racecourse and there is no doubt this is a well run course, as most of the Yorkshire tracks are. It has an informal atmosphere but provides an excellent standard of racing. **Edward Gillespie**, who is **Clerk of the Course, Christopher Tetley** the **Manager** and the **Secretary, George Hanson** can all be contacted through **Wetherby Steeplechase Committee Ltd., The Racecourse, York Road, Wetherby, Yorkshire. Tel: (0937) 582035.**

Travelling to the Course
The course is one of the most accessible in the country, being close to the A1 and thereby providing an excellent route for both north and southbound vehicles. Wetherby is 200 miles from London and close to Leeds, Harrogate and York. The B1224 is the most direct route from York. The M62 runs from the west of the country and it connects with the A1 at junction 33, ten miles south of Wetherby. There is a railway station in Harrogate about nine miles away and a bus station in Wetherby which is one and a half miles from the course. Leeds, 12 miles distant, followed by the bus is probably a better bet. Car parking is ample and is provided free of charge.

Major Races and Charges
Fixtures for 1994 have not yet been finalised but the course usually has two bank holiday Meetings and several Saturday Meetings too. A number of local Yorkshire trainers send good horses to Wetherby and a generally high standard of racing can be expected. The crowd is both vocal and knowledgeable and this generates a superb atmosphere coupled with the traditionally hearty voices of a Yorkshire crowd—always entertaining for southerners!

The Membership subscription for 1993 was good value at £65. Associate Membership for married couples was also fairly priced at £105. Daily Membership rates were priced at £12, Tattersalls at £7 and the popular Course Enclosure imposed a £2.00 charge reduced to £1.00 for pensioners. Cars to Centre of Course £6 (including up to 4 adults). Admissions for 1994 will be similarly priced.

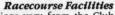

Racecourse Facilities

The racecourse buildings vary from the Club Stand constructed in 1967 to the more interesting number board which dominates the Paddock. The course has a restaurant and a number of bars which provide snacks to quell those irritating hunger pangs that inevitably occur between the fourth and fifth races. The Paddock and Course Side bars have recently been refurbished. The course does not have boxes or conference areas but four luncheon rooms are available

and these can cater for up to 30 people. Other facilities include a children's playground in the Course Enclosure, and viewing facilities close to the winning post for disabled people. There is no racecourse bank but there are public telephones and a betting shop which is located in the Paddock Enclosure.

All in all, Wetherby is a friendly racecourse. It may not have the prestige of some of the Yorkshire tracks but it is deservedly popular all the same. We wish its management and patrons a successful 1994.

Local Favourites

In South Yorkshire, there are relatively few hotels but many pubs. However, one of the best of all Yorkshire establishments is the splendid **Pool Court** (0532) 842288 in Pool-in-Wharfedale. The village is located near Otley and dinner is served from 630—930pm; booking is recommended. There is a tremendous wine list which complements some outstanding French cuisine. In addition to this first class restaurant, four luxurious bedrooms make for a superb place to stay while visiting any of the several racecourses nearby—a Travelling The Turf favourite.

It seems a crying shame to discuss Leeds in almost the same sentence as Pool-in-Wharfedale but many a suffering businessman should be encouraged to take in an afternoon's racing after a tough morning at the office. If you should need to stay in Leeds then the **Hilton International** (0532) 442000 is modern but comfortable. A more traditional, 1930's hotel is the **Queen's** (0532) 431323 in the city square. There are many good restaurants in Leeds but one with a definite pedigree is **Sang Sang** (0532) 468664.

If you can escape the city, then run to Harewood where the best known landmark in the village is Harewood House. Open from April to October, the gardens, collections of Chippendale furniture and superb English works of art are all fascinating. Good public houses nearby are **The Windmill** in Linton and The **White Swan** at Wighill, a marvellous country boozer. Whilst we are in the vicinity of Linton, **Wood Hall** (0937) 67271 is quite outstanding. This is a converted Georgian Manor which has every amenity your heart could desire, from saunas to clay pigeon shooting. A good guesthouse is **Prospect House** (0937) 582428—offering a pleasant welcome to the weary (or exuberant) traveller.

There are two modern hotels convenient for the racecourse, both owned by major hotel concerns offering high standards of comfort, although perhaps without the charm of independent establishments. They are the **Leeds Wharfedale Post House Hotel** (0532) 842911 and the **Wetherby Resort Hotel** (0937) 583881 in Wetherby.

Much of the countryside in Yorkshire is full of mystery, none more haunting than that surrounding the former home of Emily and Charlotte Bronte. A pub that dates well before the birth of the sisters can be found at Bardsey, **The Bingley Arms**, a mere four miles from Wetherby. A final thought, is **The Crown** (0423) 322328, in Boroughbridge, another selection that will not disappoint.

Wincanton is a really worthwhile establishment to visit and win or lose you will surely enjoy a good day out. **Mr. Ian Renton, Clerk of the Course** and **Jenny Michell, Racecourse Secretary** have the enviable task of running this most popular of jumping courses. They can be contacted at **The Racecourse, Wincanton, Somerset, BA9 8BJ. Tel: (0963) 32344.**

Travelling to the Course

The course itself lies just off the A303 by-pass, on the B3081 and like many racecourses on racedays is signposted by the good old AA signposts. If you are travelling from London some 110 miles away, then the M4 and the M3 both trek in that westward direction. Equally satisfactory is the old A4. Wincanton itself lies on the A303. Travellers north and south should note the A357 and the A37 respectively. Although a public bus service winds its way to Wincanton, the nearest railway stations are at Gillingham on the Waterloo line seven miles away or at Castle Cary on the Paddington route; there is a taxi service from both stations but taxis at the latter need to be ordered in advance. There are large car parks available and there is no charge for parking. Finally, helicopters may land in the centre of the course by prior arrangement with the management.

Major Races and Charges

On your arrival, there will inevitably be some fairly competitive racing, the Boxing Day meeting being the most popular. The course's leading races include the Kingwell Pattern Hurdle, The Jim Ford Challenge Cup, The Badger Beer Chase, The Desert Orchid S.W. Pattern Chase, and the Silver Buck Chase. In 1993, the first National Hunt auction race was staged here and this will be run again in 1994. These races often attract excellent horses and local trainers use them as 'prep' events for more prestigious races later in the year.

In 1993, visits to Wincanton cost £11.50 for a Member's badge, £8 for Tattersalls and £4 if you were happy to enjoy racing from the Course Enclosure. The price of an Annual Member's Badge in 1993 was £90 and the price remains static for the 1994 season. A car pass is thrown in which gives you preferential parking plus 9 reciprocal days racing at various tracks around the country including; Ascot, Salisbury, Newbury, Taunton, Devon and Exeter, Bath, Sandown and Cheltenham. If one wishes to gather a group of friends together then a 20 per cent discount can be received for parties in excess of 10 and if you are taking a really substantial number then further discounts can be arranged.

Racecourse Facilities

Bigger parties may wish to make use of the private rooms available, ranging from 30 to 120 people. Companies or individuals wishing to take advantage of these facilities should contact the racecourse. The course has seven boxes which are let annually, although it is sometimes possible to sub-let these. It's really a question of luck as to their availability. Sited on the top floor they offer splendid views of the course. Another plan for a party at the races is to arrange for your own marquee—an area near the parade ring is ideal. If you like the idea of lunching whilst you fill out your bets, then the Members' Restaurant overlooks the Paddock and should serve you well; bookings can be made through the course office. The three course luncheon will cost £12.00. The racecourse caterers are Parkers Catering at Milborne Port, tel:(0963) 250368. Alternatively, there are the snack bars and a picnic area in the Course Enclosure. People who wish to park cars in the Course are charged £3 for the privilege. An additional £3 is then required for each occupant. This is a great way to get the best out of racing, particularly for newcomers to the sport.

There is a Tote betting shop behind Tattersalls. Under 16-year-old punters are admitted free, however, they have no other facilities provided for them. There are plenty of telephones and excellent disabled viewing in the Hatherleigh Stand. Special discounts can be made in advance for disabled people on written application to the course. Wincanton offers exciting and competitive racing with welcoming staff who will ensure you have a happy and, hopefully, a successful day at the races.

Local Favourites

Some excellent pubs to try include **The Bennett Arms** (0747) 830221 in Semley, which has a pleasant atmosphere, good bar snacks and a number of bedrooms. In Hindon, one finds **The Lamb** (0747) 89573 with some good bar food. As the road diverges one has the choice of Warminster or Mere. In Mere you should visit **The Old Ship** (0747) 860258 which has a pleasant bar with appetizing snacks. The town also houses the highly recommended **Chetcombe House Hotel** (0747) 860219 and **The Talbot Hotel** (0747) 860427. And in Warminster you have an excellent proposition in the form of **Bishopstrow House** (0985) 212312, an outstanding Georgian mansion. The hotel is a delight in which to stay and the restaurant is of a similarly high standard. In Shepton Mallet, Blostin's (0749) 343648 enjoys an extremely good following, while **Bowlish House** (0749) 342022 is much recommended for a pleasant evening after a successful day at Wincanton races. Nearer to Wincanton, several places should be mentioned. Bruton offers **Truffles** (0749) 812255, a restaurant of note. Two Bulls now, one in Brewham, the other in Hardway—good bar food here. And nearby Stourton proves a worthy diversion with a Palladian mansion and superb gardens. **The Spread Eagle** (0747) 840587 is the local to note and it has some accommodation if required. In Bourtons, neighbouring Wincanton, **The Hunters Lodge Inn** is well-situated for the racecourse and is popular with racegoers. Wincanton itself offers the charming and good value **Lower Church** (0963) 32307, while in Holbrook, **The Holbrook House** (0963) 32377 is the ideal place to stay. Not quite so convenient but most appealing is **Bonds Hotel** (0963) 50464 in Castle Cary, which has delightful bedrooms and a fine restaurant. South of Wincanton, perhaps on your way to the Dorset coast, there are two places to note. In the village of Barwick, **Little Barwick House** (0935) 23902 is most accommodating and offers an outstanding dinner, the specialities being fish and game. Nearby, a handy pub for the A30 is **The Queen's Head** (0963) 250314, at Milborne Port, which has excellent value accommodation and some good bar snacks. A number of these hotels, pubs and restaurants will double for racegoers visiting Salisbury, and one excellent example is the **King's Arms** (0747) 89523 in Fonthill Bishop. The bar food here is first class and there is some unpretentious accommodation for those wishing to stay.

Windsor is a friendly busy racecourse, renowned for its mid-summer evening races. The Clerk of the Course at Windsor is Hugo Bevan and he can be contacted at Royal Windsor Races, The Racecourse, Windsor, Berkshire. Tel: (0753) 865234/ 864726.

Travelling to the Course

The racecourse is on the A308 between Windsor and Maidenhead. West and eastbound traffic on the M4 should leave the motorway at junction 6. The M3 traffic from the south should leave the motorway at Interchange 3 and follow the A332 to Windsor. Travellers from the north and the east will find a combination of the M25, M4 and the A308 the best route. For those who might prefer a slight change from the normal mode of transportation, why not travel by river bus. The summer boat leaves Windsor Promenade opposite the Thamescourt Hotel and takes racegoers to the racecourse jetty, close to the Paddock. The journey takes about ten minutes and there is a bar on board. For further information contact French Brothers (0753) 862933/ 851900. There are frequent rail services from Waterloo and Paddington to Windsor and Eton (Riverside) and Windsor and Eton (Central) respectively, both two miles away. The Green Line bus terminus is one mile from the course. The car parking facilities cost £1, £1.50 and £2 and coaches just £5.

Major Races and Courses

There are 21 days of racing at Windsor and they should follow the 1993 pattern with eight meetings over the sticks. The New Year meeting (3rd January 1994) is a really excellent raceday. Most flat racing here is run on Monday evenings with a brace of Saturday evening meetings as well. These occasions are enormously popular with owners and this assures good support from some of the country's leading stables which in turn guarantees huge crowds. A simple formula and a great success! These evenings often precede the year's major flat meetings and serve as an excellent aperitif for the week's principal attractions. What better way to spend a summer evening? However, the traffic out of London is so congested that an early start is strongly advised.

In 1993, Membership Badges for Royal Windsor Race Club were priced at £100 each. Daily badges were priced at £12 for the Club, £8 for the Tattersalls and Paddock Enclosure and £4 for the Silver Ring. The course encourages advance bookings for the Tattersalls Stand and the Silver Ring, for which 25 per cent discounts are offered for advance bookings for parties of 20 or more.

Racecourse Facilities

The executive also encourages the reservation of the Churchill Suite and private boxes in the Paddock Pavilion, overlooking the finishing straight. Lunch and dinner can be reserved by contacting the course caterers, Letheby & Christopher (0753) 832552. The potential for company and business entertainment is particularly interesting when one considers the evening meetings. Corporate hospitality is organised by the racecourse office. It is also worth noting that children under 16 are admitted free and there are public telephones available but no banks are in attendance as yet. Disabled people are well looked after with a special viewing stand and reserved paddock viewing. Admission for wheelchair users is free of charge which is excellent.

All in all Windsor has great appeal. Although viewing is not ideal from the Members' Enclosure. Critical investment in new facilities for upgrading the Silver Ring and Tattersalls in 1994 and 1995 is planned and we very much hope this signals a new era of improvement at this pleasant course.

Local Favourites

If you do wish to stay in the area then a hotel that is worthy of recommendation is **Fredrick's** (0628) 35934 on Shoppenhangers Road—the bedrooms are comfortable and the restaurant, excellent. The menu changes frequently and one is treated to some splendidly imaginative cooking. A similarly outstanding hotel and restaurant double is to be found along the Windsor road—it is an absolute pearl and its name is **Oakley Court** (0628) 74141. All manner of facilities are complemented by excellent service, gracious surroundings and beautiful grounds. The restaurant, **The Oak Leaf Room** is another great pleasure. For people who do not wish such extravagance then **Sir Christopher Wren's House Hotel** (0753) 861354 is less expensive but excellent; **The River Room Restaurant** has a splendid setting and is definitely one to sample. A further example of good fayre and good value service is **Melrose House** (0753) 865328.

In Eton, on the High Street to be precise, The **Christopher Hotel** (0753) 852359 has comfortable bedrooms and a palatable selection of real ales. This is also a good base for exploring the antique shops of Eton if this happens to be to your liking. The **Eton Wine Bar** (0753) 854921 is also reported to be good. Returning to Windsor, a number of suggestions arise. There are several excellent pubs that nestle beneath the magnificent castle, **The Castle** (0753) 851011 being a particularly notable example. Another well known landmark in Marlow is The **Compleat Angler** (06284) 4444. Its setting on the Thames is renowned as being one of the most superb spots. **The Valaisan** restaurant is also outstanding and visitors can enjoy marvellous views of the river. In Hurley a superb inn is **Ye Olde Bell** (062882) 5881—excellent comfort and once again an elegant formal restaurant.

People looking for a less formal evening meal should consider **The Walnut Tree**, in Farly, an excellent pub, well worth a peep, and in Cookham **The Royal Exchange** is also well worth a trip. Also in Cookham, **The Bell and Dragon** in the High Street is good—there is a fine restaurant to be found here. Elsewhere in Cookham lovers of oriental cuisine should seek out the **Peking Inn** (06285) 20900—where booking is advisable. **The Long Barn** in Cippenham, also offers good food and great character. In Dorney **The Palmer Arms** (0628) 666612 is also excellent serving really tremendous bar meals. Slightly further afield one finds a fine Inn, **The Chequers** (06285) 29575. It offers good accommodation and some excellent bar food—a commendable addition to a fine field of local favourites.

143

RAM Racecourses Ltd have revolutionised racing at Wolverhampton and while some details need to be finalised it is clear that life at Wolverhampton will never be the same. The Clerk of the Course, Ashley Bealby and the Racecourse Secretary, Carol Morgan can be contacted at **Wolverhampton Racecourse, Dunstall Park, Gorsebrook Road, Wolverhampton, WV6 0PE. Tel: (0902) 24481. Fax: (0902) 716626.**

Travelling to the Course

The course lies some 16 miles north west of Birmingham, close to Tettenhall, and the area is well served by motorways. Lancastrians should follow the M6 to junction 12 and thereafter the A449. Racegoers from the south-west should pursue the M5 to junction 2 followed by the A449 and A41, whilst Welshmen should aim for Wellington and the M54, then follow the A464 and the A41. London racegoers will find the M1 and the M6 most useful—by-passing the charming hamlets of Birmingham, West Bromwich, Walsall and Dudley! The course is approximately 130 miles distant. The nearest railway station is in Wolverhampton—take the train from Euston and then grab a taxi for the five minute journey to the course.. There is a bus station in the town centre and buses run to the course and there is a bus service from the railway station to the course on racedays. Ample free parking is provided for cars with over 1,500 spaces to be precise and there is also room for coaches. Helicopters can land at the course but please contact the racecourse management in advance if you wish to land your whirly bird here. Light aircraft should head to nearby Halfpenny Green.

Major Races and Charges

Fixtures for 1994, although not presently available, will hopefully include about 50 meetings. The introduction of floodlit racing adds another dimension to racing here and makes for a superb evening out. Membership to the Club Enclosure within the new stadium will cost in the region of £125. Access to the Club Enclosure will be for Annual Subscribers, owners, trainers, executive boxholders and invited guests. The emphasis will be on providing a consistently high level of facilities for every category of the racing fraternity. The new 370 seater tiered viewing restaurant offers panoramic views of the racetrack for all racegoers and the latest betting technology is available at each table. Other restaurants include the Scales Bar and various franchises, including an excellent Indian Delhi Bar. All facilities are close to the stands and paddock. Admission to the racecourse will be £6 for all areas other than the Club Enclosure and discounts are available for group bookings.

Racecourse Facilities

The eight private boxes accommodate parties of 12–80 and are let on a daily basis. Packages will be tailored to include hire of box, menu, admission charge and car parking. The price for 1994 will be approximately £35 a head—good value really. Mind you, that is before you lose a few bob on the horses. Discounts will be available for companies making multiple bookings and the Exhibition Hall can accommodate 500 guests. Marquees can also be organised.

Childen under 16 are admitted free if acompanied by an adult. There is an adventure playground and creche at the course. Both floors are purpose built for the disabled with a lift, viewing platform, loos and reserved parking.

Wolverhampton is an amazing achievement. Some £15.7 million has been invested to create an all weather track, floodlights, a new Grandstand, boxes and a 370 seater restaurant on the top floor. Not to mention a 53 bedroomed hotel. New sponsors, an extended fix-ture list and a real willingness to champion the cause of racing—I very much hope the rewards are as plentiful as they are deserved.

Local Favourites
The most obvious recommendation is the **Racecourse Hotel** (0902) 24481. The 53 rooms are all en suite with TV, telephone and tea maker. Budget accommodation starts at £35 per night. Another local idea is **The Railway** pub in Wolverhampton itself—a recent winner of a national pub award.

One of the best known leisure centres in the country is situated at Wishaw: **The Belfry** (0675) 7470301—a whole host of pursuits can be enjoyed here aside from golf. The hotel's restaurants promise nou-velle cuisine as well as English fare. Alternatively, you may wish to visit **The Moor Hall Hotel**, Sutton Coldfield (0213) 083751 which also has strong associations with the nearby golf course and is a most welcoming place to stay. Another Hall also can be found at Sutton Coldfield, **New Hall** 021-378 2442. This is an outstanding establish-ment with an inspiring setting and a fine restaurant—just two good reasons for staying here. If any or all of the above have the irritating no vacancies sign up then another good place to try is the **Standbridge Hotel** (0213) 543007.

In Birmingham, one finds some massive hotels. **The Albany** (0216) 438171 is extremely good and has a distinguished restaurant—The Four Seasons. Similarly, **The Holiday Inn** (0216) 312000 offers excel-lent leisure facilities. A little way from the city centre **The Plough and Harrow** (0214) 544111 is an excellent hotel/restaurant double. The cosmopolitan nature of Birmingham reveals a whole variety of restaurants. Chinese food is the focus at **Chung Ying Garden** (0216) 666622, a firm favourite for lovers of the Orient. Advocates of Indian cooking should try **Rajdoot** (0216) 438805. Finally, a French emphasis can be discovered at **Sloans** (0214) 556697 in Edgbaston, excellent. Slightly further afield at Waverley, the proprietors of **Bearwood Court Hotel** (0214) 299731 offer a warm welcome to every guest.

Chaddesley Corbett also offers an establishment of distinction in **Brockencote Hall** (0562) 777876. The house, restaurant and grounds are all worth a pre-race inspection, combined they make up a great favourite. Finally, on the hotel front, another sporting hotel with great appeal is **Patshall Park** (0902) 700100, where the accent is on an excellent golf course. To complete our section on a rather bizarre note, visit **The Crooked House** (0384) 238583.

The gentlemen in charge of the course at Worcester are J.H.A. Bennett, the Racecourse Manager and Hugo Bevan, the Clerk of the Course. The course address is; Pitchcroft, Worcester, WR1 3EJ. Tel: (0905) 25364/23936.

Travelling to the Course

To reach the racecourse, which lies some 120 miles west of London and 20 miles from Birmingham, one might use any one of the following routes. From the west, the M5 (junction 6) and thence the A449 and the A38 provide a winning combination. The course itself rests between Broadheath and Herwick. The A58 from Birmingham provides a smooth route for racegoers from the West Midlands. The M5 (junction 7) is another route which benefits from the A38. From the Cotswolds, the A44 is a pleasant trek - the A443 is a help here. People who consider this to be the age of the train, should note the Paddington line. One advantage is that the station is within walking distance of the track. If the proverbial Flying Horse is preferred to the so-called Iron Horse - then phone the manager in advance who will inform you where to land your chopper. Car parking is free, except for picnic parking where a £2 charge is made.

Major Races and Charges

The 1994 season is likely to be a similar fixture list to that of 1993, which included some excellent evening meetings. There are several Wednesday afternoon fixtures, of great appeal to the farming community who are so much the backbone of the National Hunt game. A wet and windy Wednesday at Worcester may not immediately appeal but even when the elements are against us it offers so much more than your average day out. If you are keen to become an Annual Member at the racecourse then you will be disappointed for there are none. The form is to visit on a day to day basis. Members' Badges were priced at £12, entrance to Tattersalls £9 and the Silver Ring £4. One thing that really is worth noting are the discounts. Twelve is the number to aim for and discounted prices of £9, £7.50 and £3 are given for Members, Tattersalls and the Silver Ring respectively. Badges can be purchased from the Manager's Office but must be paid for at least seven days in advance.

Racecourse Facilities

What also sounds great fun is the river boats moored behind the Grandstand for parties numbering between 30 to 150. The Worcester management team are clearly refusing to give in to the ravages of the Severn, and are instead harbouring its beauty for their own ends. For landlubbers there are of course the usual boxes and a superb sponsor's room capable of holding up to 120 people.

We have mentioned the various facilities on offer. Punters please note that the Croft Suite also has a restaurant for which reservations can be made, tel: (0905) 25970. It is clear that there is plenty of scope for all sorts of additional entertainment and this is reflected in the fact that the racecourse has the support of numerous sponsors. It appears that the course, despite its lack of Annual Members, or perhaps because of it, is a rapidly improving arena - resulting in some excellent National Hunt racing. Other advantages of coming to Worcester are that children are admitted free before their 16th birthday and have a special play area. Disabled people have special viewing facilities and lifts. Telephones can be found adjacent to the Grandstand where the course betting shop is also located. Make no mistake this is a delightful racetrack, its facilities are good and a day's racing here is to be thoroughly recommended.

Local Favourites

The ancient cathedral city of Worcester, which is delightfully peaceful, is famous for two things; firstly, its sauce and secondly, its china. It also has some excellent antique shops and a great variety of hotels and restaurants should you be anticipating a large gamble coming off.. The **Giffard Hotel** (0905) 726262, overlooking the cathedrals precincts, is modern while **Browns** (0905) 26263 is a splendidly converted corn mill, ideal for lunch and dinner and situated beside the cricket ground. Returning Cathedral-wards, a thirsty fellow should find **The Farriers Arms,** a traditional public house. A converted glove factory makes for another noteworthy hotel, with good accommodation and a fine restaurant, called **Fownes** (0905) 613151. One suggestion for a less extravagant room is **The Barbourne Guesthouse** (0905) 27507.

Outside the city itself, amid the fruit trees and the whiff of hops, one finds a feast of delights, starting with the racecourse. In Colwall, **The Colwall Park Hotel** (0684) 40206 stands in front of the old National Hunt course and is a tremendous place to stay. The hotel offers English cooking and the Edwardian dining room is backed up by an extensive bar menu. Some lovely places can be found in and around Great Malvern. In Malvern Wells, **The Croque-en-Bouche** (06845) 65612 is one of the country's finest dining places. Alternatively, visit the **Cottage In The Wood Hotel** (06845) 73487. A really wonderful place to stay, it also has a highly regarded restaurant which is open to non-residents. One commendable hotel in Malvern is **The Foley Arms** (0684) 73397, a charming Georgian edifice in which to slumber. Another great place to stay with a good restaurant is **The Elms Hotel** (0299) 896666 in Abberley. Where next? Try Bromsgrove and **Grafton Manor** (0527) 579007 where tradition and luxury combine to make yours a delightful stay. For a less glamorous but still comfortable place to stay, try the **Phepson Guesthouse** (0905) 69205 in Himbleton. Whilst in Droitwich Spa, **The Chateau Impney** (0905) 774411 is yet another good idea for those of you seeking refined stabling when visiting these parts.

In Wyre Piddle, **The Anchor** is a grand pub cum restaurant. **The Talbot** at Knightwick is also a tremendous inn with good-value accommodation. Followers of the Archers might care to make a pilgrimage to **The Old Bull**, Inkberrow. And don't forget Ombersley, where **The Kings Arms**, **The Crown** and **Sandys Arms** provide good food and warm hospitality. A fitting treble for visitors to Worcester racecourse.

The men in charge of Yarmouth are **David Henson** who is **Clerk of the Course** and **Tom Prior, Manager.** They can be contacted at **The Racecourse, Jellicoe Road, Great Yarmouth. Tel: (0493) 842527.**

Travelling to the Course

The journey to Yarmouth by road has now been made much speedier by the opening of the new southern by-pass around Norwich and by the many new sections of dual carriageway on the A11 and A47. From London, the following treble is advised; the M11, A11 and A47. The A12 via Colchester, Ipswich and Lowestoft however, will certainly prove a more stimulating option. And were you to make a seafront promenade the night before, you would note that a bus runs regularly from the seafront to the racecourse. Furthermore, the local blue bus routes run from each of the town's holiday centres. The nearest railway station is in Yarmouth itself and although no bus runs directly to the racecourse from here the track is only a leisurely 15 minute walk away. London racegoers should use the Liverpool Street line. Back on the roads, the A47 via Norwich serves the racegoer travelling from the north and west of the country. There is plenty of room for car parking, for which there is a £1 charge. Limited space is reserved for coaches if pre-booked with the course. Helicopters can land by prior arrangement with the heliport across the road.

Major Races and Charges

Average attendance here is around 4,000 and meetings in 1994 will follow the same pattern as last year, the highlight being the three-day September meeting. The extremely successful evening meeting in July will be repeated in 1994. The great Mtoto won his first race here and some superb two year olds make the short trip from Newmarket for their racecourse debut. If you only want the odd day's racing here a daily membership is the ticket and £12 is the asking price. If you wish to be near to the bookmakers then Tattersalls is the answer and this cost £8.50 in 1993. Alternatively, the Course Enclosure will cost you £4.50 for the day. An Annual Members' badge cost £90 in 1993 and the racecourse also operates a good policy whereby an additional badge can be bought for only £70—a good incentive to get a friend to join. Membership includes a carpark label and three reciprocal meetings (jumps) at Huntingdon and Fakenham. Discounts are also available; a party of 20 or more being admitted at a reduced rate.

Racecourse Facilities

The racecourse is eager to combine business with the leisure market and there are four hospitality boxes ideal for corporate entertainment. The boxes can be hired by the head and prices range from £15. Catering is then organised on top of this. All the boxes are fitted with close circuit television screens and are located in the centre of the course. Should you wish to arrange for a private room or even a marquee, then contact the racecourse caterers South Norfolk Caterers (0953) 788197. Smaller and more discreet festivities can be organised through the Club restaurant, while the more rushed yet equally hungry may get snacks from numerous points around the track. The young, under 16 years, are admitted free if accompanied by an adult. Indeed, Yarmouth are focusing their attention on families and a fully staffed adventure playground has recently been created. There are playgrounds, sideshows, bouncy castle, train and pony rides. One point you should remember is that there is no bank, so have enough readies to hand. And if you wish to bet at the on-course betting shop, you'll find them in Tattersalls and the Course Centre. There are good facilities for the disabled in all enclosures which is excellent to report. British resorts are increasingly having to compete with exotic holiday spots abroad. They need to offer the visitor a good time—and such offering is a day at the races and in this respect the local Yarmouth community are well served. We wish them a bumper season in 1994.

Local Favourites

A particularly traditional seaside hotel is **The Carlton** (0493) 855234 which features the informal Penny Farthing Bar, an ideal meeting place prior to the races. A strong local recommendation comes for the **Furzedown Hotel** (0493) 844138. The hotel has a great atmosphere and is another popular haunt of racegoers. Two local favourites, noted by the racecourse management include; **The Burlington Hotel** (0493) 844568 and **The Star Hotel** (0493) 842294. They are certainly worth a pre-race inspection. Two fine restaurants are **Friends Bistro** (0493) 852538 and **Seafood Restaurant** (0493) 856009 on the North Quay. The latter is fairly pricey but is a great favourite of the Newmarket trainers—a recommendation in itself. Following Yarmouth's attractive coastline southward one arrives in Gorleston-on-Sea. Here, **The Cliff Hotel** (0493) 662179 is an extremely comfortable and well appointed establishment—ideal when visiting Great Yarmouth. East of the town, in South Walsham, one finds a very English mansion, **South Walsham Hall** (0605) 49378. The hotel is beautifully situated for the Norfolk Broads. A short journey away, but well worth it all the same is Framlingham Pigot, where the **Old Feathers** (0508) 62445 is a restaurant in which great culinary delights are found—try the fresh seafood.

Norwich itself is a delightful city, over 1,000 years old. The better hotels in the city include the **Hotel Norwich** (0603) 787260 a friendly, modern place and **The Maids Head Hotel** (0603) 761111, a 13th century building ideally situated near the cathedral. If you enjoy good fish then **Greens Seafood** (0603) 623733 is excellent, while splendid Italian cuisine can be found at **Marco's** (0603) 624044. Three stayers of merit outside the town include the **Petersfield Hotel** at Horning, the **Kingfisher Hotel** at Stalham and **Church Farm Hotel and Country Club** at Burgh Castle. If you are wishing to journey further westwards then try **The Park Farm Hotel** (0603) 810264 in Hethersett. Good facilities and restaurant make this a most appealing place to stay. A number of good boozers can be found either on the coast or amongst the Norfolk Broads. In Hickling, **The Pleasure Boat Inn** has a charming waterside setting as has the **Eels Foot** in Ormesby St. Michael; both of these serve good food. In appropriately named Horsey, **The Nelson's Head** is a pleasant coastal pub, while at Winterton-on-Sea, **The Fisherman's Return** (0493) 393305 has some comfortable bedrooms and also does good bar food:- ideal for escaping the throngs when racing at Yarmouth

York

The man in charge here is the extremely capable **John Smith** who acts as **Clerk, Manager** and **Secretary**. He can be contacted at **The Racecourse, York YO2 1EX. Tel: (0904) 620911. Fax: (0904) 611071.**

Travelling to the Course

The course is located just a mile outside the town centre of the beautiful Cathedral city which itself lies some 200 miles from London. The York railway station is a mile from the racecourse and is on the speedy Kings Cross line. There are frequent buses to complete the journey to the track, only five minutes ride away. They still haven't solved the traffic problem in York and as with many major racecourses, this can cause raceday congestion. The A1 and York city centre are particularly susceptible. The A19 and the A59 north of York and the A64 and the A19, south of the city provide routes to the course. A combination of the A1079 and the A64 is the answer for eastbound visitors. There are numerous car parks which are well organised and free, unless you choose to park in the county parks and you are not a member of the course where you will pay £2. One way of avoiding the traffic is to come by helicopter and land at the course—I don't suppose you will find a long queue in the skies over York. Landing facilities for light aircraft also exist close to the course, at Rufforth. Full details are available from the Racecourse office.

Major Races and Charges

Races which are particularly valuable include the Dante Stakes, the Musidora Stakes and the Yorkshire Cup run in May—the platform for racing of the highest calibre including two Classic trials. In August, the Ebor Festival includes some of the most impressive racing of the year with the Yorkshire Oaks and Gimcrack. The overriding popularity and good feeling of the summer meeting is superb but less crowded fixtures can be enjoyed in June, July, September and October. In all, the course offers a total of 15 days racing with over 25 million in prize money.

Daily charges for the August meeting in 1993 were £28, £12, £4.50 and £2.50 for the Members, Tattersalls, Silver Ring and Course Enclosures, respectively. On other days, the charges were £16 (a £2 extra charge is made for Members during the May meeting), £9 and £4 respectively. Three Day badges are available for the May and August meetings and further details of these are available from the Racecourse. Senior citizens are given discounts in the Silver Ring and Course enclosures—an excellent policy. Annual subscriptions for 1993 were £102 for a single badge and £175 for a family badge. These prices are likely to rise for 1994 but have not yet been set. It is also important to note that there is a waiting list for those applying for senior badges. There are also reciprocal arrangements included with daily membership at Haydock, Newcastle and with Yorkshire County Cricket Club! Junior membership (17-25) was also good value at £58. Party organisers should also note that the racecourse offers concessions for all meetings except the August Festival and Saturdays when parties of 20 or more are booked in advance.

Racecourse Facilities

Fifteen boxes are available for hire—catering for between 12 and 40 people and with prices ranging from £550 to £2,000. Company and party entertaining carries on in the tented village which has marquees for 40 guests. Larger events take place in the Shirley Heights Suite in the Grandstand. Luncheon requirements can be met in the Gimcrack Room on the first floor or the Carvery restaurant on the fifth floor or the Seafood restaurant by the superb parade ring.

There is a self-service restaurant as well as a carvery in Tattersalls. Further details with regard to catering can be addressed to Craven and Gilpin at the racecourse, tel: York (0904) 638971. The Silver Ring and the course enclosure have numerous places to feed and sup. Yearly subscribers have the Annual Members Bar and County Stand. Regulars will know about the Alcoves Bar. Bookmaking and telephone facilities are also close at hand. John Smith is keen to attract families to race meetings—a great idea as long as places are provided for young children away from the action. Incidentally, champagne enthusiasts should note that the York racecourse offers a different brand on sale at each meeting at a bargain price. This point will be noted by many—the amount of champagne drunk has trebled in only three years—extraordinary in a declining market.

There is no doubt that York is one of the most successful and best run racecourses in the country. It is thoughtfully managed and immensely popular. Witness the excellent shop facilities, information kiosk and disabled facilities. Visitors should try to see the Museum (4th floor, main grandstand) which superbly illustrates the rich history of the Knavesmire turf. Memories of Eclipse, Hyperion, Pretty Polly, St. Simon, Steve Donoghue, Lester Piggott can all be seen. The Knavesmire has a glorious past; it also has a sparkling future. The August Festival is one of the most popular in the calendar and this is fully reflected in the prices charged. Some say that the north is starved of top class racing—those who proclaim this have surely never visited York. Top class sporting events are becoming more difficult to attend, and this is a great pity. To miss the August Festival is surely to miss one of the highlights of the sporting summer, and it must be remembered that there are a whole variety of less expensive enclosures.

The racecourse has managed to combine the new stands with the more traditional features really well. The atmosphere here is wonderful and York is without doubt an impressive racecourse. York City has so much to offer; the racecourse, the Castle, the Minster and it's many quaint streets which now house some super shops. The Shambles is perhaps the best known of these - a delightful warren with tiny lanes running into each other. More recent additions to the city include the Yorkshire Museum, the Jorvik Viking Museum and the National Railway Museum. For racing fanatics looking for a suitable place to 'ditch' loved ones whilst at the course, York is without doubt the most complete choice.

Local Favourites

The city's hotels really capture the imagination, however, in order to make the most of the visit, rooms should be booked well in advance. The City's leading establishment is **Middlethorpe Hall** (0904) 641241 which is set in superb grounds and overlooks the race-

course. Another excellent hotel is found within two beautifully kept William IV houses, **The Mount Royale** (0904) 628856. One of the highlights here is the charming dining room which overlooks beautiful gardens. This hotel is a real favourite and is strongly recommended. Another listed building is the excellent **Judges Lodging** (0904) 638733—superbly stylish and do visit the 18th century wine cellars which now house an exquisite cocktail bar. For a prime position opposite the Minster, the **Dean Court Hotel** (0904) 625082 is the one to opt for—very comfortable too. The city straddles the Ouse and a most modern hotel which overlooks the river is the **Viking Hotel** (0904) 659822. Two further additions to the Yorkshire stable are the huge and modern **Forte Posthouse Hotel** (0904) 707921 and the **Grange Hotel** (0904) 644744 in Clifton. York has something to offer every taste and pocket, and those planning a flutter well beyond their means may wish to save a little on their accommodation. If so, they should try the still excellent but relatively modestly priced **Hudsons Hotel** (0904) 621267, the **Town House** (0904) 636171 or the equally relaxing **Grasmead House Hotel** (0904) 629996.

Restaurants in York are not as strong as the hotels but pay special attention to **Oat Cuisine** (0904) 627929, an established vegetarian restaurant. An excellent venue for a pre-race brunch or post-race tea is the famous **Bettys** in the centre of York—renowned for its truly moreish cream cakes.

Dining in the various hotels is invariably worthwhile, particularly so at **Middlethorpe Hall**. York is unsurprisingly riddled with pubs. **The Black Swan** on Peaseholme Green offers a lively atmosphere and some good value bedrooms. For a riverside setting try the **Kings Arms**. There are a number of pubs beside the Ouse which appeal and for a more central location try the **York Arms** in Petergate.

In Easingwold, **The George Hotel** (0347) 821698, an old coaching inn, offers excellent restaurant and bar food and also has some good value accommodation. In Crayke, more bar snacks can be enjoyed in the **Durham Ox** (0347) 21506. Do also note the separate restaurant. A trip to Malton would never go amiss: after all this is one of Britain's major racing towns. Here, **The Talbot** (0653) 694031 is a comfortable inn overlooking the River Derwent. If passing through Hovingham, meanwhile, do not overlook **The Worsley Arms Hotel** (0653) 628234 another great favourite and secluded Nunnington contains the well-known **Rydale Lodge** (04395) 246. Little more than a brisk gallop away at Low Catton, lies the comfortable **Derwent Lodge** (0759) 71468.

The Bilbrough Manor (0937) 834002 in Bilborough is also a splendid hotel and restaurant double. **The Crown** (0423) 322328 at Boroughbridge is another racing favourite, and rightly so, drawing race-goers from all the Yorkshire courses. **Fairfield Manor** (0904) 670222, is also well positioned for the many who choose to visit the Knavesmire. Heading off towards Beverley, an inn of great character is the **Feathers**—an ideal choice if your trip is on a more restricted budget. A first class racing haunt which offers a friendly welcome and good food is the **Bay Horse** (0423) 770230 - a bit of a drive but well worth the effort. There are many people who visit York for the races but it has many other attractions, as a result do try and book in advance.

Travelling the Turf in Ireland

In 1995, *Travelling The Turf* will be enlarging its Irish section considerably to include a number of the feature meetings and racecourses in more detail. This year, however, I hope you will find the information here of interest.

There has been much deliberation over the Irish racing calendar, particularly with regard to Sunday fixtures. While this has inevitably caused much concern to the racing authorities matters now seem to be getting settled. This is splendid to report because I cannot recommend more highly the real entertainment of racing in Ireland and the opportunity of a long weekend to enjoy some excellent racing is too good to miss. We wish the authorities all the best in their efforts to establish a fixture list for 1994 which befits the excellence of this most spectacular sport. A good source of general advice is the marketing and promotions department of the Racing Board, tel: (01) 2892888.

If you are considering a trip to Ireland I would strongly recommend that you contact the Irish Tourist Board who are extremely helpful and if you are wanting to book a group or perhaps even sponsor a race, then Racing Promotions are the people to contact.

Underneath the thick mat of Irish turf beats the heart of the thoroughbred world. The Emerald Isle offers a whole variety of charms for its visitors and a huge choice for the racing enthusiast. The gallops of Ballydoyle, the stud farms of Arab Sheiks, the Aga Khan and many more lie here. This is racing country.

There are an abundance of courses to visit in Ireland and some night spots which make the average village local look more like a church fete. Ireland is rich in its racing heritage as well as good humour, a visit here could not be more highly recommended.

There are 27 courses spanning the length and breadth of the country. It is fair to say that some of the facilities at the racecourses are far from glamorous, but they certainly have character. Racing in Ireland is also dramatically less expensive than its equivalent in Britain, despite a higher cost of living in Eire. This is one good reason for a visit, but there are so many more!

It would seem sensible to start our summary of Irish racing at the leading flat course, the **Curragh. (045) 41205**. The racecourse is situated in County Kildare some way from the Irish capital. However, beautiful scenery en route makes the journey well worth while. The track is actually 29 miles south west of Dublin on the main Dublin-Cork-Limerick road.

For all the major meetings, £10 was required in the Reserved Enclosure and £6 in the Grandstand. For the Derby, these prices rose to £22 and £8 respectively. At all other meetings where the

Grandstand and Reserved Enclosure are combined, then the entrance fee is £5. Naturally, the more prestigious the race, the higher the price. Children under 14 are admitted to the Grandstand and Reserved Enclosure (when the two are combined) for just £1. For other meetings they are restricted to the Grandstand and for the Derby their entrance fee is raised to £2. The disabled also have special facilities.

Naas (045) 97391 is situated on the Dublin side of the town, a mere 30 minutes drive from the centre of the city. There is a special bus service from Dublin on racedays. Naas has seen a celebrated array of outstanding horses and continues to provide excellent racing. Corporate entertaining can be arranged and there are a number of bars, a restaurant and good facilities for children. The racecourse stages both flat and National Hunt racing and everyone flocks into Naas after these meetings.

Fairyhouse (01) 256167 is also close to Dublin and although racing here is mixed, the course is best known for jumping, particularly as the host of the Irish Grand National. The three day Easter Festival, which features the Grand National, is the major event of the year and a pleasure to attend. The course is clearly one of the best in Ireland. Day badges range from £5 to £7. As with all Irish racecourses there are an abundance of bars in which to make merry.

One of Ireland's best run racecourses is **Leopardstown, (01) 2893607**. Leopardstown racecourse lies just six miles from the centre of Dublin off the Dublin-Bray road. For those wanting to travel by train, the suburban line from Dublin is the answer and there are bus links from all the city's train stations. Dublin airport is twelve miles away. The Holyhead/Dun Laoghaire car ferry terminal is only three miles away too. The racecourse stages an impressive number of races throughout the year with several top class flat and National Hunt races. Admission prices are good value. Last season, entrance to the Members' was £7 and Tattersalls £5. Saturday and Bank Holidays are more expensive at £8 and £6 respectively. Children are well catered for here too. After a small entrance fee there is a supervised playground with a inflated 'bouncer' and magicians—sounds fun.

Kilbeggan (0506) 32176 in County Westmeath is a National Hunt course on the Dublin-Athlone road, the nearest train station being Tullarmore. Dublin is about 50 minutes away. Although the racing is not of the highest quality, the betting market is second to none and with the Irish that means some turnover!

Punchestown (045) 97704 in Naas, Co Kildare is certainly worth a visit and the course is only 20 minutes from Dublin by car. The nearest station is Newbridge off the Dublin to Naas road.

The racing here is tremendous. Punchestown sits amidst the rolling countryside of Co Kildare and the three day April Festival here is becoming bigger and brighter each year. Indeed, the course is endeavouring to become the last leg of the Spring treble of festivals following Cheltenham and Aintree. Facilities at Punchestown are constantly being upgraded. There will also be all manner of novel attractions for the visitor and British racegoers are warmly welcomed. The 1993 Festival was a great success and the Irish are surely developing a potentially excellent fixture in an already distinguished calendar. I hope many will make the effort to visit in 1994.

Slightly further afield in Navan, Co Meath is **Navan Racecourse (046) 21350** where one finds both flat and National Hunt racing. Navan is 35 miles from Dublin and can be reached via the N3.

Moving down from Dublin, we come to a splendid park racecourse; **Gowran Park (056) 26110** in Co Kilkenny whilst in the far south east of the country, both **Wexford (053) 42307** and **Waterford and Tranmore racecourses (051) 81425** are to be found.

Wexford offers competitive racing and is well worth a visit. The course is easily accessible form Britain via the Fishguard/ Rosslare and Pembroke/Rosslare sea routes. The terminal is only eleven miles from the track so it has to be on the shortlist for Britain's racegoers seeking pastures new.

At Waterford and Tranmore, races such as the Waterford Crystal Chase are staged during its short, nine day season. The nearest station is in the main town but, if travelling by car, the course is just off the A25, about 100 miles south west of Dublin. ·

If it's a drink and a good crowd you are after go straight to Loughlin's a pub in Gowran, after the races. It is always packed to the hilt and this is the place where the Gold Cup was passed around by the local Mullins family after Dawn Run's memorable Cheltenham triumph. If you are heading south after the racing, head out of the city on the Callan road and stop off at Mickey's pub in Callan. Not quite the sort of place where you could eat off the floor, it is full of character and even sports Christmas decorations all year round! Plenty of champagne has flowed in here too and you'll usually find a trainer and jockey or two inside having heated exchanges with the landlord whose views on Irish racing are remarkably refreshing. These are just a few examples of the vast number of splendid bars to enjoy.

County Tipperary offers Clonmel at Powerstown Park, **Clonmel (052) 22611** located between Waterford and Cahir, close to Clonmel station. This is a charming little track. McCarthy's pub is another landmark in Irish racing. This pub, which also provides an undertaking service, it is famous all over the country, and there is no such thing as a quiet night here. Many famous race wins have been celebrated within these four walls as Mouse Morris and Edward O'Grady both train nearby, with Coolmore Stud in between.

Further inland, in County Tipperary, is **Thurles (054) 22253** which, like Clonmel, stages both National Hunt and flat racing. If you are heading straight back to Dublin from Thurles, stop off at Morrissey's pub in Abbeyleix, where you can also buy your groceries. This is the place where many of the Horgan clan's parties have kicked off, notably after the successes of Don't Forget Me and Tirol in the Irish 2,000 Guineas. You don't have to pay extra here for the special atmosphere in this marvellous pub.

Tipperary Racecourse (062) 51357 or **(01) 893607** is situated at Limerick Junction. The town of Tipperary is two miles away and the course itself is off the N24. It is also handy for Limerick Junction station just 200 yards away.

West Cork is one of the most spectacular areas of Ireland and the racecourse at **Mallow (022) 21565**, Mount Ruby nestles amongst this splendour. Racing here is mixed and the best route to the course is via the A20 Cork to Limerick road. The nearest train station is one mile away at Mallow.

Moving along into Co Kerry, three racecourses are to be found; Killarney, Tralee and Listowel. **Killarney (064) 31125** racecourse is magnificent and the racing festival in early July is superbly organised. For those staying in the area, it is fantastic golfing country—a sportsman's paradise.

Tralee (066) 26188, set amidst more gorgeous scenery, is at Ballybeggan Park, off the A21. Its highlights include good racing and

a beauty contest; The Rose of Tralee Festival, held at the end of August and featuring many a fair filly. On an historical note, Dawn Run won her first race here.

Listowel (068) 21144 is the last of the trio. The course, a traditional holiday meeting place for farmers, offers mixed racing and a fun atmosphere. Described fondly as 'an annual ritual of fun and socialising' the festival takes place in September. To reach the course, turn off the A69. The nearest train station is in Tralee. There is also plenty of music in all the pubs in the town—just a short walk across from the bridge, away from the racecourse.

As we move northwards around the coast, we find **Limerick Racecourse (061) 515440**. On the road back to Limerick City is the Punch's Pub—the place to be after racing if you don't mind crowds. Try and explore Bunratty Castle and enjoy a drink in the renowned Durty Nelly's.

Galway Racecourse (091) 53870, Ballybrit in late July and early August is a must. The meeting takes place over a week and offers a

mixture of both flat and National Hunt racing. On some days, racing takes place in the evening. This really is of little consequence—the atmosphere is merry throughout, the crowd cosmopolitan and the serious betting which takes place all day is replaced by even more serious card playing at night. The scenery is marvellous. Golf, fishing and dog racing can all be enjoyed....the place is a must for lovers of the sporting life!

Ballinrobe (092) 41052, a little further north in Co Mayo, may not be the most famous racecourse in the world but it is worth a visit for the scenery alone. The course hosts both flat and National Hunt racing.

Before heading into Co Sligo, a slight detour takes us to **Roscommon Racecourse (0903) 26261** at Lenabane. Situated off the A61, the course is one mile out of town on the Castlebar road. The nearest station is Roscommon and racing features both flat and National Hunt events. The course has modern stands which inevitably provide a number of bars. There is plenty of room for parking here and the course is at it's busiest on Sundays. There are a total of nine fixtures here and admission charges are good value.

Sligo Racecourse (071) 6244840 is at Cleveragh. This is one of Ireland's most scenic courses in the suburbs of Sligo City off the A4. The nearest station, not surprisingly, is Sligo.

Laytown, Bettystown, Bellewstown and Dundalk all lie close to the Northern Ireland border. **Laytown (041) 23425** is a flat racing track and the only survivor of the once frequent meetings held on the beaches of Ireland. Racing began here in the 1890's and takes place now in either July or August, depending on the tides. To reach the course, turn off the N1 at Julianstown, some 25 miles north of Dublin. There is plenty of room for parking at this annual race day which draws huge crowds and commands a great atmosphere. Charges of approximately £5 should be expected but children are admitted free of charge. Bellewstown also offers just one meeting, a three day affair which takes place in the first week of July. Once again, admission is £5. Dundalk (042) 34419 at Dowdallshill is situated off the main Dublin to Belfast road. National Hunt and flat racing is again the form.

I certainly hope this piece whets the appetite for a few excursions to the Emerald Isle. It would not have been possible to produce anything like the flavour of this piece without the help of Claire Barry and several of Ireland's friendly racecourse managers. Finally, there are a number of general points that we should remember when visiting this spectacular racing land.

The Irish are a wonderful race but they are renowned as the worst time keepers in the world so don't expect your dinner at 8 o'clock sharp. On the other hand, their sense of wit is incomparable and they have a charm unlike that found elsewhere in the world.

In Ireland, racing and socialising are totally inseparable and even if you only know half of what a horse should look like, you'll feel very much at home. And if you are buying a horse you will be even more welcome!

Sign posting here is not the best so you are advised to head vaguely in the right direction and ask the rest of the way. If you stop at a pub be warned, you might never leave as someone is bound to start chatting. You might even get caught up in a wake, although hopefully not your own! The standard of cuisine in Ireland has improved dramatically of late and prices are generally cheaper than the British equivalent. Seafood is particularly renowned. Drinks on the other hand are more expensive but shorts are the equivalent of doubles. You have been warned! The standard and variety of accommodation in Ireland seems to improve each year and the Irish Tourist Board in London and their regional offices are very helpful. Country House Hotels of excellence are found and away from the more racey hotels, the delightful B&B's are tremendous value. What is more, you will get more sympathy for your hangover here! It is to be anticipated that some of the prices quoted here will increase for the 1994 season. Racing in Ireland, however, remains good value.

There is something quite marvellous about racing in Ireland. The Irish have supported our festivals for years and I hope that soon, more British racegoers will make the effort to visit this remarkable country. This is only a brief extract and taste of the real flavour of equestrian Eire but the true pleasures can only be found in a visit. One which will surely last a lifetime—win or lose.

Local Favourites

Many of Ireland's stately homes have been renovated into sumptuous hotels and restaurants. In contrast, there are also many bed and breakfast establishments and numerous smaller hotels which have great appeal to those travelling on a budget—as more and more of us are at this time of economic discomfort. That is not to say, however, that we can not find a winner or two on and off the turf.

The Irish Country Houses and Restaurant Association (010 353) 4623416 produce an excellent brochure called The Blue Book which is well worth a pre-race inspection. The Blue Book is available at no charge and includes information on many of the better country house hotels in Ireland. Other examples of splendid Irish hospitality can be found by consulting Elegant Ireland (010 353) 1 751665 who have a selection of some beautiful houses which can be hired by the week. These houses do not come cheap but are of an excellent standard and are strongly recommended. Less pricey but often equally enchanting accommodation can be found by requesting the Hidden Ireland brochure (010 353 1) 686463. These houses are more akin to small bed and breakfasts and provide welcoming accommodation, often in glorious countryside. The local Irish Tourist Boards are always helpful and we suggest that you contact them in advance of your visit. I have gathered together a list of warmly recommended hotels and enough information on each to thoroughly whet the appetite.

A recent addition to the outstanding collection of Ireland's hotels is the Kildare Hotel, Straffan. If ever a hotel was bound for excellence this has to be one. It is owned by the Smurfit Organisation and boasts tremendous facilities. It is pricey but is something quite special. The restaurant, The Byerley Turk, offers outstanding cuisine and a special heritage which will appeal to all lovers of the turf. The leisure facilities, including a Palmer designed golf course, are excellent.

An altogether different, but no less remarkable, establishment is Kildare's Kilkea Castle. An edifice which delights historians as well as weary travellers. The hotel is both charming and comfortable and offers a unique location in which to while away a few hours before, or after racing. One of the most celebrated of Irish racing hotels is Rathsallagh House. It is situated amidst 500 acres of Parkland and remains the home of the O'Flynn family. There is a welcoming atmosphere and an excellent dining room. A warm favourite in any field. Rathsallagh is close to the Irish National Stud, the Curragh, Punchestown and Naas Racecourses and is also handy for Goffs sales. Another popular racing rendezvous is the Hotel Keadeen in Newbridge. The Hotel is extremely handy for the Curragh and provides an ideal location for racegoers.

The city of Dublin could well be your chosen destination when racing at any one of the outstanding tracks within its environs. The Irish Tourist Board will happily provide details of a whole range of hotels. Some of the more celebrated haunts include The Berkeley Court, the flagship of the Doyle Group. The Westbury, from the same stable, is also an excellent choice with a first class restaurant as well as many mod cons which go to make up a first rate hotel.

159

The Burlington is Ireland's largest hotel and the President's Bar is particularly atmospheric. An ideal place to meet after a successful day at the track.

There are all manner of excellent restaurants in Dublin which can be a touch pricey- still you're only young once! A great favourite is Le Coq Hardi, one for racing lovers.

A similarly warm recommendation can be made of Moyglare Manor in Maynooth, standing amidst the stud farms west of Dublin. Peat fires and modern comforts together with an excellent restaurant combine to make this a worthy candidate for any visit to Ireland's principle racetrack. One final thought for those of you who love fish, visit the King Sitric Restaurant on the quay in Howth.

South of Dublin you will find another relative newcomer, Mount Juliet in Thomastown. The hotel boasts a very fine golf course and many other facilities whilst the bar will give an insight into the exploits of one former owner's passion and should also interest the racegoer.

Travellers heading to Waterford should visit the Waterford Castle Hotel which enjoys an idyllic setting. The hotel is owned by a passionate racing family and if you have a few pounds hidden away this is the place to blow it all. The restaurant here is particularly good. A similar appraisal fits Cashel House another first class hotel in every respect.

I could not recommend a trip to Killarney and Ireland's West coast more highly—it is a delight to behold. Two hotels in Kenmare almost defy belief such is their excellence; The Park Hotel and Sheen Falls Lodge. The former a Victorian edifice with a great deal of charm and a pleasing restaurant, the latter a luxurious hotel in a majestic setting overlooking the falls. The restaurant revels in its position and also offers outstanding food. Another great favourite near the race-course is Aghadoe Heights, not the best looker but a great hotel nonetheless. Some way north of here, we find Dromoland Castle, A popular 'deluxe' hotel with great style.

It is without doubt that many of the hotels mentioned here are a touch pricey, but they are all first class establishments. Next year we will be adding more 'economy' hotels, but in the meantime, if you are travelling on a budget, contact the tourist boards for advice and information, they are very helpful. If you do find a 'good'un' please let us know.

Racing in Ireland is in the blood of the people and the very roots of the country. The Irish are a welcoming race and they love a flutter, a visit to this delightful country is highly recommended

A Summary of the Irish
Racing Calendar

The Irish racing calendar is immensely rich in its variety and its quality ranges from the outstanding classics of the Curragh to the less celebrated but nevertheless entertaining country meetings. The Irish racing year starts with good meetings at Fairyhouse, Naas, Punchestown and Leopardstown to name but four of the courses. Many of these races are prep races for Cheltenham's National Hunt Festival and this trend continues into February. Other courses which offer February racing include Clonmel, Thurles, Navan and Gowran Park.

The focus in March is of course centred on Cheltenham but Leopardstown also hosts some excellent racing and as the twilight of the month looms, the Curragh is found busy with ambitious trainers, each striving to find classic winners. The National Hunt calendar is far from lost in April, however, and there are two outstanding meetings this month. The Fairyhouse Festival in April, runs over three days from Easter Monday and is a truly tremendous event. Featuring the Jamieson Irish Grand National, it offers a thoroughly entertaining three day's racing. The same can be said of the Punchestown Festival which takes place towards the end of the month. This event can not be recommended more highly. It offers an excellent standard of steeple chasing and hurdling. It will take time for any Festival to challenge the likes of Aintree or Cheltenham but this meeting has proved to be a worthy final leg of a thrilling treble of National Hunt sport, unsurpassed anywhere in the world. To be at all three events brings a huge smile to the face, although the liver is perhaps trembling at the thought!

The Killarney Spring Festival in early May is another delight to be a part of. If you fancy a little golf and racing amidst marvellous countryside you'll be in seventh heaven here. With the flat season beginning to boil, the focus returns to the Curragh, via Leopardstown and other stalwarts of the flat racing scene. Mid May offers the Airlie Coolmore Irish 2,000 Guineas with the Goff's 1,000 Guineas held a week later. In this period, a large number of very well attended evening meetings are held. The racecourses here seem to be working for their own best ends, not merely those of the bookies. What a contrast to Britain.

An enjoyable three days can be spent at Gowran Park in mid-June and on the final Sunday of the month we see the Budweiser Irish Derby. The biggest meeting of the year is held on a Sunday. I wonder when Britain will be able to host such a race on the Sabbath.

More evening meetings prevail throughout June and there are a number of summer festivals that veritably warm the cockles of your heart. Bellewstown, Killarney and Galway are three especially entertaining events. The Kildangan Stud Irish Oaks is another event to savour early this month.

Leopardstown hosts an excellent standard of racing throughout the year and their two day meeting in August featuring the Heinz 57 Stakes is well worth attending. More festivals at Tramore and Tralee take place in August and both are fabulous occasions.

The Curragh is rarely without a good fixture in the summer months and in September it offers the National Stakes, the Moyglare Stud Stakes and the Jefferson Smurfit Memorial Irish St Leger. Try and stay for the Listowel Festival, but bring plenty of loot as racing here is extremely competitive.

The autumn and winter months offer more entertaining racing at various courses. Leopardstown, Punchestown and Fairyhouse offer particularly good sport. The year ends in style with a Christmas jamboree at Leopardstown. So if you're bored with the idea of yet another Christmas with the mother-in-law why not pop over to the Emerald Isle—you won't be disappointed!

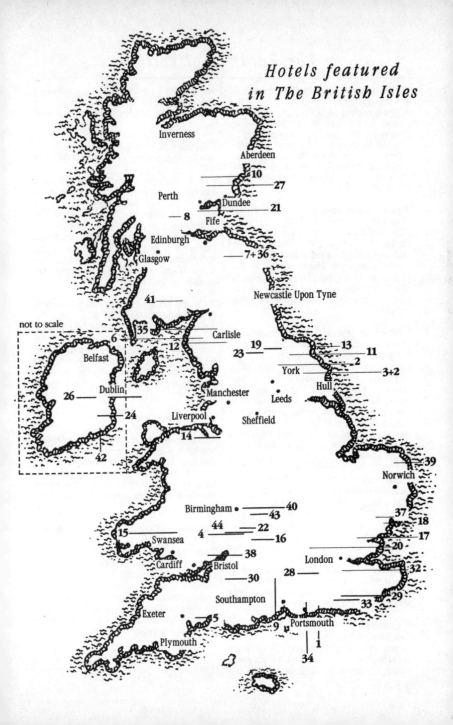

Hotels featured in The British Isles

not to scale

The Racing Collection

**1 Bailiffscourt, Climping, West Sussex.
Tel: (0903) 723511**
A 1930's replica of a 13th century court-house which has been cleverly constructed from derelict properties from all over the South of England, this hotel offers many facilities. Basing itself on a medieval manor it is furnished accordingly with four poster beds and open log fires.

2 Bay Horse Inn, Harrogate, North Yorkshire. Tel: (0423) 770230
This delightful, ivy clad inn dates back to the 18th century. It is family owned and as such provides a welcoming and friendly service. There are local race meetings at Ripon, Thirsk, York and Wetherby for which the hotel specifically caters, organising Racing Breakfasts.

3 Bilbrough Manor Country House Hotel & Restaurant, Near York, North Yorkshire. Tel: (0937) 834002
Bilbrough Manor, originally the ancestral home of the Fairfax family, was transformed into a lovely country house hotel in the mid 80's. Renowned for its friendly and professional service, excellent food and homely atmosphere, the Manor is situated on the edge of a leafy conservation village five miles west of York.

4 Cheltenham Park Hotel, Cheltenham, Gloucestershire. Tel: (0242) 222021
The Cheltenham Park Hotel is a beautiful recently extended Regency Manor House with luxury bedrooms set in nine acres of landscape gardens. The Hotel's Lakeside Restaurant and Bar overlook both the trout lake and adjacent Lilleybrook Golf Course. The Cheltenham Park Hotel is only two miles from the town centre and a very short drive from the Racecourse.

5 Combe House, Gittisham, Devon. Tel:(0404) 42756
A peaceful and secluded 14th century Elizabethan mansion set in its own estate. Guests with an interest in racing are spoilt for choice as there are several National Hunt courses within easy reach and the hotel also owns racehorses.

6 Cottage In The Wood Hotel, Malvern Wells, Worcestershire Tel: (0684) 573 487
Just 30 minutes from Cheltenham and 10 miles to Worcester, this superb hotel and restaurant has one of the finest views in Britain. The vista below unfolds across 30 miles of the Severn Vale to the Cotswolds. John and Sue Pattin own and run this comfortable 3 star hotel (all major guides) which has warmth and atmosphere allowing you to unwind and relax.

7 Crosby Lodge Hotel, Crosby-On-Eden, Cumbria. Tel: (0228) 573618
An elegant country mansion combining a tasteful collection of antiques with fine furniture in both private and public rooms. The restaurant serves delicious food and is open to non residents. Nearby racecourses include Carlisle and Hexham.

**8 Cross Keys, Kelso, Borders.
Tel: (0573) 223303**
Kelso is one of Scotland's marvellous border towns. The Cross Keys is one of the country's oldest walking inns and one of its most welcoming. This is an ideal point from which to explore the Borders or even attend the races at Kelso.

9 Culcreuch Castle, Fintry, Stirlingshire. Tel: (036 086) 228
This beautiful castle has been lovingly converted by its present owners the Haslam family into a comfortable, friendly country house hotel. The eight individually furnished bedrooms are all en suite and have full modern facilities. There is a wide range of activities in the area and the hotel is central for the racing circuit.

10 Donnington Valley Hotel & Golf Course, Newbury, Berkshire.
Tel: (0635) 551199
Set in the beautiful countryside of Royal Berkshire and conveniently situated for Newbury Races, Donnington Valley Hotel is a unique venue, blending charm and elegance with the luxury and personal service expected from an individually designed, privately owned, four star hotel.

11 Dunkeld House Hotel, Dunkeld, Perthshire. Tel: (0350) 727771
The Dunkeld House Hotel has an enviable position on the banks of the River Tay and offers a warm welcome to guests. This is an excellent base for touring and offers a wide range of sporting and leisure facilities.

12 Fairfield Manor Hotel, Skelton, York.
Tel: (0904) 670311
Tastefully extended and refurbished Fairfield Manor Hotel retains the gracious atmosphere of a classical country house hotel. The 90 bedrooms provide superior accommodation, with private bathroom and all modern comforts. Situated only three miles from the historic city of York, guests are assured of elegant surroundings, superb cuisine and professional, friendly service.

13 Farlam Hall Hotel, Brampton, Cumbria.
Tel: (06977) 46234
Dating back to the 17th century, Farlam Hall is set in four acres of grounds with a lake and offers great comfort. It is ideally located for visiting Hadrian's Wall, Naworth Castle and Lanercost Priory. For racegoers, Carlisle, Hexham and Newcastle racecourses are all within easy driving distance.

14 Feversham Arms Hotel, Helmsley, North Yorkshire. Tel: (0439) 70766
A luxuriously modernised, historic coaching inn set in over an acre of walled gardens, this hotel offers every comfort and is perfect for exploring the Moors, Dales, East Coast and the medieval city of York.

15 Frogg Manor, Broxton, Chester. Tel:

(0829) 782 629/280
Not far from the madding crowd. A superb Georgian Manor House recently refurbished using traditional decor and period furniture to combine modern comfort with the grace of the Georgian era. An atmosphere that is pure romance.

16 Gliffaes Country House Hotel, Crickhowell, Powys. Tel: (0874) 730371
Dating from 1885, this distinctive hotel is set in 29 acres of private gardens offering stunning views of the surrounding National Park and River Usk. The hotel is elegantly furnished although the atmosphere is distinctly informal and the owners maintain country house standards of the old order.

17 Halewell Close, Withington, Gloucestershire. Tel: (0242) 890238
Situated on the edge of the pretty village of Withington and within reach of Cheltenham, Stratford and Warwick racecourses this delightful Cotswold stone house hotel is set in 50 acres of private grounds. The six large bedrooms provide every modern comfort and convenience.

18 Hanbury Manor, Thundridge, Nr Ware, Hertfordshire. Tel: (0920) 487722
From beamed ceilings and oak panelling to fascinating tapestries this hotel is nothing less than impressive and is to be savoured. With its huge range of facilities Hanbury Manor caters for nothing less than the civilised aesthetic. The mansion itself has been lovingly restored offering elegant bedrooms and a choice of three dining rooms. Guests can relax and be pampered at this splendid hotel.

19 Hintlesham Hall, Hintlesham, Suffolk.
Tel: (047387) 334
The Georgian facade faces the front, while the Tudor rear part overlooks gardens and lawns. Effortless luxury is the air of this highly impressive hotel. The adjoining restaurant is equally gracious.

20 Jervaulx Hall, Masham, North Yorkshire. Tel: (0677) 60235
A 19th century manor house adjacent to the ruined 12th century Jervaulx Abbey. Offering a high standard of comfort and cuisine, it is ideally situated for visiting Middleham Castle, Bramham Park, Castle Howard, Harrogate, Ripon and York.

21 Le Manoir aux Quat' Saison, Great Milton, Oxfordshire. Tel: (0844) 27881
The history of this outstanding manor dates back 750 years. Set in 27 acres of beautiful landscaped gardens and woodland this is an internationally acclaimed hotel. Each one of the 19 elegant bedrooms has been individually designed and the bathrooms are equally luxurious. Le Manoir is widely acknowledged as Britain's finest restaurant and the superb cuisine is complemented by an extensive wine list.

22 Lomond Hills Hotel, Freuchie, Fife. Tel: (0337) 57329
The Hotel is set in the heart of Fife in the charming village of Freuchie where courtiers from the nearby Falkland Palace were banished to when out of favour, hence the saying 'Awa tae Freuchie and eat mice' . Character and comfort combine to make a stay at the Lomond Hills extremely enjoyable.

23 Lygon Arms, Broadway, Gloucestershire. Tel: (0386) 852255
The Lygon Arms is a magnificent Tudor building meticulously restored to retain its wealth of original features, such as 17th century oak panelling and minstrels gallery. Offering numerous leisure facilities, it is well based for racing at Stratford, Cheltenham, Warwick and Worcester.

24 Miller's House, Market Place in Wensleydale, Middleham, North Yorkshire. Tel: (0969) 22630
Nestled in the heart of the Yorkshire Dales the elegant Georgian Miller's House is an ideal base from which to explore the 'Herriot country'. Breathtaking views across Coverdale and Wensleydale with a backdrop of Middleham castle and racehorses from the many local racing stables exercising over the low moor. Award winning restaurant.

25 Mount Juliet, Thomastown, County Kilkenny. Tel: (010 353 56) 24455
One of Ireland's premier hotel and sporting estates set in 1500 acres of unspoiled parkland in the south east of Ireland. In addition to the estate's own stud farm, once the home of racing legends such as The Tetrach and The Tetratema and now home to over 100 thoroughbreds, Mount Juliet also boasts one of the top equestrian centres in Ireland.

26 Mount Royale Hotel, York, North Yorkshire. Tel: (0904) 628856
The elegant combination of two beautifully restored William IV houses with an acre of old English gardens has created this gracious hotel only minutes away from the historic city of York. There are several race meetings in the area and guests can also explore this wonderful city.

27 Moyglare Manor, Maynooth, Co Kildare Tel: (010 353 1) 6286351
The modern amenities and diversions available at this handsome Georgian house have detracted nothing from the ambience of the past and the splendid era of Irish country living and hospitality that Moyglare evokes. Ideal for the racegoer as the Manor is in the heart of Irish racing country.

28 Murrayshall Country House Hotel and Golf Course, Scone, Perthshire. Tel: (0738) 51171
Recently refurbished to give the atmosphere and style of a Country House Hotel and set in 300 acres of parkland this is an attractive venue whatever brings guests to this area of Scotland. The Old Masters Restaurant offers a wide variety of dishes with the emphasis on wholesome fayre.

29 Oatlands Park Hotel, Weybridge, Surrey. Tel: (0932) 847242
Set in acres of parkland and overlooking the Broadwater Lake this is the ideal location for business and pleasure alike. The elegant high-ceilinged Broadwater Restaurant offers a wide range of dishes to cater for every taste. The bedrooms have all been tastefully furnished to a high standard of comfort and have all modern conveniences.

30 Ockenden Manor, Cuckfield, West Sussex. Tel: (0444) 416111
A 16th century manor house set in 9 acres of gardens, this hotel retains some striking period features including wood panelled public rooms. Ockenden Manor is famous for its modern English cuisine and outstanding cellar of 300 bins.

31 Priory Hotel, Bath, Avon. Tel: (0225) 331922
This well run former private residence has retained many of the early 19th century gentleman's necessities - croquet lawn, orangery, lovely furniture. There is also a wonderful and widely acclaimed restaurant featuring local produce. The 21 tastefully appointed bedrooms are enhanced by antiques and works of art. Many have views over the superb garden.

32 Rathsallagh House, Dunlavin, Co Wicklow, Ireland Tel: (010 353 45) 53112
Converted from Queen Ann stables which burnt to the ground in 1798, this large comfortable farmhouse is situated in 500 acres of peaceful parkland, surrounded by some of the most beautiful countryside of eastern Ireland. The addition of modern comforts has done nothing to spoil the traditional splendour of the house.

33 Selsdon Park, Sanderstead, Surrey Tel: (081) 657 8811
Set high in the rolling hills of the Surrey countryside, Selsdon Park combines the ancient virtues of hospitality and courtesy with the modern attributes of efficiency and friendliness. For those guests who are travelling the turf, Lingfield and Epsom racecourses are close by.

34 South Lodge, Lower Beeding, Hampshire. Tel: (0403) 891711
An elegant country house with one of the finest Victorian rock gardens in England. The light and spacious bedrooms have fine views over the South Downs and the hotel is well situated for Glyndbourne, Chartwell, Goodwood and Leonardslee.

35 Spread Eagle Hotel, Midhurst, West Sussex. Tel: (0730) 816911, Fax: (0730) 815668
The Spread Eagle is one of England's oldest hotels dating from 1430 and has been beautifully restored in keeping with its past. It is an ideal base for visiting Chichester Cathedral, Fishbourne Roman Palace and Downland Museum as well as the racecourses of Goodwood and Fontwell.

36 String of Horses Inn, Carlisle, Cumbria. Tel: (0228) 70297
A late 17th century inn, the String of Horses is a must for antique lovers, it is a true Aladdin's Cave of furniture. There is a well equipped leisure centre and the hotel is only a short distance from Hadrian's Wall and racing at Carlisle.

37 Sunlaws House Hotel, Kelso, Roxburghshire. Tel: (0573) 5331
Owned by the Duke of Roxburgh and resting in 200 acres of beautiful gardens beside the Teviot, this hotel boasts a fine library bar with open log fire and leather bound tomes. The 22 bedrooms have all been furnished with care and include every modern comfort. This is the perfect base from which to explore the Borders or pursue a wide range of sporting and leisure activities.

38 The Black Lion, Long Melford, Suffolk. Tel: (0787) 312356
Situated on the green is this fully restored 17th century coaching inn. Guests will find a family run hotel, where nothing is too much trouble. A veritable home from home, famed for its 'Countrymen Restaurant'.

39 The Crown at Whitebrook, Nr Monmouth, Gwent.
Tel: (0600) 860254

Remotely situated one mile from the River Wye on the edge of the Tintern Forest this is the ideal place to get away from it all. The bedrooms are comfortable and are all en suite. The chef specialises in creating original dishes from fresh local ingredients and to compliment these there are fine wines from the interesting cellar.

40 The Old Rectory, Great Snoring, Norfolk Tel: (0328) 820597

A 16th century former manor house nestling contentedly beside the church. Old fashioned charm with a homely warmth and friendliness. Wonderful tranquillity, good food, fine breakfasts and courteous service all make this the ideal place to stay. For those seeking total privacy enquire about the superb Sheltons cottage suites.

41 Three Swans Hotel, Market Harborough, Leicestershire. Tel: (0858) 466644

A warm welcome traditional hospitality and excellent service awaits you at this historic 14th century coaching inn. Centrally situated in this delightful market town. Comfortable lounges, bars and conservatory. Dine in our elegant Swans Restaurant, renowned in the county for its superb cuisine. Ideally located for business purposes. Conference facilities for up to 75 persons. Large free car park. Special weekend rates available.

42 Turnberry Hotel, Turnberry, Strathclyde. Tel: (0655) 31000

Set in 360 acres overlooking the islands of Arran and Ailsa Craig this world famous resort has been extensively restored and offers luxurious accommodation for the most discerning individual. Best known of course for its excellent golfing facilities the hotel is also ideally placed for nearby racecourses.

43 Waterford Castle, The Island Ballinakill, Co Waterford, Tel: (010 353 51) 78203

Set on a private 310 acre island and reached by ferry, this 18th century castle is beautifully tranquil and impressively decorated inside with stone walls, old panelling and a gorgeous ribbon plastered ceiling. The hotel is ideally situated for several major racing fixtures in the area.

44 Woodhouse Hotel, Princethorpe, Nr Rugby, Warwickshire. Tel:(0926) 632303

A privately run hotel and restaurant offering a personal service tailored to the needs of their guests. Ideally placed to use as a base from which to take in the races at Warwick, Stratford and Cheltenham. All 17 bedrooms are well equipped and guests are invited to make use of the outdoor heated swimming pool and tennis courts. A superb range of cuisine is served in any one of the three uniquely located restaurants.

45 Wyck Hill House, Stow-on-the-Wold, Gloucestershire.
Tel: (0451) 31936

Set in 100 acres and dating from early 1700's, reputedly on the site of a Roman settlement, the interior of this hotel is furnished with antiques. The cedar-panelled library is a particularly peaceful room. Ideally situated for the many racecourses of the area this is also an excellent base for touring this beautiful region.